Policies Into Practice

National and International Case Studies in Implementation

Policies Into Practice

National and International Case Studies
in Implementation

Edited by
David Lewis and Helen Wallace *Civil Service College*

 Heinemann Educational Books · London · Exeter (NH)

Heinemann Educational Books Ltd
22 Bedford Square, London WC1B 3HH

Heinemann Educational Books Inc
4 Front Street, Exeter, New Hampshire 03833

LONDON EDINBURGH MELBOURNE AUCKLAND
HONG KONG SINGAPORE KUALA LUMPUR
NEW DELHI IBADAN NAIROBI JOHANNESBURG
EXETER (NH) KINGSTON PORT OF SPAIN

British Library Cataloguing in Publication Data

Policies into practice.
   1. Politics and government
   I. Lewis, David   II. Wallace, Helen
   354   JF1411

   ISBN 0-435-83488-6
   ISBN 0-435-83489-4 Pbk

Typeset by The Castlefield Press, Moulton, Northampton
Printed by Biddles Ltd, Guildford, Surrey

Contents

Preface

This book is a contribution to policy studies. By 'policy studies' we mean analysis of the ways in which policies are formulated, implemented and evaluated, with the hope that this will help to make the procedures involved more efficient and the outcomes superior. In this context, implementation has a crucial importance.

Policy studies have proved to be a particularly fruitful approach to the study of government. However the literature on implementation has important limitations. It has been impossible to know whether conclusions reached from examining one field of policy apply more generally. And from the British point of view, there is the limitation that a large proportion of the literature deals with American conditions.

We believe that there are indeed insights and understanding available from academic analysis which can increase the capabilities of practical administrators, and thus of governments and nations. We also believe that, to achieve quality and realism, academic analysis needs to maintain close links with the practical world. We hope this book goes some way to realise these ideals, and will be of value both to an academic audience and to people in administration and government.

All but one of the contributors to this book are current or recent members of the teaching staff of the Civil Service College, which can be regarded as a focus for dialogue between the two worlds. Its aims are to improve the efficiency of civil servants in their work by providing that training which is more effectively or more economically done centrally; and to carry out research in support of its training programme. This book is the outcome of a decision to make the implementation of policies one of the main subjects for research in what is now the College's Directorate of Policy and Administration Studies.

We have brought together a collection of case studies within an integrated framework. We hope the individual cases are sufficiently self-contained to be of value to people whose interest is in the particular events described or in the relevant field of policy. However, the real aim of the book is to bring together a wide range of cases so that contrasts and comparisons can be drawn about implementation in a variety of settings. We think this variety is unique, and it is also intended to redress an imbalance (towards social policy) in the fields covered in the previous literature. In selecting the cases, there was an emphasis on the interactions between separate organisations at different levels of government. As an extension of that, and breaking new ground, there are three examples of the implementation of policies across national boundaries. Three chapters deal in whole or in part with the USA.

The backgrounds of the contributors, and the methodologies of the case studies, also show a wide variety. Two of the contributors are administrators and four others have experience of working in government administration. The academic disciplines represented are political science, international relations, organisational analysis, social policy, sociology and social anthropology. Some of the case studies are based wholly or partly on direct participation or observation, others on interviews and written sources; but we have deliberately not included full descriptions or discussions of methodology. Where references are given at the end of each chapter, they are confined to secondary works, or else to generally available published works.

The overall framework for the book is also of particular importance. This is the evolutionary model of the policy process which Masood Hyder presents in Chapter 1. It resulted from dissatisfaction with the theories and models available when the contributors started work on the subject, and a strong desire to find a framework within which the case studies could be profitably discussed and analysed. Even if the ideas incorporated in the evolutionary model are not in themselves novel, they have not previously been applied systematically to implementation, and we hope the book will therefore make a significant contribution to theory. In that respect, the intention has been to make it stimulating rather than exhaustive; and the model has not been elaborated, or applied to individual cases, in great detail. We have also tried to make the language of the book simple and accessible, especially to people in the practical world.

The structure is as follows. Chapter 1 discusses alternative perspectives on implementation and the implications of the contemporary environment in order to place the evolutionary model in perspective. Part I (Chapters 2–7) consists of studies of the implementation of national or sub-national policies. Chapter 6 deals with California, Chapter 5 compares parallel policies in California and the UK, the other chapters deal with the UK. Part II (Chapters 8–11) is concerned with the implementation of policies across national boundaries. It is introduced by a general discussion (Chapter 8) of the considerations and issues which arise in situations of that kind. The other chapters are case studies: Chapters 9 and 10 from the European Community, Chapter 11 from US–UK defence collaboration. Finally, Chapter 12 tries to elucidate, in the light of the cases and the evolutionary model, why implementation is problematic, what constitutes 'successful' implementation, and what can be done to increase the probability of success.

We are grateful to all those who helped this project towards completion, especially Andrew Dunsire, Lewis Gunn, Christopher Hood and Les Metcalfe. We are also grateful to all those, civil servants and others, who have read and commented on drafts of individual chapters. Needless to say, no statement made or opinion expressed in this book should be ascribed to any government department or other body. In all cases they represent the personal views of the author.

We owe a special debt to those who have expertly typed very numerous drafts and papers over several years. Most of this fell to, and was cheerfully fulfilled by, Marie Walsingham and her team at the London Centre of the College. Our thanks, too, to Ron James and his colleagues for all their work in handling manuscripts.

As well as costs of research met by the College, Chapters 2 and 7 draw on research carried out when the authors were supported by, respectively, a research studentship and a research grant from the Social Science Research Council. Chapter 4 has appeared in a different form in *Public Administration*, and we are grateful for the Editor's permission to include it here. Chapters 1, 3 and 8–11 are wholly, and Chapters 2, 5, 6 and 7 are in part, Crown copyright and appear here with the permission of the Controller of Her Majesty's Stationery Office.

David Lewis
Helen Wallace
May 1983

Notes on contributors

R.A. Blanche worked in local government before going to university, and is now Lecturer in Public Administration at the Civil Service College

Dudley Coates was Lecturer in Public Administration at the Civil Service College from 1978 to 1981, on secondment from the Ministry of Agriculture Fisheries and Food

Gaynor Cohen is Lecturer in Social Policy and Administration at the Civil Service College, and spent the academic year 1979/80 on leave of absence in California

Masood Hyder is a Senior Research Officer at the Civil Service College

David Lewis was Director, Public Administration and Social Policy, at the Civil Service College from 1978 to 1980, on secondment from the Department of the Environment

J.L. Metcalfe is Lecturer in Public Administration at the Civil Service College, and was previously a Senior Research Officer at the London Business School

Jaqi Nixon is Senior Lecturer in Community Studies at Brighton Polytechnic, and was previously a Senior Research Officer at the Civil Service College and in the Department of Health and Social Security

F.F. Ridley OBE is Professor of Political Theory and Institutions in the University of Liverpool, and was Chairman of the Merseyside Board for the Job Creation Programme

Helen Wallace is Lecturer in Public Administration at the Civil Service College, a visiting Lecturer at the College of Europe, and worked for a period in 1979–80 in the Planning Staff of the Foreign and Commonwealth Office.

1 Implementation
The evolutionary model
Masood Hyder

Why study implementation?

Implementation is about putting policies into practice. It is the often complex process of planning, organisation, coordination and promotion which is necessary in order to achieve policy objectives. As an *activity* implementation constitutes an important, even a central, phase in the policy process. As a *concept* it has proved somewhat elusive. The importance attached to the study of decision-making has often diverted attention from the fact that the initial decision is merely the starting-point, and it is the ensuing interaction between policy, organisations and interests that actually determines who does what, when and how.

The problems of implementation emerged as a topic of general interest following the failures of the great social welfare programmes of the Johnson era in the USA. Previously consideration of inputs and intended outputs had rarely extended to the workings of the intervening institutions, and the ways in which these determine efficiency and effectiveness. The easy assumption prevailed that, once a decision had been taken, its execution was a simple and mundane affair that did not merit a great deal of attention.

Even the discipline of public administration had little to say directly on the subject. This prompted Pressman and Wildavsky to claim in 1973 that no previous literature on implementation existed, whereas in fact insights could have been gained from many studies in politics, economics and social administration; and there was a very substantial literature on such topics as the planning and management of change, and organisational development. What was lacking, certainly, was an attempt to analyse a phenomenon characterised and defined as 'implementation'. At best there existed lists of steps in implementation, devoid of any explanatory power, like that by Le Breton (1968):

Receipt of approved plan; obtaining an understanding of the technical components of the plan; interpretation of ramifications of plans; determination of role of implementor; organising implementation staff and assigning responsibility; preparation of an implementation plan; taking action and making necessary commitments; notifying organisation members of the new programme; interpretation of operational plans to subordinates; instruction of subordinates in their control assignments; gathering data on progress of plan; taking corrective action when necessary; report of progress to authorised personnel.

This enumeration merely describes, without enhancing our understanding of the process, and fails to alert us to the difficulties we might encounter on the way. Implementation was apparently not regarded as a major problem.

Over the years a greater wariness has crept into treatments of the subject, and with it a greater depth of analysis. Consider a list of searching questions drawn up more recently (Gunn 1978):

Are there likely to be insuperable physical, political or other external constraints upon the programme? Will sufficient time and adequate resources be available? Will the necessary combinations of resources be available when required? Are there any relatively inflexible stocks of resources likely to be in short supply? Does the policy seem based upon an adequate understanding of the problem to be solved? Is the policy response perhaps over-elaborate, requiring too many links of assumed cause and effect to be forged? How dependent is the programme on getting the co-operation or consent of other agencies and powerful groups – and how many of them are likely to be involved? Are those who must participate in the programme all aware of, and agreed upon, its objectives? Have such aids been employed as are available to identify and sequence the detailed tasks needed to carry out the programme?

The literature on implementation, as well as being more sophisticated, is now also substantial in volume. But to what extent has it influenced practice? While the aim of policy studies is to improve the results achieved from the policy process, and preferably contribute to the training of administrators (Gunn 1980), the actual practitioners of the art and craft of policy implementation, especially civil servants, remain sceptical about the relevance of theorising and question its utility to them. Practical administrators want to take the right decisions in particular, usually complex, situations; they are not interested in implementation in general. They may argue that they already know a great deal about putting policies into practice, because they have been doing it all their working lives: what can an academic approach teach them?

First, academic analysis can help the practical man widen his horizons, and increase his ability to cope with new situations: 'Very often the "practical man" tends to emphasise only one administrative problem or solution which has been important in his own experience, excluding other types of problem' (Hood 1976: 4). One difference in circumstances which is very important in shaping our perceptions of implementation is the level of organisation in which we happen to be located: by focusing on different levels, as the case studies in this book do, academic analysis can help us understand what happens at other levels apart from our own. Secondly, academic analysis can be a more effective way of acquiring understanding, even about the problems we have ourselves encountered: in life, the long time-span between an initial action and the emergence of a clear result handicaps us in learning from experience; and there are always strong psychological pressures to adapt experience to the tacit theories we already hold about the world in preference to modifying the theories. Above all, academic analysis holds out a possibility that we may be able to avoid the costs and pitfalls of learning from experience by choosing in advance methods that suit the requirements of a particular policy and situation. In other words, it holds out the promise that we may be able to select the most appropriate strategy of implementation.

In order to do that with confidence we would need to have an adequate model of the implementation process. The practical man acts on the basis of a mental picture of the process acquired over a number of years, and possibly a very adequate one. However it remains largely unarticulated, unquestioned and untested; and it therefore runs the risk of being incomplete, and possibly in conflict with reality. The academic analyst proceeds in a fundamentally different way, by generalising, deliberately simplifying, and organising the data into significant patterns. In this book we have set out to discover such patterns.

This chapter reviews briefly some of the perspectives which have been adopted by previous writers on implementation, and in so doing illustrates the kinds of difficulty that can arise in implementing policies. It then considers the current environment for implementation, which provides the basis for putting forward a model of the policy process, *the evolutionary model*, which we consider to be particularly suited for coping with the problems of implementation in the harsh world of the 1980s.

Alternative perspectives

Implementation as an inter-organisational process

The classic post-mortem on the failures of the Johnson era, already mentioned, is Pressman and Wildavsky's study (1973) of 'How great expectations in Washington are dashed in Oakland'. Their approach, in other words, was to take a major, real-life case and identify the points where things actually went wrong. They focus on the relations between organisations: implementation frequently involves exchanges between organisations at different levels of government, or between centre and periphery, or between public and private sectors. Central government is frequently not the executant of its own policies, which are carried out by local authorities, public corporations, firms or other agencies. The divisions and distances between such organisations render implementation complicated and uncertain. The difficulties are exacerbated by growth in the scale of government, which causes the interrelationships within government to proliferate. Pressman and Wildavsky show how, even when a policy is relatively straightforward and uncontroversial, and everyone involved is reasonably committed to it, the sheer number of the linkages which have to be made is likely to undermine effective action. Apart from the mathematical improbability that all the linkages will operate favourably, an extensive process of bargaining, negotiation and interpretation is needed in order to bring about the necessary exchanges of information and resources between the numerous organisations involved.

The over-riding characteristic of this process is that it is played out in the defensive mode. Each actor is more concerned about what he might lose than about the prospect of collective gain. And he sees no reason to put a particular issue at the top of his priorities when he has nothing discernible to gain from co-operative behaviour (Bardach 1977: 37).

Inter-organisational relations loom large in a number of the case studies in this book, but especially in Chapter 3 on race relations policy, Chapter 5 on education, Chapter 6 on public expenditure cuts, and Chapter 7 on industrial policy. Can the challenges they set be overcome, and if so how? There is no unanimity of view. Pressman and Wildavsky took a 'top-down' view of such policy-making, but this has been challenged by a 'bottom-up' view. The top-down view rests on two traditional assumptions in public administration: that 'policy' and 'administration' can be neatly separated from each other; and that policies have fairly clear goals. On this view the study of implementation must be an account of the mistakes, delays and deviations that occur as administration translates policy goals into action. In contrast, the bottom-up view denies these two traditional assumptions and sees implementation not so much as conformance with the previously laid-out policy, but as 'the art of the possible' (Barrett and Fudge 1981: 21). On this view it is only right, and inevitable, that the outcomes should reflect the interactions and negotiations between the interests involved. That is even more true when policy-making moves beyond national boundaries, and it ceases to be possible to identify a single hierarchical chain of authority.

This disagreement carries echoes of old and well-rehearsed themes: rational analysis versus disjointed incrementalism, scientific management versus organisational development. However the two views are not only different ways of looking at the same policy, but have emerged partly because different writers have looked at different types of policy, which vary in a number of ways: in scope; in the certainty of their outcome; in the demands they make upon the resources of government; in the degree of coordination they require between various agencies; in the attention they attract; in the controversy they arouse.

Neither view is valid for all types of policy. In designing *strategies* for implementation, therefore, the nature of the particular policy, and the organisational context, must be taken fully into account. Berman (1980) identifies two basic strategies, 'programmed' and 'adaptive', and the types of situation for which each is appropriate. In broad terms, a programmed strategy seeks to prepare carefully, in terms of defining goals, assigning responsibilities, and laying down clear and detailed programmes of the activities necessary to achieve the goals, so that implementation can proceed without any great need for subsequent changes or adjustments. An adaptive strategy on the other hand deliberately leaves the content of the policy flexible, and gives the implementers scope to adapt the policy to varying circumstances, and perhaps in so doing to clarify its goals. Selecting the correct strategy for a particular policy should enable problems of inter-organisational relations to be minimised. In practice, many policies require strategies which combine appropriate elements of the programmed and the adaptive.

Implementation in a bureaucracy
Because analysis of all the complexities of real-life cases was slow to produce a full-blown explanatory theory of implementation, some writers tried a quite different approach. As often happens in the social sciences, they dealt with the problems of complexity by narrowing the focus and examining one selected aspect of the subject with the greater analytical rigour which this approach made possible. Hood (1976) and Dunsire (1978) tried to form an ideal picture of implementation, in fact an 'ideal type' (Weber 1949) derived from the classical theory of bureaucracy as a rational form of human organisation. Whereas 'Pressman and Wildavsky are pathologists', Dunsire claims he is interested in 'the physiology of the normal process'. The assumption was that failure can best be avoided by identifying the conditions under which policy objectives are successfully translated into action.

To achieve simplicity and rigour, Dunsire concentrated for this purpose on the structures and processes within a single organisation. He makes a clear distinction between policy and implementation and devotes little attention to the external environment. By these means, he is able to expose clearly certain administrative *limits* on the capacity of a large organisation in any sector, which therefore place constraints on the ability of governments to implement policies. Furthermore, he is able to show that these limits derive from the essential nature of bureaucracy. For example, even under perfect conditions, all information passing upwards in a bureaucracy is subject to 'uncertainty absorption' and awareness of the context of that information is lost; rules are always subject to non-uniform application because there are always borderline cases; and so on.

Dunsire also excludes policy variables and differences in bureaucratic structure. This deliberate simplification enables him to identify, among other things, a common source of difficulty in implementation. He observers that the 'organising principle' on which implementation proceeds may be in conflict with the structure and functioning of the organisation involved, which represents another 'organising principle'. This is a point to which we refer frequently. Chapter 3 describes how the Home Office, a predominantly 'regulatory' body, found it difficult to cope with a race relations policy requiring promotion and innovation. Chapter 9 describes how existing structures in Whitehall and townhall were adapted to deal with new conditions in the field of food standards, where policy is increasingly made at the supranational level. Chapter 11 is the story of a pioneering exercise in project management. The Polaris Executive was established specifically to carry out a particular decision; consequently, the organising principles of the implementation process and those of the Executive were in close accord.

Of course the exponents of the ideal approach also deal with other aspects of implementation. For example, Dunsire draws a distinction between 'developmental' and 'aggregative' implementation which has parallels to the programmed and adaptive approaches mentioned earlier. In aggregative implementation, the available 'stages' exist before the implementation process starts. They are like the activities of officials in a Ministry, which go on all the time, but are orchestrated in a particular way to carry out a specific policy. In developmental implementation the nature of each succeeding step is uniquely determined by the nature of the preceding step. The process is analogous to organic growth (oak from acorn). In carrying out a given policy both types of implementation may well occur, but in different contexts (Dunsire 1978: ch. 4).

Once we have become aware of the limits on the implementation process, we can try to take steps to avoid them or compensate for them.

In a sense, the result is adaptation, but of a quite different kind from that envisaged by Berman. Instead of 'adaptive generalisation', a divergent and creative process, it would be 'adaptive specialisation', a much more limited exercise to produce a better bureaucracy for the purpose of particular tasks.

Implementation as a political process

A third type of factor highlighted by some writers is the wider and more diffuse political setting within which implementation takes place. Political constraints have been discussed by Hood under the title of 'quasi-administrative limits', and he distinguishes several types of case. Multiple or ambiguous political objectives may 'prevent administrative success'. Or objectives may change, so that success in terms of last year's criteria turns out to be failure in terms of this year's criteria. 'The publicly stated objectives may turn out not to be the real objectives.' Or administrative requirements may be deliberately sacrificed, because 'administrative logic is subordinate to some other type of logic.' He concludes that such political constraints are present in some form in almost all cases: 'In none of the cases which we have studied was an administrative "failure" divorced from political manoeuvring' (Hood 1976: 12, 193).

However, political factors need not always be a hindrance, they can also facilitate implementation. For example, there is often a need for active political support for a policy or programme from groups representing those closely affected (Sabatier and Mazmanian 1979). A government organisation which recognises this fact may itself play an important role in ensuring that support is forthcoming and that appropriate networks of people and contacts are established (Rose 1977). This is the opposite of Hood's quasi-administrative limits. Both involve interaction between administration and the political context; but in the latter situation such interaction is, or should be, welcomed or encouraged by those responsible for administration, as a positive influence.

The cases in this book include contrasted examples of the political factor in implementation. Chapter 3 identifies the lack of sustained political support as a factor which impeded the success of race relations policy. Chapter 5, on the other hand, emphasises the extent to which political support was actively and successfully cultivated by the California State Superintendent of Public Instruction in support of his policies and in support of continuing funding for education.

In the light of these two cases, we might say that political support, or the lack of it, and the degree of prominence or saliency that a policy achieves, has an impact on the manner or *style* of its implementation.

Independently of the choice of strategy, there will be a considerable difference of style between an everyday policy (such as food standards, discussed in Chapter 9) which is uncontroversial and attracts little public attention, and one (like the UK Polaris programme in Chapter 11) which has great priority and very strong ministerial support. The whole way in which the latter is managed will be quite different because the political context is different. Where the objectives of a policy are concealed or perceived as liable to change (to take some of the situations Hood envisages) the style of implementation will be different again, reflecting the difference in the political context.

Implementation across national boundaries

One feature of the literature on policy implementation is the tacit assumption that there is a high *degree of insulation*, which contains the process within national boundaries. Little attention has been paid to the question whether international obligations alter the parameters of the domestic policy process, nor the extent to which such obligations may specifically constrain implementation. The rather separate body of literature on foreign policy analysis has not included implementation among its central preoccupations. Some authors have focused on the ways in which domestic politics and policies may circumscribe external actions, but the impact of external pressures on domestic policies have barely been treated in theoretical terms. Yet it is striking how studies in this field echo the themes already raised in this chapter. Here too inter-organisational processes are crucial, but with the special complication that the organisations involved are often, but not exclusively, national governments. The consequences of bureaucratic behaviour for foreign policy outcomes emerged as a major focus in the 1970s with the attempts to criticise and to refine the conclusions of a pioneering study of the Cuban missile crisis (Allison 1971). There has been a running debate over the importance of political factors in influencing both the foreign policies of states and the results of international negotiation.

A distinctive feature of this book is the discussion in Part II of some of the analytical issues raised by the web of obligations amongst governments to implement agreed policies (Chapter 8), and the three case studies which follow (Chapters 9–11).

The environment for implementation

If, as suggested above, circumstances are crucial in determining the nature of the implementation process, then it is also crucial to diagnose accurately the circumstances which apply in the 1980s, and the types of policy which are likely to characterise such a period. We shall look in turn at four important ways in which the environment has altered, and then proceed to examine the implications of our analysis.

From overload to less government

In the mid-1970s a number of writers (King 1975; Rose 1975) argued that the UK had become harder to govern. The range and respon- sibilities of government had expanded over the previous decades; the environment had become more complex, interactive and unpredict- able; and the capacity of government to deal with problems had therefore declined. It was a pessimistic analysis: even if we tried to make better sense of the environment, we would continue to be out- paced by the rapid rate of change. They concluded that the solution could not lie solely in better management, but in making governments less ambitious: 'Political scientists have traditionally been concerned to improve the performance of government. Perhaps over the next few years they should be concerned more with how the number of tasks that government has come to be expected to perform can be reduced' (King 1975: 296).

Acceptance of such arguments changes the way in which difficulties over implementation are regarded: they may now be interpreted as evidence that it would be preferable for government to withdraw from the field in question. In fact such arguments have been influential on both sides of the Atlantic. Chapter 6 deals with this phenomenon in California. In the UK there have been critical reviews of the ranges of services provided by government and strong pressure to transfer serv- ices to the private sector. However, privatisation does not necessarily reduce, still less remove, the difficulties of implementing policies. First, it alters the set of instruments which are available for implement- ing other policies. Secondly, it may make inter-organisational relations in a given field still more complex and difficult. And last, it is in itself a long-term government policy with a wide field of application which requires to be implemented.

Inter-organisational turbulence

Although the complexity and unpredictability of inter-organisational relations enter into the argument about 'overload' they have also been analysed as a factor in their own right. The basic ideas are expressed by LaPorte (1975):

> We are caught somehow in spreading webs of dependence. These networks become increasingly hard to understand. We act, supposing that the conse- quences of our actions will be acceptable. Yet our actions often prompt reactions unforeseen and unwanted. We seem to have unfamiliar connections to others, connections whose strength and locus change frequently.

The more complex the system of relationships, the greater the dependence of each organisational unit on the co-operation of others, the more the performance of individual organisations depends on that of other organisations. The term 'causal texture of organisational environments' (Emery and Trist 1965) was coined to describe different patterns of interdependence between organisations. As organisational interdependence increases, the 'precarious but predictable pattern of environmental restraints' may be undermined. As larger numbers of diverse organisational units are linked together, individual units become more dependent on the co-operation of other units which hardly perceive their community of interest, and the causal texture becomes 'turbulent':

> The distinction between a disturbed–reactive environment and a turbulent environment is marked by an increase in environmental complexity such that the performance of any one organisation is much more dependent on external events it cannot predict or control than on intra-organisational processes. In turbulent conditions, each organisation can veto the stability of the system as a whole, but none can restore it or manage macro-level change. (Metcalfe 1978: 44)

The development towards inter-organisational turbulence is a long-term one, but there has certainly been a perceptible shift since the early 1970s. By contrast many earlier studies of implementation have started from the assumption that the inter-organisational relations involved are stable and predictable.

Economic restraint

Another feature of recent western life is economic restraint, which has implications for public expenditure. Sustained growth in public expenditure presupposed sustained economic growth, and in the UK 1974–5 marked the end of an era in both respects. Since then there has been a general climate of restraint and substantial cutback in some public expenditure programmes. However the engrained assumptions of growth are difficult to remove. Public sector bodies are used to 'decremental cuts', and are experienced in coping with them. Such cuts are (usually) small, temporary and can be tolerated without removing the possibility of future growth. Increasingly, cuts have become 'quantum cuts', larger in size and more permanent in nature. The strategy evolved by organisations in response to cuts that are presumed to be temporary has been described as 'defending the base' (Glassberg 1978). This involves nothing more serious than gathering in slack, making miscellaneous housekeeping economies, and sacrificing future capital expenditure plans (on the assumption that they were likely to be restored eventually).

The strategy of 'defending the base' is only a rational response to what are likely to be temporary disequilibria. When it becomes impossible to sustain existing policy, a major reappraisal becomes necessary. Since quantum cuts require major shifts of policy, the incremental approach may now be much less useful and valid.

The transnational dimension

It is a cliché to describe the world, and therefore individual states, as having become increasingly interdependent, economically, industrially and militarily. Political systems and policy processes are more and more 'penetrated' by influences from abroad, and the old orthodoxies about the boundaries of the state need re-examination. Nowadays, governments compare their performance in particular fields with that of other governments: in terms of the broad objectives of policy; in terms of the results achieved; and in terms of the methods used. A yearning to emulate the apparent 'success' of others can be a very potent factor in the policy process. The efforts made since about 1960 to reformulate British industrial policy have generated a succession of recommended models drawn from other countries. Often there has been a lack of appreciation of the political, social and economic conditions peculiar to another society, or a lack of knowledge of the actual mechanisms and procedures whereby other governments implement their policies. Such gaps can be cruelly exposed if an attempt is actually made to copy the policies of another government. Comparison, emulation and the use of foreign models have a longer and more extensive history in defence than in other fields: Chapter 11 describes a major case from the 1960s in which the UK government sought to meet its defence needs by using an American model, adapted to British requirements.

A further important feature of the last two decades has been the trend towards bringing more and more areas of activity within the framework of international agreements. The tentacles of international co-operation now spread deep and exceedingly wide, but its impact depends on how far the agreements negotiated are actually put into effect. The attempt to do so gives rise to distinctive problems of implementation, because of the absence of an established legal and political framework. With the great increase in the number and significance of international agreements, such problems have now assumed a much greater relative importance, and are discussed in detail in Chapter 8. However, it would be misleading to imply that the implementation of internationally negotiated norms is always necessarily problematic. In a highly specialised area like food standards, examined in Chapter 9, implementation proceeds smoothly and effectively, despite the extensive external aspects of the policy process.

The European Community presents an extreme, but highly relevant instance because it is specifically in the business of complementing, supplementing and even replacing the individual policies of its member states. Chapter 10, which examines the UK experience in operating Community funds, illustrates all three kinds of intervention, each of which leads to somewhat different results in terms of the character of implementation. Even in this case, however, as Chapter 8 argues, we cannot satisfactorily identify an autonomous and transnational policy process. Community membership alters and renders more complex the way in which British civil servants pursue their tasks.

The implications

The combined impact of these major changes in the environment within the last two decades has significant implications for implementation, which can be described in terms of the four approaches identified earlier in this chapter, and discussed in terms of degree of national insulation, administrative limits, strategy and style.

The degree to which policy implementation in one country can be *insulated* from external influences has been significantly reduced. Community involvement is significant in this context, especially the way it blurs the distinction between policy formulators and policy implementers. Moreover, the compulsion on governments to control the interactions between the national and Community levels makes the management of some areas of policy more awkward politically. While international commitments outside the Community may often be less stringent, they are none the less very significant. This does not suggest a need for a separate model of transnational policy implementation, but emphasises that our model of implementation within the state must be capable of encompassing the transnational dimension.

Secondly, *limits*. In the early 1970s, when the classical theoretical frameworks were constructed for implementation, resources were assumed to be relatively plentiful, so that the quality of management and the degree of foresight were seen as the key factors in ensuring that the necessary resources were available and avoiding bottlenecks. This did not mean that temporary shortages would not occur, but they would be remediable if management was improved and the priorities were properly defined. In an era of economic restraint, when we need to accept scarcity of resources as the normal situation over the medium term, this factor has in itself placed important additional limits on the capability of a public sector body to implement policy. Moreover, as we have noted, it has been difficult for such bodies to learn to cope with the management problems of a different character associated with economic restraint. Cutback and privatisation create novel problems of implementation. (The impact of a major cutback in public services in California is analysed in Chapter 6.) Thus new problems have emerged, posing different challenges and exposing further limitations of bureaucracies.

Thirdly, there are implications for the *strategy* of implementation. The classical theoretical frameworks relied heavily on a static and predictable view of organisational interaction. There was a more or less confident belief that an individual organisation could successfully formulate a 'rational' strategy and put it into effect. That is not possible in a 'disturbed–reactive' or 'turbulent' environment. If the whole constellation of relationships between governments, interest groups and other organisations is in change and flux, the fate of individual organisations increasingly comes to depend upon other organisations and extraneous factors. The probability that the appropriate strategy for implementation will be an adaptive one is considerably greater.

Finally, there is the *style* of implementation. Economic restraint and greater turbulence can be expected to lead, by various routes, to a higher level of politicisation: Chapters 5 and 6 describe such a development in California. The increased importance of international factors is a further influence in the same direction: where any issue has an international dimension, the national government becomes more fully involved, and often the issue is drawn more forcefully to public attention. Thus political factors have become much more important in implementation, and we are more likely to encounter a style of imple- mentation appropriate to a politically salient policy. However there is a finite supply of political support: the fact that a policy requires support for its implementation does not guarantee that such sustenance will be forthcoming when required; and, if not, then implementation will suffer all the more from its absence. Likewise, if *all* policies have priority, then none of them can have any genuine priority.

Perhaps more important therefore as an environmental influence on the style of implementation is a sad change in the terms on which political support is available, as a result of the more circumscribed and pessimistic view about the functions and capacities of governments. The early growth of policy studies, including the study of implementation, was linked with a determinist and progressivist view of the world which was widespread in the early 1970s. It was often assumed, if only implicitly, that sufficient information could be obtained in the early stages of the policy process to allow a policy to be designed in detail. The policy process could be improved by increasing the accuracy of forecasts and by anticipating whatever difficulties could arise in implementation. This made monitoring and evaluation useful extras rather than key components. If policies still tended to have unintended consequences, that was a residual problem rather than an endemic one.

Now, in an era of less government, a much more modest view is taken of our ability to predict and control the world. The implications are nowhere more clearly seen than in the retreat from the idea that policy analysis has a major contribution to make to government (Lindblom and Cohen 1979; Wildavsky 1979). In so far as scope is still seen for government action, the remedies are suitably modest: policies must be open to correction and modification at all stages. As we cannot foresee all the incidental difficulties in advance, and undesirable side-effects cannot be eliminated, we must therefore seek to minimise the latter and overcome the former by constant monitoring of the implementation process. We must take decisions which are 'corrigible' and adopt policies which are 'robust' (Collingridge 1980). This ought to lead eventually to a different style of implementation.

The evolutionary model

In the harsh world of the 1980s the approach to implementation must be flexible and experimental, and pay the fullest attention to the environment. If the outcome of a policy is uncertain, then we must expect to have to adjust its content from time to time; to become as it were more systematically tentative in our approach to policy-making. In short, to regard the policy process as an evolutionary one.

Emphasising flexibility and experiment is not the same as advocating a totally reactive or unplanned approach. Implementation is in the fullest sense 'a policy-action continuum in which an interactive and negotiative process is taking place over time, between those seeking to put policy into effect and those upon whom action depends' (Barrett and Fudge 1981: 25). In particular, the process of implementation must leave scope for innovation and correction. The whole policy cycle can be regarded as a learning process, just as politics itself is regarded as a means of social learning (Deutsch 1966). In the periodic repetitions of that process, a policy is continually clarified or altered or expanded during the various stages, from initial definition of the problem to final evaluation; and implementation is perhaps the most crucial stage, together with monitoring and evaluation. Let us now develop this approach by looking in turn at each stage in the policy cycle.

Problems usually exist unperceived, partially perceived or mis-perceived, and it is difficult to define them clearly at the beginning of the policy process: it is much easier to say what precisely the problem was, with hindsight, *after* it has been solved. The problem to which a policy-maker addresses himself is usually much larger and deeper than he or she realises. However, the only way to get a realistic estimate of a problem is to try to solve what one currently takes it to be.

But a policy is only a tentative solution to a problem. That is all it can be in fact, however convinced its particular advocates might be of its effectiveness, for we cannot be certain of the policy's results in advance. The policy or hypothesis has to be tested against reality, and its effectiveness evaluated and subjected to correction. Furthermore, policies are created by us, and our intention in creating them is finite and specific. But they are open to interpretation by others, and not just by their creators; they have unintended consequences, and they give rise autonomously to new problems. Policy is often a hypothesis bound up in uncertainties.

Implementation is the working-out in practice of the hypothesis. It is the attempt at realising policy, its trial solution. It is more than the mechanical carrying out of policy. The process of implementation is capable of affecting policy or altering the policy process itself. The study of implementation often assumes fully formed, complete policies as the starting-point. Most policies that are to be implemented are in fact unclear, tentative and subject to negotiation, and it is precisely because of their unsettled and unfinished nature that the implementation process has a close and creative interaction with policy. Thus the whole process may be regarded as evolutionary.

The attempt at realisation of policy, or implementation, comes before any critical comparison or evaluation and correction: 'making comes before matching' (Gombrich 1960). In this view the policy cycle is not complete until the process of criticism and evaluation is carried out. Until then we do not know how efficient implementation was, and whether policy has actually been implemented. The cycle is completed by the recognition of a new or redefined problem, and the formulation of a tentative solution to it, a new hypothesis.

This model of the policy process can be formulated as follows:

$$P_1 \rightarrow H_1 \rightarrow I \rightarrow E \rightarrow P_2 \rightarrow$$

where P is the problem, H is the policy (or 'hypothesis'), I represents the implementation stage, and E the evaluation/correction stage. H_2 follows P_2, then I, E, P_3, and so on. The model is evolutionary because, through the process of implementation, the initial policy H_1 takes on a new form H_2, H_2 becomes H_3, and so on. The fact that change takes place does not mean that there is an automatic process of improvement. H_2 is not necessarily superior to H_1, but is a response either to the process of implementation acting on the environment, or to extrinsic changes in the environment. The changes may be smooth and gradual, or they may in some circumstances be sharp and sudden. In either event, no problem is ever so completely solved that P_1 is not followed by P_2. The policy process is a running argument, a chain of linked problems and tentative solutions (Popper 1979).

This model of the implementation process, which we have called *the evolutionary model*, provides the framework for the present book. There are two possible objections to it which may suggest themselves. The first would be that there is nothing novel about the evolutionary model because it is simply a restatement of the classical 'incrementalist' view of the policy process (Lindblom 1959). However, nothing in the model implies that changes in policies are normally, or ought to be, gradual: discontinuous change may be caused either by feedback from within the policy process or by external factors. In fact, it was argued above that an era of quantum cuts may make discontinuous changes more necessary than previously. The evolutionary model could be regarded as an attempt (Etzioni 1968: 283–306; Gunn 1980) to bridge the gap between incrementalist and rationalist views of the policy process. In crude terms, it could be regarded as representing the pursuit of rational ends by incremental means. In fact an evolutionary approach, an adaptive strategy, can be regarded as particularly appropriate to an innovatory policy, for example an innovatory policy in the social field which can amount to 'a new way of perceiving society and the rights and duties of its citizens' (Donnison 1978: 49).

However, if the evolutionary model is not simply incrementalism, an alternative objection would be that the stress on an experimental approach is politically unrealistic, or more specifically is inconsistent with the British constitutional doctrine of ministerial responsibility. If something is an experiment, then there is a possibility of failure. But (in contrast to the USA) if it was done by or in the name of the minister, that failure will be a more or less serious political defeat for him or her. Certainly the term 'experiment' can carry an implication of detachment, even of an absence of political support: Harold Wilson began to describe the Department of Economic Affairs as 'an experiment' only three months before it was abolished. The fact that Chapter 4 portrays an experimental approach operating in the activities of the Manpower Services Commission is not really a counter-example because that is a quango rather than a ministerial department. A more convincing reply would be to point to the long-term changes in attitudes towards government, noted above, which have led to identification of the need for corrigible decisions and robust policies, pointing towards a different approach to policy-making and implementation.

Rather than develop it in detail at a purely theoretical level, we have used the evolutionary approach in analysing and comparing a number of cases from a wide variety of fields, and a broad range of international activity. Reality is always richer than the theoretical models we invent to comprehend it. However, it is important to see whether, and to what extent, these cases were in practice affected by the changes in the environment identified above, and if so whether the results and implications were as predicted. At a theoretical level, we can ask whether implementation did indeed take the form described by the evolutionary model. Or, if not, we can nevertheless ask whether implementation would have been more successful if it had done so. Finally, Chapter 12 will review the evolutionary model in the light of the preceding chapters, and will seek to elucidate both the processes by which policies evolve in the course of implementation and the nature of success in this context, in order to suggest ways of improving implementation. In that way, we shall complete the circle, from theory back to practice.

References

Allison, G.T. 1971, *Essence of decision: explaining the Cuban missile crisis*, Boston, Little, Brown

Bardach, E. 1977, *The implementation game*, Cambridge, Mass., MIT Press

Barrett, S. and Fudge, C. (eds) 1981, *Policy and action: essays on the implementation of public policy*, London, Methuen

Berman, P. 1980, 'Thinking about programmed and adaptive implementation', in Ingram, H.M. and Mann, D.E. (eds), *Why policies succeed or fail*, Sage Yearbooks in Politics and Public Policy, vol. 8, and London

Collingridge, D. 1980, *The social control of technology*, Milton Keynes, The Open University Press

Deutsch, K.W. 1966, *The nerves of government*, New York, The Free Press

Donnison, D.V. 1978, 'Research for policy' in Bulmer, M. (ed.), *Social Policy Research*, London, Macmillan

Dunsire, A. 1978, *Implementation in a bureaucracy: the execution process*, Oxford, Martin Robertson, vol. 1

Dunsire, A. 1980, 'Implementation theory', in *Implementation, evaluation and change*, Course D336, The Open University, The Open University Press, Milton Keynes, pp. 5–55

Emery, F.E. and Trist, E.L. 1965, 'The causal texture of organizational environments' *Human relations*, vol. 18, pp. 21–32

Etzioni, A. 1968, *The active society: a theory of societal and political processes*, New York, The Free Press

Glassberg, A. 1978, 'Organisational responses to municipal budget decreases', *Public administration review*, vol. 38, no. 4, pp. 325–37

Gombrich, E. 1960, *Art and illusion*, London, Phaidon Press

Gunn, L. 1978, 'Why is implementation so difficult?', *Management services in government*, vol. 33, no. 4, pp. 169–76

Gunn, L. 1980, 'Policy and the policy analyst', unpublished paper, PAC Conference, York

Hood, C.C. 1976, *The limits of administration*, Chicester, John Wiley

King, A. 1975, 'Overload: problems of governing in the 1970s', *Political studies*, vol. 23, nos 2–3, pp. 284–96

LaPorte, T.R. (ed.) 1975, *Organised social complexity*, Princeton, N.J., Princeton University Press

Le Breton, P. (ed.) 1968, *Comparative administrative theory*, London, University of Washington Press

Lindblom, C.E. 1959, 'The science of muddling through', *Public administration review*, vol. 19, no. 1, pp. 79–88

Lindblom, C.E. and Cohen, D.K. 1979, *Usable knowledge*, New Haven, Yale University Press

Metcalfe, J.L. 1978, 'Policy making in turbulent environments', in K. Hanf and F.W. Scharpf (eds), *Interorganisational policy making*, Sage, London, pp. 37–55

Popper, K.R. 1979, *Objective knowledge: an evolutionary approach*, Oxford, Oxford University Press (rev. edn.)

Pressman, J.L. and Wildavsky, A. 1973, *Implementation*, Berkeley, University of California Press

Rose, R. 1975, 'Overloaded government: the problem outlined', *European studies newsletter*, vol. 5

Rose, R. 1977, *Managing presidential objectives*, London, Macmillan

Sabatier, P. and Mazmanian, D. 1979, 'The conditions of effective implementation', *Policy analysis*, Fall

Weber, M. 1949, *On the methodology of the social sciences*, Glencoe, Ill., The Free Press

Wildavsky, A. 1979, *The art and craft of policy analysis*, London, Macmillan

PART I

2 Education

How Humberside went comprehensive

Robin Blanche

The Education Act 1944 created both a Ministry of Education (later to become the Department of Education and Science), and a tripartite system of education for children aged 11 and over in England and Wales. The three types of school were intended for children of different abilities, and were called respectively grammar, technical and secondary modern. However, there were relatively few technical schools, and the proportion of grammar school places also varied considerably in different areas.

The powers of the Minister of Education (later to become the Secretary of State) were considerably greater than anything previously available to central government. For example, while the 1944 Act retained the 'local' nature of educational administration, the minister had sole power, under section 13, to change the character of a school; the local education authorities (LEAs) could make proposals, but final approval rested with the minister. This was important, and became increasingly so during the 1960s and 1970s.

In 1965 the Department of Education and Science (DES) invited local authorities, in Circular 10/65, to submit proposals for the reorganisation of secondary education on comprehensive lines, so that all children of a given age would attend the same type of school, irrespective of ability. This had been foreshadowed in the 1964 election manifesto of the Labour Party. The rate of progress towards this objective varied considerably in different areas. There were also local differences of view about the desirable age ranges for schools. As a result of all these factors there was considerable diversity in the secondary education systems existing in England and Wales in the early 1970s, a diversity fostered by a general belief in local autonomy in education. At national level the Labour Party was in favour of general reorganisation, whereas the Conservative Party, while supporting comprehensive schools where appropriate, opposed their introduction both on a compulsory basis and where existing grammar schools were well regarded by the local people.

A new factor then came into operation: the changes in local government areas in 1974. This chapter looks at what was now to become the area of a major new local authority, the county of Humberside. First, it reviews the stage reached there by 1974 in the implementation of the original national policy. Then it examines the implementation of the policy of the new county council (contained in the election manifesto of the majority group) to establish comprehensive education throughout its area. It goes on to describe how the issue of 'banding' arose in the city of Hull and was resolved. Finally, it analyses the nature of the implementation process in this case, in the light of the particular characteristics of education as a field of policy, and in the light of the evolutionary model of implementation advanced in Chapter 1.

Events prior to 1974

The county of Humberside occupies an area of approximately 1350 square miles on both sides of the Humber estuary, in the middle of the east coast of England, with a population at the time of this case study of 849 000. It comprises:

> a) on the north bank, nearly the whole of the former East Riding of Yorkshire plus the former county borough of Hull; b) a relatively small area previously in the West Riding of Yorkshire; c) on the south bank, part of the former administrative county of Lincolnshire (parts of Lindsey), in which the main urban areas are Cleethorpes, Scunthorpe, Barton and Brigg, plus the former county borough of Grimsby.

On 1 April 1974, when the new local authorities took over their functions, the position in Humberside was a complex one. As in the country as a whole, Labour-controlled authorities had been more inclined than Conservative authorities to comply with Circular 10/65. The most populous authority in the area, the county borough of Hull, had been controlled by the Labour Party and had responded quickly: it had already built one comprehensive school before 1965 and others were planned. Intensive consultations were held with all interested parties, and within a year the authority was able to submit proposals for complete reorganisation of all its secondary schools. It suggested a two-tier system, operating from ages 9–13 and from 13 upwards: this was approved by the Secretary of State six months after submission. Implementation of the scheme began in 1969.

Things were not so clear-cut in the rest of East Yorkshire, which had been administered by the East Riding County Council. The Riding had always been dominated by Independents. In 1945 it had had four grammar schools and three senior elementary schools, the remaining 80 per cent of its pupils attending all-age elementary schools. By 1963 all the all-age schools had either been discontinued or converted into secondary schools of various types. However, the East Riding had never been particularly fond of secondary modern schools: at no time did it have more than three. This was at least in part a consequence of the population structure of the county. Being largely rural, the East Riding was very well suited to a system that drew all the children within a given radius into one school, which made for economy in school provision. Thus after 1945 it mainly planned and built 'bilaterals', that is, schools with two streams of ability. The first was opened in 1947, at Withernsea. However, by 1965 it also had two fully comprehensive schools and several more were planned.

Not surprisingly the East Riding welcomed Circular 10/65. As with Hull, it rapidly held consultations and discussions, and within a year had submitted its proposals. Broadly, these involved transfer at the age of 11 from primary to non-selective secondary schools, with age ranges up to either 16 or 18 according to their facilities. Pupils at a school with a range to 16 could, when they reached that age, transfer to a school offering sixth-form facilities.

The Secretary of State gave approval to this scheme. However, the governors of Beverley Grammar School were strongly opposed to its reorganisation on comprehensive lines. Governors of a state school are appointed by the local authority, but in the case of a school originally established by a church or foundation (a 'voluntary aided school'), that church or foundation has the power to appoint a majority of the governors. Beverley Grammar School was a 'voluntary aided' boys' school; its character could not be changed unless the governors agreed to put statutory proposals to the Secretary of State (and they were not prepared to do this), and the governors themselves could not be changed by the county council. This difficulty had not been resolved by 1973, when almost all other areas within the East Riding County Council's jurisdiction had gone over to the comprehensive principle and thus ceased to operate selective tests for entry to secondary education. In short, unless the LEA proposed to the Secretary of State that it ceased to maintain the school, there was nothing that could be done to resolve the problem unless or until the governors could be prevailed upon to change their collective mind.

Selection also still remained at Bridlington, the other main town in the East Riding. But there the matter was at least capable of resolution by the county council. The governors of the boys' grammar school (a state school) did not want to abandon selection, but if necessary they could be replaced; the hold-up in reorganisation was caused by a lack of decision as to the exact form comprehensive education would take in the town.

The area previously in the West Riding effectively meant, in educational terms, the Goole and Snaith areas. Here comprehensive schools on two-tier lines (the Hull system) had been planned by the West Riding, which had responded swiftly to Circular 10/65. The schemes for Goole and Snaith were approved by the Secretary of State before Humberside came into existence; no date for implementation had been set, but that could quickly be rectified.

On the south bank of the river schemes for fully comprehensive secondary schools had also generally been approved prior to 1974. The county borough of Grimsby was ready to put its proposals into full operation, and September 1974 had for some time been fixed as the date for their implementation. As with Goole and Snaith, the incoming county council had merely to put into effect the existing plans. These too were for a two-tier system, although with different ages of transfer: 8 and 12, instead of 9 and 13.

Scunthorpe was an 'excepted district' in the Lincolnshire (parts of Lindsey) area. (Excepted districts were large boroughs within a county which for historical reasons had the right to administer their own education service.) Scunthorpe was already operating a fully comprehensive system, and had been doing so since 1968. At the age of 11 all pupils went to non-selective secondary schools and at 16 transferred to a sixth-form college.

Elsewhere on the south bank, reorganisation was not so far advanced. Like the East Riding, Lindsey was controlled by Independents, but unlike the East Riding it was rather suspicious of new-fangled educational theories. It had never been opposed to comprehensive schools where these seemed not to clash with existing selective schools, and in fact it had two in operation by the beginning of 1968. However, where there were grammar schools which worked well and were popular locally, it was reluctant to alter things; and this situation prevailed at two places: Barton and Brigg. Lindsey's belief in established grammar schools was very strong; the full council had vetoed its Education Committee's proposal to introduce comprehensive education to Barton in 1971.

This was the situation which faced the new Humberside County Council. It was taking over the responsibilities of six authorities, all of which had at least partly introduced at least partly comprehensive systems. However, only two of those systems, at Hull and Scunthorpe, were complete and only two, Hull's and the West Riding's, were exactly similar. Neither the East Riding nor Lindsey was fully comprehensive, and powerful interest groups were seeking to ensure that they did not become so; the educational (and usually though not always the political) Right increasingly saw the grammar schools of

Beverley, Bridlington, Barton and Brigg as representing something if necessary worth saving. Conversely the educational (and usually though not always the political) Left saw them as an undesirable collective obstruction to a necessary educational advance. The battle lines were being drawn up.

Predictably enough the creation of Humberside as an administrative county and an LEA quickened the pace and the intensity of party involvement. The merging of the various LEAs into one meant that it became both easier and more necessary for each side to concentrate its attack: the grammar schools, hitherto dispersed among different authorities, had become Humberside's grammar schools; and the issue had become a party political one, as part of a national trend which included such controversial cases as Enfield, Tameside and Sutton. In large parts of what had become Humberside, party conflict had until now hardly mattered; in the East Riding and Lindsey Independents had dominated, and the Labour Party had never been in a position to dictate policy. With the inclusion of the predominantly Labour areas of Hull and Grimsby, however, there was clearly a good chance that the party would win control at the first election, especially as this would be held midway through the Conservative government's period of office, and thus when it was likely to be at a trough in terms of popularity. It was with this in mind that party policy for that election was decided at a series of meetings held by the different constituency Labour parties in the area during 1972. In the context of education, it was settled that, in accordance with national party policy, a Labour-controlled council would end all selection for secondary education; the party duly fought the election in April 1973 on that basis.

Humberside County Council and its policy

The Labour Party won the election, although with an overall majority of only three, and began at once the process of organising the end of selection within the new county. It had no substantive functions until 1 April 1974, but its planning for the exercise of those functions could begin immediately. Many of the old authorities' members had been elected to the Humberside County Council, and the staff that council now proceeded to appoint were largely those who had served, and of course were still serving, the old authorities. Such a situation was complicated, but had the advantage of providing a high degree of continuity: for example, in September 1973 John Bower, County Education Officer of East Riding, was appointed as Director of Education for Humberside.

It may be useful at this stage to clarify the Humberside County Council's administrative structure. Like most authorities created under the Local Government Act 1972, the council modelled itself along the lines recommended by the Bains Committee, which had reported in 1972 on management structures in local government. Thus it placed great importance on a corporate approach to policy-making. It continued to have committees for different services, and in fact was legally required by the 1972 Act to establish an Education Committee. However, between the committees and the full council came the Policy and Resources Committee, responsible for overseeing the work of the other committees and making recommendations to the council about policy and the overall allocation of resources. Like all committees and sub-committees, the Policy and Resources Committee had a majority of members from the controlling (Labour) group, although the Conservative and Liberal groups, and Independent councillors, were also represented on it.

The Education Committee was very important to the extent that in educational matters its view was almost always accepted, but it could not make final decisions, only recommendations. These had to be accepted by the Policy and Resources Committee and thereafter by the full council, although following usual local authority practice this was normally a formality.

In the matter of reorganisation of secondary education, the new Education Committee quickly decided on the approach it would take: where reorganisation was necessary, this would take place on a geographical basis, different areas being dealt with every year until the process was complete. It appointed a senior officer with the title of Forward Planner and the task of producing a development plan for education in Humberside. It also set up a special sub-committee, and this in turn established consultative bodies in each area. The purpose of these bodies, which were not overtly party political, and were composed of parents, teachers and governors, was to act as a two-way channel of communication between the county council and local people. Their task was to examine all aspects of reorganisation in their area, and to make suggestions and recommendations accordingly. This was seen as helping the council in its objective of implementing reorganisation, and at the same time enabling local people to understand what was being done and why, and to assist in its coming about.

From the outset the Education Committee approached its task in an awareness of the need to reconcile different interests as far as possible. Consultation was not merely a coincidental aspect of the system, or tolerated because it was unavoidable; it was deliberately built into it, and can now be seen to have been a major factor in the eventual success of the policy.

There was never any real possibility that a single system of secondary education, common to the whole of Humberside, could be imposed by the county council. The financial cost alone would have been very high, but at least as important was the potential effect on public opinion. Every area was already at least partly comprehensive, and changing any area to a different system would inevitably have alienated the residents. Humberside faced a big enough credibility problem as it was. The populations of north and south Humberside can be said to be united only by common possession of a large river, a bridge across it, and a common dislike for the people on the other side. In 1974 they lacked the bridge. It was by no means clear to large numbers of them that Humberside needed to have been created at all, at least in that form. If the county council's plans were to have any chance of long-term success, they needed to be sold to the voters.

The Labour group had come to power at a period of unpopularity for the Conservative government, but with a majority of only three. It was always possible that such a majority could disappear at any time, and certain that it could be overturned at the next county council election in 1977. Thus in education, as in other matters, the county council worked to get public opinion on its side. With that, it might be possible to implement its policies within three years; without it, it probably would not.

The implementation of the policy
The basic approach described above, however, was not by itself sufficient for success; given that the Conservative government was in favour of the retention of grammar schools where these were believed to be desirable, it was always likely that, at least in a few places, tougher tactics would also be needed. In Beverley, for instance, the opposition by the governors of the boys' grammar school to the Independent-controlled East Riding was hardly likely to lessen when faced with a Labour-controlled Humberside. In fact, bolstered by what appeared to be the Secretary of State's sympathy for their cause, the governors continued to refuse to join any scheme based on unselected entry to secondary education; and took the war to the enemy's camp. A notice inserted in the local press in June 1973 stated that any parent who wished to exercise 'his lawful right' should ask the LEA to conduct selection tests for entry to the school as laid down in statute, which it had not yet done for the educational year due to start in September.

At this point the LEA was still the East Riding; and in fact it was trying to avoid conducting selection tests. Without tests there could be no selection, and thus entry to the school would become *ipso facto* non-selective. This tactic was, it must be said, both delightfully simple and of doubtful legality. The dispute dragged on throughout the summer. In July the East Riding at last reluctantly administered tests: only 7 of the 55 entrants passed. The governors, faced with a first-year intake so small that it was practically invisible, promptly accused the LEA of 'fixing' the tests by altering the catchment area for the school. Shortly afterwards, at the end of July, the Secretary of State announced that she approved proposals to turn the girls' grammar and secondary modern schools in Beverley into comprehensives, but that she did not approve any change in the character of the boys' grammar school. In September the new educational year began, and the selected seven started their secondary school careers. The school intensified its representations to DES, and a month later the Secretary of State recommended that new selection tests for the school should be held, and that all those who had previously failed should be allowed to sit again. A *Hull Daily Mail* editorial described the boys involved in the dispute as 'unfortunate pawns'.

The Secretary of State made a similar decision about Bridlington: that the boys' grammar school must remain selective. However, the Labour group on Humberside County Council was not too cast down by either of these decisions. A statement in November stressed that the council would press for an early end to all forms of selection in the county. The Conservative group, responding quickly to the challenge, pledged its support to the county's grammar schools, describing them as 'oases of academic excellence and discipline'. This was the first statement of support ever issued officially by the Conservative group. However, there was little the group could actually do, for it could not rely on the support of either the Liberals or the Independents on this issue.

By January 1974 time was running out for the existing LEA; increasingly it was the policies of the incoming Humberside authority which attracted attention. The Beverley Grammar School governors began to hold regular discussions with its leading members and senior officers. These went on notwithstanding the second series of selection tests for the school which were held in January and turned out to be highly significant: none of the boys who took them passed. This is perhaps less surprising than it first appears. Entrance to the tests was not automatic, but by parental choice. Parental love may, if not blind, then at least tend to colour perception: of the 33 boys entered fewer than half had IQs over 100, and several scored in the low 80s. The justification, on both human and educational grounds, for submitting such children to such tests is difficult to understand.

The governors were understandably shaken by the results. The chairman said he was 'shattered' by them, and added that they left the question of the school's future 'wide open'. Within a few weeks, the governors announced that the school would accept a non-selective intake in September. Their statement 'regretfully concluded' that they could no longer maintain the school as a selective grammar school. They blamed what they called the 'combined strength' of the LEA and the government. In fact the latter was suddenly more important than the former: a Labour government had been returned in the general election held at the end of February. The governors knew that they could no longer rely on the support of a sympathetic national government; thus they conceded defeat.

The governors' decision came a fortnight before Humberside County Council took over its functions, and got the new Education Committee off to an easier start than it could have expected. Full reorganisation in Beverley was now straightforward and was completed in September. The LEA had already divided the town into catchment areas. Children were allocated to the school appropriate to their areas, but where the parents so desired, there was scope for a child to attend a different school. It was easy to bring the boys' grammar school into this system.

There were teething problems however. The first non-selective intake contained 22 boys who could not read properly. The LEA made appropriate resources available to the school, but at least as important was the attitude shown by the existing teachers. Such pupils were in educational terms unlike anything most had experienced, and this might have led to an insensitive or uncooperative attitude within the school. In the event, that did not happen. In their first year those boys made an average gain in reading age of 21 months. Once again, Humberside County Council's strategy of carrying with it as far as possible the interest groups involved (in this case, the teaching unions) was shown to pay dividends.

Grimsby had for some time been scheduled for full reorganisation in 1974, and this was implemented accordingly. It was necessary for considerable sums of money to be put into the schools, but this had the beneficial effect that it helped convince people on the south bank that the new county was a reality and treated both sides of the river as of equal importance.

This approach also worked in Goole. The West Riding County Council had planned for reorganisation there, but had not set a date. Humberside County Council decided to put the existing plans into force in September 1974. Despite initial problems of overcrowding at the former boys' grammar school (which were referred to in terms of unusual bitterness by the headmaster at the annual speech day in the following year) reorganisation in Goole took place with general smoothness; the completion of extensions to the school within a year eased the overcrowding and also helped facilitate acceptance of the new authority in the western part of its area.

Humberside County Council now turned its attention to Snaith, Barton and Bridlington. In Snaith, as in Goole, the West Riding's plans were accepted as they stood, and put into effect in September 1975. They could have been implemented a year earlier, but the Education Committee sought as far as possible to avoid reorganising areas in the same vicinity at the same time. It was concerned not to be seen to be attempting too much too soon. It consciously created an impression of a systematic approach to a major task, in the correct belief that people would thereby accept more readily what was being done.

Barton too was reorganised on comprehensive lines in September 1975. Here however the former authority, Lindsey, had not wished to end the selective system. The Barton consultative body was set up in 1974, and within a few months had reported its recommendations to the Education Committee's special sub-committee. As a result the grammar school was combined with the secondary modern school to form one split-site school. DES were not very happy about its size. This was not merely a reflection of the developing view in educational circles at the time that very large schools were undesirable, it was also the result of local pressure from those opposed to reorganisation in any form. Mainly as a result of local representations, DES stipulated that Humberside County Council must ensure that it remained aware of the 'dangers' inherent in schools of too great a size; and must, if it proved necessary in the future, carry out a further reorganisation in Barton. It is worth noting that the upper limit was set by DES at 1500; the school roll has never been more than 1300 and it seems extremely unlikely, given declining secondary school rolls throughout the 1980s, that any further reorganisation will be necessary.

In Bridlington, reorganisation was also achieved in 1975, but only after a number of difficulties had been resolved. One problem had arisen over the selection of boys for secondary schools. Of the 60 or so boys who had taken the tests for entry to Bridlington School in September 1974, only ten had passed. As at Beverley, there were complaints that the LEA had in some way cheated in administering the tests; but, as at Beverley, there was no real evidence to support this. Seven boys who had failed the tests nevertheless presented themselves in full school uniform on the first day of the autumn term; a spokesman for their parents said that they were exercising their rights under section 76 of the 1944 Act, which stipulates that in general children are to be educated in accordance with the wishes of their parents. The boys were not admitted. Ironically they had disqualified themselves for entry: to sit the tests was in no way compulsory, but their results were binding on those who took them, and it was useless thereafter to say (or imply) that they had no validity or relevance. The boys continued to present themselves at the school every Monday for the next few months. In the mean time they received tuition at the home of one of them. The LEA considered prosecuting the parents for the children's non-attendance at school but eventually, having satisfied itself that they were indeed being educated, took no action.

In November the Bridlington consultative body reported. It recommended that the two grammar schools in the town should become co-educational, but it was evenly divided as to whether or not they should merge into one school. The Education Committee decided eventually that they should be merged, for individually they were too small to be viable; but that the merger should be delayed until 1977. It was felt that to make three changes simultaneously (two schools into one, single-sex to co-educational, and selective to non-selective) was altogether too far-reaching. Again there is apparent the conscious awareness of keeping public opinion favourably disposed towards the county council's policies. Thus, when Bridlington was reorganised in 1975, the existing secondary modern school became a comprehensive, and the two grammar schools became single-sex departments of a second comprehensive. The full merger duly took place in 1977.

In fact, the decision to merge the two grammar schools was of doubtful legality, because the Secretary of State had not approved it. In 1973 she had confirmed that the boys' school would remain selective; and thereafter nothing could be done unless the governors of the school decided to change its character and submit proposals to that effect through the LEA to the Secretary of State. To facilitate this, Humberside County Council dismissed and replaced a number of the governors; and the reconstituted body duly approved the change in character. The Conservative group on the county council complained, but really it was inevitable that the Labour group would eventually act as it did. Technically this was not enough in itself, however, for it was still necessary to obtain the Secretary of State's approval, which had not at that stage been given. However, it was always likely to be forthcoming eventually, as there was now a Labour government: the LEA merely anticipated the decision.

Of the previously selective areas, only Brigg was now left. Consultation did not begin until January 1975, and it was not until March 1977 that details of the schemes were announced. Two grammar schools and one secondary modern school would become, in September 1977, two comprehensive schools with a joint sixth form. This scheme, modelled on one at Banbury in Oxfordshire, was not self-evidently an ideal answer, but clearly reflected the county council's desire to achieve a solution within its self-imposed deadline of September 1977.

Hull, and the banding issue

The Brigg scheme meant that the last piece of Humberside's jigsaw had been fitted into place on time. However there was one major issue that had not been foreseen affecting an area in which comprehensive education had already been established before 1974: the Hull division's system of 'banding'. Briefly, this entailed ensuring by a number of means that all senior (from 13 upwards) comprehensive schools had as representative as possible a social and academic mix of pupils; in effect, schools in declining inner city areas were allocated a proportion of middle-class and high ability pupils from outside their normal catchment areas. In the USA similar practices have been the cause of considerable educational and political discussion, largely though not wholly because of racial overtones. In Hull there were no such overtones; the ethnic minorities in the city are very small and relations very harmonious, and in any case race was not a consideration in the allocation of children to schools. Nevertheless, banding became politically problematic for the county council.

A believer in the principle of comprehensive education is also likely to hold that its achievement is particularly necessary in a city like Hull, in which the various areas correspond so obviously to groupings of social classes. But in these circumstances the concept of the 'neighbourhood school' is tinged with irony. Without measures like banding, some schools in Hull would have found it impossible to run a sixth form, with a detrimental effect on both staff and pupil morale in schools in which the pupils were anyway likely to feel either consciously or unconsciously disadvantaged. Equally some schools in middle-class areas would have become neo-grammar schools, except that selection would have been solely on the basis of place of residence. The Labour group on Humberside County Council, pledged to establish a truly comprehensive system throughout the county, therefore continued with the banding system bequeathed to it by the former Hull county borough.

Even with banding, more than 85 per cent of children attended the senior comprehensive school of their parents' choice. However, inasmuch as banding placed a constraint on parental freedom of choice, it was likely to be opposed by those who placed a high value on such freedom. The Conservative group on the county council opposed it on those grounds, and accused the Labour group of engaging in 'immoral social engineering'.

The issue came to a head in February 1976. The new Education Bill, when introduced into Parliament, included a clause specifically forbidding banding. (As the purpose of the Bill was to abolish all forms of selection for entry to state secondary schools, and banding clearly involved selection of a kind, that was hardly surprising.) This caused Humberside what the chairman of the Education Committee called 'considerable consternation'. The county council, together with the local branches of the teaching unions, began at once to make forceful representations to DES that the end of banding in Hull would be disastrous for the city in educational terms. These were listened to, and in April the Secretary of State, conceding that Hull's circumstances were unusual, and made more so by an intensive slum clearance programme, announced that the Bill would be amended, and that Humberside and a small number of authorities elsewhere in the country would be allowed to retain their banding systems.

How the policy process operated

Overall, it can be said that Humberside County Council did a good job in implementing its policy. The fact that the various parts of the new county had different systems of comprehensive education is unimportant. They all conformed to the accepted criteria of 'comprehensive'. The county council had faced and overcome a number of problems: public antagonism towards the concept of 'Humberside', the Labour group's small majority, and (related to that) the short time-scale it had set itself.

The concern to complete reorganisation within three years proved to be justified. In the 1977 election Labour lost control of Humberside to the Conservatives. By then, however, educational developments had moved too far to be reversed. More accurately, they had moved too far to be reversed given a relative lack of enthusiasm for reversal. The county council had consulted interest groups at all stages in the reorganisation, taken note of their views, and as far as possible incorporated them in its policy. The strategy adopted for implementation was adaptive rather than inflexible.

Additionally and importantly, the county council thereby acted upon (rather than merely nodded at, as so many administrations both local and national tend to do) one of liberal democracy's most important values. Only where it felt there was no alternative, as at Bridlington, did it stray from its normal approach. The benefits of that approach, from its own point of view, were obtained over the long as well as the short term. By making effective use of local opinion (and in counties like Humberside there are many local opinions: Grimsby shares little in common with Beverley) the county council was able to win that opinion, or rather the opinion-formers, to its side. Thus it was able to implement its policies quickly, and in such a way that it would be very difficult for an incoming Conservative administration to make wholesale changes. So it proved. The Conservative group in control from 1977 to 1981 made relatively few amendments to the system of comprehensive education in the county, despite what the group's members had said while in opposition in 1974–7. Even Hull's banding system was altered only slightly.

The evolutionary model of the policy process is a valuable analytical tool for understanding what the county council was doing, why it was appropriate to the particular circumstances, and why it resulted in successful implementation. The details of the policy were worked out in a creative process of consultation extending over several years, and in a manner that would be difficult to represent in terms of any simpler and more conventional model. The problem of achieving the objectives of comprehensive education in a large and heterogeneous city like Hull was more complicated than the Labour group had realised; but in this instance a solution lay readily to hand in preserving the banding system introduced by the previous LEA. There was a risk in spacing out reorganisation over the period, in that teething problems in one part of the county might have become known in other parts and prejudiced reorganisation there. In the event however the county council made sufficient resources available to mitigate teething troubles and prevent any adverse reactions of that kind.

It may be that an adaptive strategy is especially well suited to educational policy. Education is an unusually pluralistic world in terms of the number and significance of both statutory bodies and interest groups. It is difficult to think of a single innovation in the last hundred years or so that did not start spontaneously at the periphery as the result of the activities or interactions of such bodies. Certainly this is true of the 'comprehensive movement', if it may be so phrased. Reinforcing this situation is the importance of values, in our political and social cultures generally, and particularly with regard to education. One of these values is that local people, by and large, know best what they want; and thus education has since 1870 been the responsibility of local government. Central government, recognising the variety of local circumstances, has limited its role to the laying down of policy guidelines, backed when necessary by the statutory sanction of Parliament (and of course the provision of much of the money with which to put those guidelines into effect). These principles of variety in education and local autonomy are enshrined in the 1944 Act. They justify the viewpoint adopted in this chapter, in which comprehensive education is treated as a policy of the LEA, irrespective of the changing policies of national government. They account for the fact that Humberside County Council inherited such a confusing variety of systems of secondary education; but equally they provided the framework within which it was able to solve its problems and put its own policy into effect.

3 Race Relations Policy

The role of the Home Office

Jaqi Nixon

This chapter examines the implementation of the policy on equal opportunity for ethnic minorities expressed in the 1975 White Paper, Racial Discrimination (Cmnd 6234), and the Race Relations Act 1976. This policy sought to alter the context and framework within which a variety of instruments could be deployed to ensure equal opportunity. Its success depended on the involvement of both public bodies, at several levels, and a variety of other organisations. Only with their co-operation could it be possible to develop appropriate responses over a sufficiently long period to achieve objectives set out in the Act. Moreover the policy was not only ambitious in itself but it also presupposed cumulative changes in the environment. Implementation would thus require an adaptive process along the lines implied by the evolutionary model of the policy process described in Chapter 1, and many of the details were left to be filled in subsequently.

This chapter concentrates on the role of the Home Office as the department of central government with the lead responsibility for the 1976 Act and its implementation. It covers the period from publication of the 1975 White Paper to the general election of May 1979. First the reasons for, and content of, the policy, and the overall position of the Home Office, are described. Then four specific roles of the Home Office in implementation will be examined in turn in order to show how the basic policy was developed (although in practice there has been some overlap between them): enforcement, co-operation at the national level, the Home Office's relationship to activities at the local level, and taking further initiatives. To a greater or lesser extent, all of these roles depended on the effective communication of the content of the policy to other organisations involved, an aspect which has been discussed elsewhere (Nixon 1980).

Earlier legislation on race relations had been largely ineffective in outlawing discrimination and safeguarding equal opportunity. This was due partly to the limited scope of the policy and partly to a weak machinery for enforcing the law. A major part of the 1976 Act is concerned with the elimination of racial discrimination in employment, education, training, and in the provision of goods, facilities and services. To that extent it represented a strengthening and extension of existing policy rather than a new and unfamiliar policy. An important innovation, however, was the introduction of the concept of indirect discrimination. This prohibits anyone from applying, whether intentionally or not, a condition or requirement which means that

(i) the proportion of a racial group who can comply with it is considerably smaller than the proportion of people not in that racial group who can comply with it;

(ii) that it is to the detriment of the person who cannot comply with it;

(iii) that the condition applied cannot be justified.

The Act also allows for positive action to improve access to facilities for education, training or welfare where this is to the benefit of a minority group which, hitherto, has been disadvantaged in these areas (Nixon and Cohen 1978). The White Paper said that the law against discrimination would need to be supplemented by a more comprehensive strategy for dealing with the related and at least equally important problem of disadvantage. The government view was that, although ethnic minorities share employment, education and social disadvantages with other groups in society, especially in inner city areas, few other groups suffer the accumulated disadvantage experienced by ethnic minorities. The section of the Act which allows positive action to be taken to redress this balance is, however, only permissive. Moreover, it was always likely that these innovatory parts of the policy could prove more difficult to implement on account of their unfamiliarity at both central and local government level (Nixon 1980).

The 1976 Act also established the Commission for Racial Equality (CRE). The CRE's statutory duties are first to work towards the elimination of discrimination; secondly to promote equality of opportunity and good relations between persons of different racial groups; and thirdly to keep under review the working of the Act. The CRE itself has been the subject of considerable and diverse criticism, some of which will be examined below. It is worth noting, however, that the Home Office had to start with existing organisations, the Community Relations Commission and the Race Relations Board, when setting up the CRE. This meant that both the strengths and the weaknesses of the former bodies were likely to persist.

How and why had race relations policy become the responsibility of the Home Office? It had long been responsible both for immigration and for law and order, two subjects which have themselves frequently been linked. This means that the Home Office played a leading role in discussions about the entry of Commonwealth immigrants, and their status and activities within the UK, in the late 1950s and early 1960s. It was, however, only in 1966 that the Home Secretary became the minister responsible for general policy on race relations and for the coordination of government activity in this field – a development reflected in the transfer of the junior minister responsible for integration policies from the Department of Economic Affairs to the Home Office. The effect was that immigration and integration were no longer separate aspects of Commonwealth relations but a 'wholly internal problem, and one of regulation: control at entry and control of the situation resulting from entry' (Rose 1969). Thus the White Paper which preceded the Race Relations Act 1968 dealt with both subjects.

The Urban Programme, developed by the Home Office in 1969, was also explicitly linked both with immigration policy and the problems arising from the concentration of immigrant communities in inner city areas. This has been made clear by Harold Wilson (1974), who was responsible for initiating the programme. Writing about his May Day speech of 1968 he explains:

> I then devoted some serious passages to explaining the facts of immigration, and immigration control, the steps we were taking to prevent evasion and the statistics. I announced new measures we had been working on to deal with the problem of areas where immigration had been at a high rate.

The government decided finally to 'disguise' the focus of the Urban Programme on immigrant areas by referring to them simply as 'urban areas of general social need' (Edwards and Batley 1978).

The location of race relations policy in the Home Office, Roy Jenkins suggested, helped to humanise the negative character of much Home Office work (Jenkins 1971), to the benefit of its image. On the other hand, an independent team which made an exhaustive analysis of events prior to 1968 suggested that responsibility for this subject should be transferred to another government department. They proposed the newly-constituted Department of Health and Social Security, because it has a more obvious social policy orientation than the Home Office, which they argued is largely a regulatory department (Rose 1969). It was later argued, in evidence to the Select Committee on Race Relations and Immigration of the House of Commons, that as the Home Office was not a spending department for a major service, it had very little real presence in the community except in so far it has responsibilities for police forces.

However, both the Central Policy Review Staff, in an unpublished report, and the Select Committee report in 1975 concluded that the

Home Office should continue, despite its somewhat inert posture on race relations since 1965, to have responsibility for government policy. One reason given was that it was closely interrelated with urban deprivation policy, and there was a continued need to coordinate the two. But, as we have noted, the Urban Programme was itself placed in the Home Office precisely because immigration and race relations were already there, and this is a circular argument. Moreover, as the programme was shifted to the Department of the Environment in 1977, where it was allowed to blossom into something much broader and aligned to policy for the inner cities, this particular case for retaining race relations within the Home Office is clearly not very sound. More logically Tom Rees (former director of the Runnymede Trust) argued that it did not matter which department had the major responsibility for race relations, as long as there was one department within central government which 'took the responsibility for prompting and nagging Departments' (HC 1974/5). From this point of view race relations policy was arguably better left within the Home Office, where there was at least a base of experience in dealing with legislation, in understanding related policy issues, and in building up contacts with both official and voluntary agencies which had responsibilities in the field. What is not clear, however, is whether ethnic minorities and the community at large might have been better served if overall responsibility had rested elsewhere in central government, where a positive approach might have developed more readily.

From this brief account of why the Home Office retains responsibility for race relations, it is not altogether difficult to conclude that it does so by default. This is a policy which lies on the edge of the major areas of responsibility of a number of central government departments. In other words, it is an area in 'policy space' which is occupied by many bureaucracies and where none seeks sovereignty (Downs 1967). Although the Home Office's position of dominance has not gone unchallenged, particularly from outside the government, no other department has sought to replace it.

Within the Home Office the responsibility is shared between two divisions: one deals with issues arising in the enforcement of the 1976 Act, and also with the Sex Discrimination Act 1975; the other deals with community relations and the promotion of race relations policy at national and local levels. It is the latter division that is therefore primarily responsible for tasks such as innovation and coordination.

Enforcement
The Home Office has largely delegated to the Race Relations Board initially, and now to the CRE, the task of enforcing anti-discrimination

legislation. The only statutory power invested in the Home Secretary is that of granting the CRE subpoena powers, and authorising it to undertake certain investigations. Otherwise, for the period we are considering, the Home Office ensured that it kept itself informed of developments, partly by way of regular contact with the CRE and partly by assessing both official and press reports of particular cases. These were usually cases which were likely to raise points of principle, and where the law may be interpreted by the courts in a significant way – which may or may not be one that Parliament intended. This distancing of the Home Office from the enforcement procedures can be regarded as justifiable.

However, a component which is essential to an equal opportunity policy (or indeed any other policy) is some system of monitoring. Prior to 1976 the Home Office had failed even to develop contingency plans in the event of the Act including provisions on monitoring. As it was, no clause to this effect was introduced, although the question of effective monitoring and record-keeping was debated during the Standing Committee stage of the Bill (HC 1975/76). Yet the Home Office might have been expected, as the lead department, to have prepared the ground by developing the basic principles of a monitoring system and an effective and acceptable method of carrying them out.

Although the Home Office already required local authorities to keep a record of ethnic origin in order to provide a basis for grant aid under section 11 of the Local Government Act 1966, it seems not to have taken advantage of this experience when more widespread discussions on monitoring got under way. Other bodies, such as the CRE, continued to stress the need for the civil service itself to be seen as an equal opportunity employer. This meant knowing, as a minimum, how many members of ethnic minority groups were employed in the civil service and at what grades. The Select Committee had already made quite clear its view on the role of monitoring: 'Monitoring is a most important element in the implementation of race relations policy and we believe that the almost complete failure to provide any monitoring system greatly contributes to the present lack of confidence.' Subsequently, in 1977, the Civil Service Department commissioned the Tavistock Institute to study the effectiveness of race relations policy within the civil service and to make suggestions for an appropriate system of monitoring (CSD 1978). The report of this study led to lengthy negotiations with the civil service unions, which had opposed earlier attempts to introduce monitoring, and these continued beyond the period under study here. This procedure was certainly justifiable in that support from the unions was essential for the operation of any record-keeping system. Indeed, even before 1976 one major government department had already managed to undertake a rough exercise with the consent of the union concerned. But government's delay in submitting proposals meant that the case for record-keeping was not made. Home Office officials saw the need for a demonstrable policy within the civil service as balanced against problems over political feasibility and political costs.

As a final aspect of enforcement we may turn to the Home Office's shared responsibility, with the Department of Employment, for government contracts. Since 1969 all government contracts had included a standard clause requiring contractors to conform to the provisions of the 1968 Act about discrimination in employment. That a more active role was required to ensure compliance with this clause was noted in the 1975 White Paper: 'The Government cannot passively assume that a formal condition in a contract is all that is required' (Cmnd 6234: para. 54). A later statement by Merlyn Rees as Home Secretary did no more than reiterate what government had already proposed in the White Paper: 'It should be a standard condition of Government contracts that the contractor will provide on request to the Department of Employment such information about its employment policies and practices as the Department may reasonably require' (Home Office 1978). The statement led to further negotiations between the Home Office and the CBI, TUC and CRE to establish procedures. And typically, this meant substantial delay before such a condition could be applied.

Coordination at the national level
The Select Committee had asked:

> Is any effort made by the Home Office to see that in the realm of race relations there is not a great deal of overlapping of effort on the one hand and on the other that areas which should be covered are not covered? Is there any conscious effort by the Home Office to achieve efficient administration? (HC 1974/5: 8)

The Home Office witness referred them to the duties of the Community Relations Commission under section 25 of the 1968 Act, which included the words 'to coordinate on a national basis'. However this duty can hardly have been intended to cover coordination between government departments; in its Annual Report for 1975/6 (p. 15) the Commission itself complained that, through lack of such coordination, departments were 'responding in an inadequate, uneven and somewhat haphazard way'. Other witnesses before the Select Committee, such as Rose of the Runnymede Trust (p. 165), criticised the Home Office for this situation, and for acting merely as a postbox in interdepartmental committees.

The reference to coordination was not retained among the duties of the CRE. The 1975 White Paper acknowledged that 'good relations require a coherent and coordinated policy over a large field involving many Government Departments, local authorities, the existing and future statutory bodies concerned with the subject and . . . many individuals in positions of responsibility or influence' (Cmnd 6234: para. 21). And it proposed the setting up of a Standing Advisory Council under the chairmanship of the Home Secretary 'to advise him on all aspects of the development and implementation of race relations policies.'

Membership of the Advisory Council includes ministers from the relevant government departments (i.e. those dealing with employment, education, housing and social services), the chairman of the CRE, representatives from local authority associations, the CBI and TUC, and members of ethnic minority groups (members from ethnic groups are invited as individuals, not as representatives of a particular association or group). The Advisory Council has met only two or three times a year. From a minister's point of view it may provide a useful opportunity to receive feedback from the field and to discuss the issues and difficulties which those in the community regard as significant. In addition, each department is called upon to submit papers on particular subjects, so that the Home Secretary and his civil servants can be kept informed about their activities. For instance, the first subject to which the Advisory Council addressed itself was racial disadvantage – the least well-understood problem and the most neglected in the legislation. Each department submitted a paper which gave an account of the action it had taken so far, and the difficulties in countering disadvantage. This exercise helped to focus the minds of departments on a particular issue, thereby prompting them to reconsider their own major programmes in terms of ethnic minority needs.

It is unlikely that the Advisory Council is well known amongst ethnic minority groups as a whole, or indeed has much credibility with those who are aware of it. Nevertheless, for outside members, especially those from minority groups, it can be useful as a means of finding out what government departments are doing. It also provides minority members with an opportunity to express their views freely to ministers on issues which they regard as important, and which others may not otherwise raise, such as immigration, or relations with the police. If such issues are taken up and pursued by the Advisory Council, then the Home Office itself has to consider more carefully its own programmes and services and whether these are sufficiently well adjusted to meet the needs of ethnic minorities.

To date the Council has tended to give consideration to issues which require a longer-term perspective. These include recruitment of ethnic minorities into the public services, communication between public services and ethnic minorities, training of ethnic minorities to bring them up to required standards for entry into the public services, and finally the collection of statistics on ethnic minorities, in terms of the purpose for which they are kept and the form which they might take. In this way the Advisory Council is able to demonstrate to its ethnic minority members not only what has already been achieved by government departments, but also in which direction they are intending to move.

Perhaps more important, the existence of the Advisory Council has provided Home Office officials with an easier entrée into other departments at a more informal level, where they can discuss the 'ethnic minority' implications of new measures. It also helps to alert civil servants in the Department of Education and Science, Department of Employment, Department of the Environment and the Department of Health and Social Security to the need to discuss with the Home Office proposed policies which may have an ethnic minority or equal opportunity dimension. That there is greater opportunity for a dialogue of this sort does not mean, of course, that the department concerned can be easily persuaded to take on board the Home Office recommendations, or will necessarily welcome intervention in an area for which another minister has responsibility. Assessing the educational performance of West Indian pupils and establishing possible reasons for their underachievement, for which the Department of Education and Science has responsibility, is a case in point.

A major aspect which requires further consideration is the division of functions between the Home Office and the CRE. Some examples of the CRE's activities (in addition to its enforcement functions) have already been mentioned: representation on the Advisory Council, participation in discussions on the terms of government contracts, pressure for action on monitoring within the civil service. However, the CRE's major concern was the difficult task of building up its own basis of support at the local level in areas with large ethnic minority populations. Not only did this have priority, it shaped the nature of its activities, and made it slow to undertake or promote any coherent activity at the national level.

Relations with the Home Office were largely on an informal day-to-day, issue-by-issue basis. They improved over time, partly because of changes in personnel and partly because of a noticeable improvement, as a result of deliberate effort, in the Home Office's knowledge of events and problems. On a number of policy issues there was a considerable convergence of opinion between the two bodies, and it is not easy to tell whose view had prevailed.

The promotional division within Home Office had day-to-day contact with the CRE. Meetings were regular but not frequent – about 6–7 times a year – though at senior levels informal contact was likely to be neither regular nor frequent. There were a number of reasons why coordination should have been improved and why it had not reached a satisfactory level. In some areas of activity both the Home Office and the CRE were involved, for instance in persuading government departments and local authorities to adjust services to the needs of ethnic minorities. Therefore, to avoid duplication and confusion it was important that each side knew what the other was doing, and preferably sooner rather than later. Yet there were difficulties which, as the Home Office was the first to point out, stemmed largely from the fact that the department was developing a new role for itself in the 'diplomatic, coordinating business', and it was one to which the officials were not really accustomed.

Finally, there were bound to be some tensions and difficulties over such questions as degree of autonomy, staffing and fiscal accountability (Smith and Hague 1971; Hague *et al.* 1975), arising out of the CRE's position as a quango sponsored by the Home Office. As one Home Office official explained:

> They obviously want more independence and on the whole the Home Office goes along with that. On the other hand they are spending public money and since the Home Secretary may have to answer for this public expenditure, the Home Office has to have an interest. Between the restraints and controls and parliamentary accountability on the one hand, and the CRE wanting more independence and more money to do their own thing on the other, there is inevitably a tension. But in the end, with luck, one works out a reasonable relationship.

The outcome of a review by CRE of its self-help scheme is an illustration of the way potential conflict was contained by compromise and by some degree of consensus over fundamental issues. Both sides concurred over the basic principles of the scheme, though there were differences of opinion about how it should develop in the future. It was agreed that extra resources would be made available and that the CRE would have greater autonomy in the allocation of funds. But, as a *quid pro quo*, the CRE would have to improve its own monitoring arrangements for the funded projects.

The local level
One vital part of implementation was the amount of pressure the government could exert on local authorities to promote equality of opportunity at the local level. Perhaps the most important issue here was the status of local community relations councils (CRCs), and

whether they should be placed under local authorities or maintain their independence, the subject of a consultative document at a later stage (CRE 1978). But there were also other aspects of the subject.

As a consequence of evidence submitted to it, the Select Committee had concluded that 'the problems of multi-racial society should be of concern to all the authorities.' It recommended, therefore, that 'to facilitate the funding of local race relations activities a statutory obligation should be placed on local authorities to promote equal rights' (HC 1974/5: para. 38). It then sought to satisfy anticipated local authority demands for more control of CRCs by proposing that local authorities should devise schemes jointly with the regional officers of the new Commission (the CRE), in consultation with the local CRC, for submission to the Home Office for approval. The Select Committee was opposed to community relations officers (CROs) being in the employ of local authorities. This, it argued, would undermine both their independence and their relations with ethnic minorities.

At about the same time, however, Alex Lyon, the newly-appointed Minister of State with responsibility for race relations, was putting forward a very different view. From his tours round the country, visiting local CROs and meeting members of ethnic communities, Lyon became convinced that legislation against discrimination was not sufficient, and that there was a need for more positive measures to counter additional disadvantages experienced by many New Commonwealth immigrant groups. As part of a broader attack on disadvantage, he argued the case for a statutory duty to be placed on county councils and metropolitan districts 'to assess the needs in their area and to claim extra resources from the Government' (*Sunday Times* 1976). It was in this context that Lyon began to consider the role of local CRC staff, and raised the question whether they would not be more effective if they operated within the local authority rather than from outside it. Even as a suggestion this idea was sufficient to create a serious threat to the survival of the whole local CRC machinery. To forestall action on such a proposal the Community Relations Commission stressed in its Annual Report for 1974/5 that 'there is general agreement among members of the Commission and in the field that the autonomy of local councils should be preserved and that community relations officers should not be transferred to the establishment of local authorities.' The Home Secretary was finally persuaded that 'the balance of advantage lies in the new Race Relations Commission taking over the present responsibilities of [the Community Relations Commission] for local community relations work' (HC 1974/5: para. 32).

It was partly because of evidence submitted to the Select Committee that Fred Willey MP introduced a clause at the Committee stage of the

Race Relations Bill (HC 1975/6) to impose a duty on every local authority 'to work towards the elimination of discrimination and to promote equality of opportunity and good relations between persons of different racial groups.' Willey went on to emphasise how important it was to realise that, in race relations, government is dependent upon the support and actions of local authorities. There followed a debate, largely between Willey and Brynmor John, the new Minister of State at the Home Office, on both the nature and the efficacy of a general duty placed on all local authorities. John argued adroitly that, as the clause was only a declaratory provision (i.e. it imposed no sanctions on local authorities which chose to ignore it), 'Disappointment might . . . occur if, when a declaratory provision had been put on the statute book, there appeared to be no remedy for a breach of it. That would engender far more cynicism and disappointment.'

The government was defeated on the amendment and the clause emerged as section 71 of the 1976 Act. Thus, as one official explained, the government's own response to the clause was one of 'hostile neutrality'; and in its first circular to local authorities it simply drew their attention to section 71 without offering further guidelines or advice (Home Office 1977; Nixon 1980).

Nevertheless, both in the Home Office and within the CRE, there was growing talk about the need to concentrate more on the role of local authorities in implementing an equal opportunity policy. Such a discernible shift of emphasis seems to indicate that the government felt that pressures upon it to do more should be eased, and that its role was secondary to that of local authorities. However, the Home Office claimed it could do no more than exhort them to develop appropriate strategies. A survey conducted by the Liberal Party showed that up to the end of 1978 only a few local authorities had responded positively to section 71, either as employers or as providers of services to the public. It was unlikely therefore that, simply by further exhortation, the government would be able to persuade the more recalcitrant ones to develop equal opportunity policies. The only alternative, other than placing a stronger duty on local authorities, which it was clearly opposed to doing, was to influence by way of example; that is, to adopt more positive measures which would make more credible its own commitment to equal opportunity.

The Home Office acknowledged that it also needed to improve its own links with local authorities. However, this was another part of the department's emerging 'diplomatic liaison' role, which was still relatively unfamiliar to its officials. It is also important to recognise that, even after the increases in its responsibilities, the division concerned with community relations had increased its complement by only one principal post, to three in all. Thus the Home Office relied mainly on information supplied by other departments and the CRE to discover what was going on at local authority level. Yet it had first to understand more thoroughly what circumstances obtained within local authorities before it could hope to offer them advice which they would accept.

The Home Office's main experience of closer coordination with local authorities was in the newly-designated inner city partnership areas. Here there was some scope for a Home Office official, assigned to the Officer Steering Group within the partnership structure, to ensure that the interests of ethnic minorities were looked after in programmes developed for the partnership areas, and to assess what impact policies would have on them. The Home Office intimated that it wished to extend to other authorities the coordinating role it had developed in partnership areas. But without a considerable increase in staff and resources, it is difficult to see how this role could ever have been effectively extended. Even so, the opportunity to establish more positive links with local authority personnel could have been better developed from the Home Office's existing responsibility for section 11 funding. Not to have taken advantage of and extended an existing network, built around a source of special funding, suggests perhaps a lack of foresight, or of awareness that effective policy implementation depends upon there being either a moral or a material incentive for the implementers (Hill 1980). If a government department wants to convince local authorities that it is also in their interests to make a positive response to a national policy, then one way surely is to indicate that extra resources are already available.

Apart from selected individuals who are members of the Advisory Council, the main direct contact between Home Office officials and ethnic communities is through local CRCs. The major responsibility for overseeing CRCs rests with the CRE. However, in view of the Home Office's important funding role, both directly to the CRE and indirectly via the CRE to local CRCs, it was considered appropriate to have a limited Home Office presence in the field and establish some contact with CRC workers. Thus one official in the Home Office had the responsibility for developing this liaising role. As a consequence, the Home Office managed to build up an impressive amount of first-hand information about minority perspectives and activities and about the effectiveness of many ethnic minority projects. But it is a little difficult, from a community perspective, to forget that the Home Office has a regulatory role too in respect of immigration. This tends to tarnish what otherwise might have been the beginning of an effective, more extensive coordinating activity. And the fact that such contacts with the field had developed from the legislative division within the Home Office, rather than from the promotional division, may not have helped to dispel community fears. The latter division would also have welcomed more direct contact with ethnic communities as well as with local authorities, though officials thought that some reserve in making additional contacts was necessary simply to avoid adding to the confused array of officials and organisations to which ethnic minorities were already directed.

Initiatives

The most innovatory part of the policy, and the part which offered most scope for new approaches, was that concerned with racial disadvantage, as distinct from discrimination. One approach favoured by some members of the government was 'positive discrimination' to ensure that disadvantaged ethnic minority groups could compete on truly equal terms with other groups. However, though familiar with the concept of positive discrimination in relation to the Urban Programme and other area-based policies (Edwards and Batley 1978), Home Office officials indicated their dislike for the term in the context of race relations. They argued that it gave a misleading impression of wanting to favour one group at the expense of another. Yet official dislike for this approach did not lead the Home Office to suggest any alternative method by which government could try to counter racial disadvantage.

The Advisory Council is the main machinery within the Home Office for introducing changes in race relations policy. As we have seen, the Home Office made use of the Council to coordinate the policies of other central government departments and to bring to the attention of other Council members what government had achieved already. However, the Home Office did not take advantage of the Council as a forum in which new ideas could be brought forward.

In practice the one significant development within the Home Office related to section 11 funding and the responsibility placed on local authorities to promote equal opportunity. Reference has been made already to the reluctance to impose a duty on local authorities and the recognition, rather late in the day, of their significance in implementing the policy. As a result of continuous pressure from local authorities, the CRE and other groups, section 11 came under review and the Home Office published a consultative document in November 1978 prior to the introduction of possible further legislation (Home Office 1978). This exercise represented an important part of the feedback process and the document proposed certain necessary innovations. It reasserted the main position of government, namely that a 'great deal of the disadvantage the minorities suffer is shared with the less well-off members of the indigenous population.' However, it did acknowledge that there was a particular problem of racial disadvantage and, moreover, that the special needs of ethnic minorities were of a 'continuing kind'. This analysis therefore demanded both a longer-term commitment and additional overall expenditure to ensure that their needs were effectively met. The main proposals of the consultative document included, first, the provision of grant aid to any local authority with ethnic minority communities within its area (not simply to those with a 10 per cent 'immigrant' population) which can demonstrate that it has a need for extra staff and facilities. Secondly, grant aid would be given for programmes in housing, social services and education. And finally, there would be no statutory restriction on the purposes for which the grant could be used, thus removing the restriction on grants for the employment of local authority staff. These proposed changes were generally welcomed by both race relations workers and the minority communities themselves, although clearly the final outcome would have depended first, upon how much extra money would have been made available and second, upon whether more local authorities would have been encouraged to take up grant aid of 75 per cent of total expenditure. It is also important to look closely at those parts of the consultative document which could have determined the final shape of section 11. For instance, although recognising the persistence of racial disadvantage, the document went on to explain that section 11 funding is largely 'to test the feasibility of particular arrangements for adapting main programmes and that the period of separate funding . . . would be short-lived.' It was to be regarded, therefore, as pump-priming money to get things moving and, eventually, local authorities would be required to adjust in whatever ways proved 'feasible' the main programmes funded through rate support grant allocation. To give further emphasis to this point, the Home Office made it very clear that approval for section 11 funding would depend upon 'the speed with which the project in question is capable of becoming absorbed into local authority main expenditure programmes.'

The Local Government Grants (Ethnic Groups) Bill, introduced at the beginning of 1979, was subsequently lost with the dissolution of Parliament. Without amendment of section 11, and at a time of great financial stringency, the implementation of section 71 by local authorities is likely to continue to be patchy and in some areas very limited indeed. Thus, a recent commitment to reform the administrative procedures for the payment of grant would appear to be a step in the right direction (Home Office 1982).

Conclusion

It was suggested at the beginning of this chapter that an adaptive strategy was appropriate for race relations policy, given its particular nature. However, Chapter 1 draws attention to the conditions that have to be satisfied if such a strategy is to be successful. The policy has to be made more precise and specific, adapted to particular situations, and negotiated with other organisations whose co-operation is required to a greater or lesser extent. Successful negotiation may well depend critically on the level of continuing political support for the policy. The organisation responsible for implementation must also communicate effectively its interpretation of the policy, to prevent other interpretations being given to it. There must be adequate channels for feedback both about the quantitative results of the policy and about changes in attitudes. These are the data against which the hypothesis represented by the policy is being tested. And there must be adequate evaluation of the data. The responsibility for ensuring implementation lay with the Home Office.

The evidence is that Home Office officials were either not aware of these conditions for successful implementation of the policy or were not in a position to fulfil them. They did not see implementation as a *creative* process, and they did not ensure that the appropriate mechanisms existed. As a result, the evolution of the policy took place only haltingly and to a limited extent.

Certainly, implementation involved a large and confusing network of interdependent organisations of the kind which Chapter 1 identified as increasingly characteristic: the CRE, other government departments, local authorities, CRCs, ethnic organisations. However, this made it all the more necessary that appropriate mechanisms should be constructed. As we have seen, there were important differences of view about the role of local authorities which it took time to resolve. The resource implications of the policy were not fully considered and no extra money was specifically earmarked for implementation at either central or local government level. However, given the nature of the policy, that was not necessarily a fatal obstacle, and in the end (abortive) proposals were made for extending the system of grant aid. More important, no attempt was made to sustain the early political enthusiasm and support which an innovative policy requires if it is going to be successfully implemented. The Home Office would probably also have done better in some respects with a rather larger staff. As for communication, it has been shown elsewhere (Nixon 1980) that the communication of the policy to local authorities and other public bodies was not always clear or supportive of positive action. At central government level, the Home Office certainly made a deliberate effort to develop its relationships with other government departments, both through the Advisory Council and by direct contacts. As other departments began seeking ways of implementing equal opportunity policies, it was able to play a useful part in comparing and contrasting what each was doing and what each had achieved. This was mainly an exercise in spreading 'good practice' on a large scale. But it was largely passive coordination and did not necessarily lead to any impetus for the further development of policy. And where departments proved more obdurate on certain policy issues (for example, on the monitoring of ethnic minorities, both as employees of the civil service and as customers of policies and programmes), it is questionable whether the Home Office was capable of providing the necessary pressure to effect any change.

The Home Affairs Committee of the House of Commons, reporting in 1981 on more recent events, concluded that 'there does not seem to be more than the most perfunctory consultation between the Home Office and other departments concerned with racial disadvantage' (HC 1980/1: xvii). This suggests that what progress had been made by the Home Office towards improved coordination has not been sustained. And, as regards the Home Office adopting a more innovatory role within Whitehall, the report took the view that only by regular coordinating meetings between officials, and by establishing a Cabinet committee, would the Home Office have an opportunity to offer 'vigorous leadership' and 'break with inhibitions about interference with other departments' (p. xviii). Clearly, the analysis of events presented in this chapter and the inquiry undertaken by the Home Affairs Committee indicate agreement on a number of important points. This gives added weight to the view that the Home Office gave too little attention to the implementation of its race relations, or more specifically its 'racial disadvantage' policy.

Finally, we can assess the provision made for feedback and evaluation. It is striking that no systems of monitoring were introduced to measure either the short- or long-term effectiveness of the policy. Feedback of a qualitative kind certainly was provided for in the Advisory Council in the direct contacts established with CRCs and local authorities, and subsequently in the consultative document on amendment of section 11. However, the situation was greatly complicated by the existence of the CRE, by the number and diversity of ethnic organisations, and by the fact that many of the issues involved the responsibilities of other government departments. In view of these complexities it must be very doubtful whether the feedback process operated effectively. Moreover the Home Office was inhibited from developing more links of its own by a wish not to aggravate the complexities, and by the unfamiliarity of its role.

Assessment of the Home Office's role in implementation is complicated by the presence of a quango, the CRE, created in that form by the 1976 Act, and with wide responsibilities. The CRE had a quite specific function of keeping the working of the Act under review. Although the CRE's own performance has not been discussed in detail here, it has already been noted that it was extensively criticised from several sides but especially for ineffectiveness in its promotional role. However the CRE's performance was itself affected by the degree of support and guidance it received from the Home Office. Although a new organisation may have 'powers that enable it to bring together the resources for implementation that were not possessed by any single previous organisation, yet it still has to relate to a world in which other agencies have a great deal of power to influence its success' (Hill 1980: 94). It can be argued that organisations like the CRE are 'creatures of the national state' and as such 'the legitimacy of the national state extends towards them' (Boulding 1973). In other words, if the Home Office itself had been taken more seriously by the public, especially by the ethnic communities, then the CRE might also have achieved greater accept- ance. As it was, there were doubts about the legitimacy of government activity in this field and the CRE had to remain excessively preoccupied with downward 'answerability' (Barker 1982: 20). It had to forestall criticism that it was too far removed from the real problems experienced by both black and white communities at the local level.

These various factors may be regarded as a reflection of the traditions of the Home Office as a regulatory, rather that a 'promotional' or 'operational' department. It is of course always a problem determining what is an acceptable pace of change and views are bound to differ about the Home Office's speed of progress. There seems little doubt that, on the information-absorbing and coordinating front, it had moved relatively swiftly from a rather poor starting-point. In so doing it outpaced sections of the CRE and led the way for a number of other departments which were themselves late-starters. However, in main- taining a noticeably neutral position on the more innovatory parts of the policy (primarily on the scope for positive discrimination) and on the more controversial action required to implement it (a system of monitoring) the Home Office leaves a lingering impression that it was still waiting for someone to fire the starting pistol.

References

Barker, A. (ed.) 1982, *Quangos in Britain: government and the networks of public policy-making*, London, Macmillan

Boulding, K. 1973, in Bursk, E.C. (ed.), *Challenge to leadership: managing in a changing world*, New York, The Free Press

CSO 1978, *Applications of race relations policy in the civil service*, London, HMSO

Cmnd 6234 1975, *Racial discrimination*, London, HMSO

CRE 1978, *The nature and structure of local work for racial equality*, London, CRE

Downs, A. 1967, *Inside bureaucracy*, Boston, Little Brown

Edwards, J. and Batley, R. 1978, *The politics of positive discrimination*, London, Tavistock

HC 1974/5, Select Committee on Race Relations and Immigration, *The organisation of race relations administration*, HC448, London, HMSO

HC 1975/6, Report of debates, Standing Committee A, 16th sitting, cols. 741–794, 24 June 1976, London, HMSO

HC 1980/1, Home Affairs Committee, *Racial disadvantage*, HC424, vol. I, London, HMSO

Hague, D.C., Mackenzie, W.J.M. and Barker, A. (eds) 1975, *Public policy and private interests: the institutions of compromise*, London, Macmillan

Hill, M.J. 1980, *Understanding social policy*, Oxford, Basil Blackwell/ Martin Robertson

Home Office 1977, Joint Circular 103/77, London, Home Office

Home Office 1978, *Proposals for replacing section 11 of the Local Government Act 1966: a consultative document*, London, Home Office

Home Office 1982, *The government reply to the fifth report*, Home Affairs Committee, Session 1980–1, London, HMSO

Jenkins, R. 1971, *Sunday Times*, 17 January

Nixon, J. 1980, 'The importance of communication in the implementation of government policy at local level', *Policy and politics*, vol. 8, no. 2, pp. 127–44

Nixon, J. and Cohen, G. 1978, 'Dimensions of equal opportunity', in Brown, M. and Baldwin, S. (eds), *The year book of social policy in Britain 1977*, London, Routledge & Kegan Paul

Rose, E.G.B. *et. al.* 1969, *Colour and citizenship*, London, Oxford University Press (for Institute of Race Relations)

Smith, B.L.R. and Hague, D.C. (eds) 1971, *The dilemma of accountability in modern government*, London, Macmillan

Sunday Times 1976, 23 May

Wilson, H. 1974, *The Labour government 1964–70*, Harmondsworth, Penguin

4 Employment
The Job Creation Programme
F.F. Ridley

Under the Employment and Training Act 1973 the Secretary of State for Employment has powers to create temporary work for unemployed people. The Manpower Services Commission (MSC), established the following year, commissioned a review of prospects and policies and, on the basis of the Mukherjee Report, recommended a job creation programme. With unemployment reaching the million mark, a figure then embarrassing to the Labour government, and with growing concern about young people, the programme was quickly accepted. The Job Creation Programme (JCP) was introduced in autumn 1975. The uncharacteristic speed with which a new idea was taken up is worth noting. Unlike most reforms, which have relatively long gestation periods, Royal Commissions, party group studies, and an ancestry of publications, there was little to go on apart from the report and brief visits to see the rather different model in Canada. Certainly, there had been no real discussion in the Labour Party, nor 'informed public debate'. For a 'response to crisis' measure with little to build on in past practice, requiring new institutional structures as well, JCP was a remarkable success. Nevertheless, it left the main elements of policy to be worked out in practice and its *ad hoc* character inevitably placed the programme within an untidy and somewhat ambiguous administrative structure.

JCP was launched in October 1975 'to provide worthwhile temporary employment for people who would otherwise be unemployed on projects which seem to provide community benefit.' It was administered by MSC, on behalf of the Secretary of State, through a central unit and ten area offices staffed by civil servants, each area having a non-executive board with ambiguous functions. MSC was essentially a rule-making, funding and auditing organisation; the actual management of job creation projects was in the hands of 'sponsors', essentially local authorities and voluntary bodies, who devised schemes within the rules and presented them for approval.

JCP started as a temporary measure, no doubt because of the difficulty of persuading the Treasury to undertake longer commitments at a time of expenditure cuts, but also because of a political reluctance to admit that unemployment on the 1975 scale was more than a temporary phenomenon. Its original small scale (£30 million for one year) also reflected its experimental character. The sums available were regularly increased, and by the end of 1977 they had reached some £166 million, accounting for 120000 temporary jobs in 13000 projects (this only means, however, that in January 1978 there were 49000 JCP jobs against 1360000 unemployed), and by then the need for more permanent measures had been accepted. New funding stopped at the end of 1977 and the scheme was wound down, to be replaced by a new, larger but more complex model: the 'Special Programmes' of MSC, with emphasis on a range of 'Youth Opportunity' components. Based on some research and planning, embodied in the Holland Report, the new model built on the experience of the old. The breach between the two (symbolised deliberately by the change of name) reflected the appeals of administrative reorganisation which have been a symptom of British governments in recent decades. This study concentrates on JCP because it can be regarded as a complete chapter, even though its policies continue in modified form under another name.

Policy

Let us start with policy – the rules made to flesh out the broad purpose mentioned above and their interpretation, turning later to questions of organisation. Note, however, that policy-making depended partly on the division of responsibility between minister and ministry, MSC with its chairman and central staff, area boards, and local staff. It also depended on which sponsors came forward: the shape of the programme, in the end, had as much to do with who volunteered to implement it as with the guidelines set out by MSC.

All three basic principles (temporary employment, worth while for employees and of benefit to the community) caused problems. Only the temporary employment rule was clearly defined: it was laid down that no job could last more than a year. There were many appeals against this and, as it became clear that the programme as a whole would last more than a year, a change might have been considered. However, the word 'temporary' appears in the parent Act and the one-year limit was said to be a legal interpretation. After a year's work, youngsters were often left unemployed again and the sense of let-down did great harm. In some projects, moreover, the year ended just as the youngster was beginning to acquire skills and this undermined training efforts. The rule had to be justified to sponsors and workers (not unduly impressed by the references to parent law or Treasury determination to limit its commitments) by appeals to principles of equity: the choice was between short jobs for a lot of people or longer employment for fewer people. But some breaches could be made. Projects were allowed to keep on a small number of adults if they could be classed as 'trainers' whose proved ability would benefit another batch of youngsters going through. The principle was adopted by the MSC central unit, presumably by fudging the rules. Similar fudging for youngsters was not obtained, though towards the end of the programme a meeting of local board chairmen did persuade MSC to permit short extensions in the few cases where formal qualifications might be acquired thereby.

Because the programme itself was defined as temporary, there was a tendency to argue at first that projects should be ruled out which required a more permanent life to make sense. This often involved the local board in such discussions as whether there was any point in mowing lawns for pensioners for a year or two or whether shopping for the disabled merely created expectations that would be let down when JCP ended. As the flow of such projects increased, however, sponsors were given a freer hand: in other words, the board either changed its 'philosophy' or became less careful as the case-load grew and the novelty of debating applications wore off.

More serious were cases where the longer survival of institutions would depend on JCP staffing (e.g. a swimming pool, hostel or playground). Community organisations argued that once they got started they would be able to mobilise volunteers or raise money elsewhere: they rarely could, and local authorities worried that JCP funding would establish subsequent claims on them. The original guidelines certainly stated that projects should be of a temporary character and this the board took to imply that one should not create expectations of ongoing aid among sponsors or their clients. Because it was almost impossible to verify claims about the future viability of schemes, policy here was interpreted in a changing and often quite superficial fashion.

The area boards developed shifting philosophies about what sort of work was worth while for participants, though there were guidelines from the centre about projects for juveniles having some training content and/or 'day-release' for further education. For adults, the problem was not too serious in building or environmental projects which involved the sort of work they might be doing anyway, while the production of teaching kits, adult literacy schemes and research provided newly-qualified teachers with quite useful experience. The growing number of community work, play group and youth club schemes were more dubious as they obviously required some mature people as well as youngsters. While sponsors argued that employees would gain useful experience, allowing them to train subsequently as youth workers, one often felt that they were pursuing ill-defined activities unrelated to any future form of employment: for some it was a worthwhile experience, for others it was merely a continuation of a 'counter-culture' way of life.

Greater concern was shown about the work offered to youngsters. Some projects clearly involved job skills related to future employment, e.g. building apprentices, trainee librarians and residential care assistants. In other cases the training element was limited, as was the relationship to future employment. This was partly an unforeseen consequence of the fact that MSC only funded wage costs plus 10 per cent of the wage bill as a contribution to other costs (transport, materials, rent, etc.). Unless sponsors had money of their own, this limited the sort of projects that could be put forward. It was inevitable that many local authority projects should be of the 'parks and gardens' type with relatively small costs. JCP tried to insist that they had an element of training, but on-job training was necessarily limited in scope and there were many complaints about the dead-end nature of unskilled manual work.

A different question arose for many schemes that involved community work. These were popular not only because they were labour-intensive but because they allowed voluntary organisations to come forward with projects expanding the activities which were their own primary concern. This factor, inadequately foreseen by MSC, caused a reinterpretation of the notion of worthwhile work. At the start of JCP the Merseyside chairman made himself unpopular with social work and community organisations by arguing that projects should offer young people 'orthodox' work – manual or clerical – related to their employment prospects; but the board had to tailor its policy to the sponsors who came forward. It then discovered the educational merit of many of their schemes. Work in small groups allowed youngsters to relate to a supervisor (a surprising number of older craftsmen found unsuspected educational talents in the process) and to a work team, and to see a worthwhile end-product to their work; they learnt not only work discipline and social responsibility, but acquired self-confidence, became more articulate, and discovered abilities that would not otherwise have emerged. In other words, such projects proved worth while in teaching life skills and at the same time made youngsters (often with poor educational records and difficult backgrounds) more employable than they would otherwise have been. Local JCP staff, as well as boards, became more favourably disposed as they watched such projects operate and got to know sponsors. Reinterpretation of policy was thus partly the result of new contacts leading to a change in values.

The guidelines came to include the criterion that projects for young people should include some training, but this again was something of an abstract formula. Certain types of work could be assumed to be training in themselves; sometimes the sponsor was asked to provide a short training element separately. Nobody was too clear about what this meant, however, and in the last resort one had to rely on sponsors. The principle that all who wanted should be entitled to – and be encouraged to take – a weekly day off work to attend further education was a little firmer. That, however, met another difficulty: while day-release can be made an obligation on employers, it was impossible to ensure that education authorities provided educational opportunities of the right kind at the right place and at the right time. This aspect of policy might have been looked at differently if JCP had been more of a joint venture between education and employment services.

Of all the principles, community benefit was perhaps the vaguest. The two words required interpreting: what was a benefit? and what was the community? The boards tried to find their own way, and case law was built up with occasional guidelines emerging from central unit. There was an assumption that most things local authorities proposed were, if not beneficial, at least acceptable. Given their composition, however, it is not surprising that boards were suspicious of the value of surveys (e.g. transport, housing), demanding assurance that they would lead to action as well as reports. Here again, board interest tended to wane and confidence in the judgement of local authorities was gradually built up. In the case of university research, Merseyside tried to distinguish between work of immediate benefit (e.g. grassing of derelict land) and more academic studies; but other boards appear to have been more liberal.

Attempts were also made to work out definitions of 'community', the general principle being that either the community at large should benefit or specially deserving categories such as youth, the aged or the disabled. Again, differences of interpretation were possible. Liverpool, perhaps over-sensitive to past religious conflicts, decided against the restoration of churches, though church halls qualified if used by community groups, as did cemeteries if these were an eyesore to passers-by; completion of the Anglican cathedral also slipped through by its definition as a tourist attraction which would help the local economy. Major football grounds were excluded because spectators were not a section of the public deserving special support.

The line was never clear, however. An open-air swimming pool employed a large JCP staff despite the fact that it charged users: the argument hinged on the sponsoring group's non-profitmaking character and its rehabilitation of a derelict site. Although private sports clubs were generally excluded, unless they allowed considerable free use by schoolchildren, an exception was made for clubs attached to factories – less because workers were considered a disadvantaged section of the community than because of the desire to get some private enterprise sponsors in the programme. Much casuistry could go into decision-making: the broad principle proved almost meaningless, and policy emerged from implementation with personal judgements reflecting the views (and backgrounds) of individual decision-makers.

The original intention was that sponsors should include the private sector of industry. A rule, reflecting most but not all board members' views, prohibited any element of profit however. A few large firms could undertake environmental work on land open or visible to the public; a few sponsored community projects totally unrelated to their business. Some argued that certain business-related schemes, not profitable unless funded by JCP, might actually be of community benefit (e.g. the reclamation of materials as a substitute for imports) but nothing came of such ideas because it always proved impossible to disentangle the element of possible gain. Schemes to repaint factory canteens similarly fell by the wayside because it was argued that firms might otherwise do the work themselves. For obvious political reasons, the 'no-profit' rule proved much harder to fudge than some others. The original intention thus became impossible to implement as a result of this secondary guideline.

Another fundamental principle was that jobs created should involve work that would not otherwise be done, otherwise JCP schemes might simply lead to employment substitution (depriving persons elsewhere of work) or become a form of subvention of sponsors (allowing them to use for other purposes funds they would have spent on wages themselves). It sounded simple, but caused a number of problems. It was often hard to verify that a sponsor would not have undertaken the work in question anyway. As JCP funded only labour costs, and building work requires a good deal of additional money for materials and equipment, it could be argued that a sponsor coming forward with a major project might, if left to his own devices, build on a smaller scale employing regular labour. The result sometimes hinged on chance. A local authority project to redecorate Liverpool airport was rejected because the authority had already decided to redecorate, with a committee minute to the effect. The temptation, generally, was to give the benefit of doubt in the voluntary sector in order to expand JCP, but union representatives on the board were uneasy, feeling that their first responsibility was to protect the regularly employed labour force.

Serious difficulties arose in the local government field. Employment of young people, helping hard-pressed staff, provided excellent training opportunities, with some possibility of regular jobs at the end, but it was difficult to argue that the work of the offices would not otherwise get done. A loophole was to invent job descriptions outside normal routine, such as classifying and making accessible old records. Guesses were made by the board about whether the work proposed would be done anyway, though in retrospect it is hard to see why this should have been regarded as an issue at all. One could have focused, instead, on whether the authority would itself have employed additional staff and, if not, allowed the jobs on the grounds that the work would surely be done better with extra hands. In other words, JCP became preoccupied with attempts to interpret the phrase 'work not otherwise done' too literally. The matter was settled, eventually, by a central guideline that local authorities should certify that the work in question would not be done for a couple of years, this statement obviating the need for inconclusive debates on particular cases.

Though never intended at the start, it soon became apparent that no project could proceed in any sector without approval of the relevant union officials because of the pressure they could bring to bear either directly on JCP or on the sponsor. In the case of local authority projects, the unions' criterion was not 'work not otherwise done', but whether the work *should* be done by the authority, i.e. by expanding its own workforce. The National Association of Local Government Officers (NALGO) reacted differently in different places, but tended to see JCP office work schemes as a way of reducing pressure on local government to employ more regular staff. A number of voluntary organisations organised teams of youngsters to redecorate the homes of pensioners and the disabled but the Union of Construction, Allied Trades and Technicians (UCATT) argued that the authorities ought to take responsibility for such work in council housing by expanding the direct labour force. The paradoxical result was that JCP teams were allowed to improve the homes of tenants of private landlords but not council tenants.

It was laid down that JCP should, where possible, employ people under 24 and over 50. It was assumed that the over 50s would have greater difficulty in finding employment than those in the prime of life, though this did not always prove the case, private employers often preferring older craftsmen. More serious problems appeared in promoting the employment of youngsters when voluntary organisations presented projects that required reasonably mature people as community workers, youth leaders, and the like. Attempts were made to persuade them to put forward schemes suitable for the 16–18 age group also. But policy-making of this sort was unrealistic as JCP in Merseyside generally had more money than applications and, unable to ration, its bargaining power was relatively weak. Another limit to policy-making was the attitude of the unions. Although this varied from area to area, unions were generally unwilling to allow projects to employ school-leavers for work that was suitable for their own members. Some trades were more effective in this than others. There was no objection, for example, to youngsters doing unskilled manual work preparing allotments, but they could not help in laying the water pipes. While UCATT officials became very helpful on home-decorating schemes in the private sector, rumblings among members persisted, either because they felt they should be doing the work themselves or because they feared that these youngsters would afterwards swell the ranks of unemployed building workers. NALGO, as we have seen, objected to JCP projects for reasons other than union membership, but the result was the same. These factors help to explain the fairly rapid shift from orthodox forms of work to community work in JCP, and raised the question, what work will workers allow their unemployed children to do? And more seriously, what is 'worthwhile work', i.e. does it have an industrial training element and is it related to future employment?

In practice the local board found itself bound by the principle of local union approval. Perhaps the problem had not been sufficiently considered by the initiators of JCP; perhaps they assumed that, as the TUC is represented on the MSC's board, unions would collaborate, forgetting that power lies in local branches.

One of the conditions of TUC support of the programme, embodied in the rules from the start, was that all projects must pay the union-agreed wage for similar work in normal employment, though this had to be within a maximum JCP wage laid down by the MSC. The notion of 'rate for the job' was sometimes hard to apply because it was not clear what the comparable job would be, especially in community work. A policy was adopted of assimilating youngsters to appropriate local government rates for social workers, youth leaders, labourers, and so on. As a result, they often earned more than they would have done in regular employment, e.g. as shop assistants or office juniors in the private sector. This was doubly difficult where youngsters were doing work they might otherwise be doing as volunteers with their youth clubs. Some of the community projects should probably not have been seen as regular paid jobs at all, not because such work does not deserve full pay when done professionally, but because those concerned were amateurs. Rates of pay that would not be matched by normal employment after the year with JCP, or by the earnings of their peer group, moreover, were not necessarily the best introduction to work. Although TUC approval of JCP depended on the principle, a slip may have been made at the start. It is not clear why JCP came to use relatively high local government rates as a general guide or why certain forms of community activity were defined as if they were identical to work done by 'professionals'; but once the precedent was set, it could not be broken. All that JCP officials could check was that sponsors had entered the appropriate union rate on their applications; and all that the board could ask was whether union approval had been given.

A firm rule limited the funding that sponsors could obtain for costs other than labour to 10 per cent of the wage bill. It reflected government policy that JCP was to create a maximum number of jobs for minimum outlay. As a result, projects either had to be labour-intensive or the sponsor had to have money for other costs. One consequence was a tendency to produce 'parks and gardens' projects involving 'dead-end work' or community work relatively unrelated to normal employment prospects. Another was equally serious: when JCP was launched, it was hoped that local authorities and voluntary organisations would put money aside to seed projects. Conscious of their responsibilities, they tried to; but the more depressed the area, the harder it was to launch worthwhile schemes despite the greater need. The 10 per cent rule caused most upset. Organisations campaigned endlessly for larger contributions to non-wage costs, arguing, for example, that training workshops required equipment and premises. The government was immovable, and no real fudging was possible to ease the rule. Some questions about allowable costs within the 10 per cent rule were asked at the beginning. One could attempt to strike out local authority claims towards apparently fixed overheads; one could argue whether record players for youth clubs or climbing-frames for playgrounds were tools necessary for employment; but this did not prevent an automatic 10 per cent becoming the norm. The point to note is that the rule, an integral part of JCP policy, affected its implementation and distorted the end-product in ways not intended.

From the range of examples above, we see that policies may have unintended effects. We see also that interpretation of policies and gradual rule-making form part of the implementation process. The opening principles of JCP were very general indeed. It was a new programme, launched with neither precedents to guide its implementation nor much detailed planning. Local boards were set up, supposedly to make policy on the ground through discussion of general principles and through individual case approvals. They, too, at the start had little to guide them, no notion, for example, about what sort of projects would come forward and what the issues would be. New offices were set up locally, staffed by people drawn from other branches of MSC and with little experience of the fields of activity involved. In the

British tradition of administrative discretion, formalised (i.e. legally binding) rules were avoided. Principles emerged, some in the form of guidelines from the centre, reacting generally to cases coming forward or problems raised, others simply to local practice and precedent. But they remained internal to the organisation, so that individual decisions still remained discretionary as far as the applicants were concerned.

What is interesting, though it will come as no surprise to students of administration, is how little one could predict from the original statement of principle. In the first place, such general principles always turn out to be ambiguous when it comes to application. They cause problems of interpretation, and interpretation turns out to be a major part of the principle. Secondly, the actual shape of the programme and, indeed, the way that policy itself develops through interpretation depends not just on the policy-makers but on those for whom the policy is made – in this case the sort of sponsors that came forward, and the sort of projects they proposed. It was influenced also by local factors such as trade union attitudes. Area chairmen, boards, managers and staff had some influence, although this diminished when it became obvious, in Merseyside at least, that the board was not in the business of rationing a scarce resource and hence could not set priorities, and because of increasing standardisation through central unit. Organisational factors discussed below also affected policy interpretation and rule-making. So did the fact that London responded to demands for equality of treatment throughout the country and to public criticism of JCP projects by tightening control. In other words, it is almost impossible to disentangle who made applied policy and how.

Organisation

Labour market administration covers a wide range of activities: unemployment insurance, placement services, vocational counselling, training schemes and special measures to relieve unemployment such as the job creation programme. The field shades into the even wider one of employment subsidies and thence to industrial policy. Employment problems are often localised and thus also relate to regional policy. It is not surprising that administrative responsibility for so wide a range of concerns should be divided between different branches and complicated by different systems of decentralisation.

The MSC was entrusted with the task of developing and operating a comprehensive manpower policy. In so far as employment depends on industrial expansion, however, the responsible ministry is the Department of Industry (DoI) rather than the Department of Employment (DE); transition from school to work, vocational counselling and the placement of juveniles in their first jobs fall within the spheres of both

DE and the Department of Education and Science (DES). Training programmes may be seen in the context of DES, DE or DoI. If one is concerned with problems of hard-core unemployment in inner city areas among disadvantaged groups, the Department of the Environment (DoE) has a stake as 'leading' ministry in the field of urban problems. There may be no correct answer to the allocation of functions between ministries, but the issues remains important because the attachment of a programme to one ministry rather than another is likely to lead to different emphases in policy. Because designed to deal with an apparent crisis of unemployment, JCP fell under the DE. Politically, this made money available that other ministries could not have obtained. One might, nevertheless, have thought of juvenile unemployment as part of a longer-term problem of occupying school-leavers, continued education or community service (not obvious MSC functions), just as training might have been thought of as primarily education-oriented (life skills) rather than market-related (work skills).

The same ambiguity is obvious when one looks at the activities funded by JCP. In so far as projects were intended to benefit the community as well as those employed on them, other ministries might have been more competent to judge their value or, more positively, to design projects and provide the necessary back-up for their implementation. One thinks particularly of inner city rehabilitation projects, the concern of the DoE. In Merseyside, JCP became a major funder of new activities in community work, culture (housing the arts, street murals), education (teaching resources, theatre for schools, adult literacy), leisure facilities (country parks, wildfowl reserve) – the list is long and varied. One could ask by what 'authority' JCP was making policy in such fields through approval of projects to create temporary employment. More practically, the question arose whether boards and local staff were qualified to assess such projects. Though most JCP projects were of community benefit, they doubtless cut across the priorities of those properly concerned with social work, youth leadership, promotion of the arts, environmental improvement, and so on.

As the introductory remarks to this section indicate, it is necessary to say something about the wider framework into which JCP fitted. The MSC is a hived-off agency (quango) run by a 'representative board', appointed by the minister after consulting with the TUC and the CBI, local authority associations and vocational education interests. Its staff has retained civil service status, however, and, in general, it operates according to civil service rules: a certain amount of flexibility appears to have been gained, but hiving-off has not made the organisation anything like as free in its procedures as, say, the nationalised industries. Somewhat problematic is the location of policy-making and responsibility for policy. In theory this remains with the ministry, but most policies seem to emerge from studies within the MSC, consultation between the MSC and interest groups, MSC board decisions – all resulting in proposals that go to the minister. To sort out where the initiative lies, and whose ideas and formulation are adopted, can only be done by case studies.

When MSC was established in 1974, the Training Services Agency and the Employment Services Agency were transferred to it from the department. They retained their separate organisational structures, staff, hierarchies and decentralised offices. A third leg of MSC – central unit – was established to deal with special measures to alleviate unemployment, including JCP. The division of functions was roughly the following. The Department of Employment was responsible for (a) general policy; (b) direct administration of unemployment benefits through special local offices (but not supplementary benefits which come under the Department of Health and Social Security); (c) direct administration of certain subsidies to industry such as Temporary Employment and Youth Employment subsidies (through its regional offices); (d) some responsibility for MSC and its special programmes, especially JCP which was carried on the ministry's budget. The MSC ran (a) the Employment Services responsible for job placement, with area offices and local Jobcentres, with the Professional and Executive Register separately organised within this system; (b) the Training Services responsible for MSC training schemes; and (c) Central Unit, responsible for JCP and other programmes.

This, however, only describes the beginnings of the complexity. Industrial Training Boards were responsible for developing training policies and running training programmes within particular industries: these are run by boards representing employers and workers, financed by levies on firms, and are not staffed by civil servants. In so far as MSC training involves courses in colleges of further education, rather than MSC Skillcentres, the local education authorities are involved. Vocational counselling for schools and the placement in work of school-leavers lies with the Careers Service – a local government function. Though careers officers are employed by local education authorities, they are paid out of direct grants from the DoE and come under the general supervision of that department rather than the DES. While there is an obvious logic in linking careers counselling with the Employment and Training Services, there are those who argue that the interests of youth might be better served by placing the emphasis on integrated school and post-school educational planning. Two philosophies are in conflict: education to serve industrial needs versus 'education for life'. From the point of view of clients, the functional division between Careers Service and Jobcentres can confuse youngsters who may use either or both, and who may be hard to plan for as they slip between the two. From the point of view of organising a training element in JCP projects, the marginal situation of local education authorities in relation to MSC administrative structures made it hard to plan coherent opportunities.

The complexity of the system became even greater locally. The Department of Employment had seven regional directors to represent it in regions far larger than any of those used by MSC. Merseyside falls in the north west and the regional director was located in Manchester. In practice, he did not impinge on JCP activities, ministerial supervision being channelled through MSC central unit. The MSC had 18 areas for employment services with 106 districts: an area manager in Liverpool ranked as the senior MSC official locally. The Training Services had ten regions with 40 districts.

For JCP purposes, on the other hand, the country was divided into ten areas. In Merseyside it was roughly that of the Merseyside development area, which coincided neither with other MSC areas nor with local government, its boundaries going beyond the county to include Warrington and Skelmersdale. The Careers Service and further education, moreover, were the responsibility of second-tier local authorities: five districts in Merseyside plus those outside the county. The local JCP office was answerable directly to London, though for some administrative (staffing) matters it was at one time placed under the Employment Services area manager in whose building it was located.

Officials of the Employment and Training Services attended JCP board meetings, but the link between the three was never very clear and there were frequent complaints about the difficulty of obtaining coordination. Indeed, the more one moved from central organisation to local level, the looser seemed to be the connection between services. In that sense, despite apparently extensive administrative decentralisation, the system as a whole could also be described as fragmented and centralised: each function tended to have its separate administrative structure with a chain of command running from London. Of the consequent problems that arose in implementing JCP, attention may be drawn to one in particular: the independent operation of Jobcentres meant that their policies were not integrated with JCP. Insufficient efforts were made to place those most in need of support in projects, and insufficient help was given to sponsors in finding specialist staff necessary for efficient management.

Let us now turn to the organisation of JCP. When JCP was established, much was said about extensive decentralisation, notably about the policy-making roles of local boards. JCP was supposed to be adapted to local needs, harness local initiatives, be run close to the ground, and avoid the bureaucracy of centralisation. It did not turn out quite like that for a number of reasons. The first relates to the constitutional position of MSC itself in relation to government and Parliament. The Employment and Training Act empowers the Secretary of State to make such arrangements as he considers appropriate for the purpose of providing temporary employment and provides for agreements with MSC under which the latter may act on his behalf. This is very different from implementing policies defined by Act of Parliament and vested in the executing agency itself. MSC operated JCP on the minister's behalf according to an agreement setting out principles; and did so on the basis of a special grant from the ministry – itself an item on the ministry's parliamentary vote, quite separate from the grant-in-aid it has for its other functions. An implication of this was that MSC was responsible for ensuring that the conditions attached to the grant were observed and that the programme was operated efficiently. In the circumstances there could be no real delegation of authority to area boards. The chairman of MSC consistently made clear that as Accounting Officer he was responsible to minister and Parliament. *De jure*, therefore, decisions had to be taken at the centre. Moreover, while *de facto* authority in individual cases might be given to area boards (their decisions ratified in London as a matter of course so long as they were within the guidelines laid down by central unit), London retained the last word because it was the chairman's responsibility that would be engaged in the event of public criticism. A second implication was that the minister remained responsible to Parliament for all decisions in JCP because, constitutionally, MSC was operating under an agreement with the minister, and not in accordance with duties specifically entrusted to it by Parliament. Parliamentary questions could be asked in individual cases, and there were a fair number of these, generally answered on the basis of briefs prepared by MSC central unit (consulting local officials but, significantly, not the local chairmen whose boards had taken the decisions). Though ministerial intervention as a result of parliamentary questions seems to have been very rare (in Merseyside he only stopped one project despite continuing support of the area board), the fact that it could occur further underlined the impossibility of real decentralisation.

Ten area boards (called Action Committees) were appointed to oversee JCP. They were originally to be tripartite, representing local authorities, unions and employers. An academic was added to the list in some areas and voluntary organisation representatives were added later. In addition to an academic chairman (probably because seen as independent), Merseyside eventually had two local authority, two union and two employer representatives, one from a voluntary organisation, and the editor of the local newspaper. Apart from the union representatives named by the regional TUC, other names tended to 'emerge' in the usual informal manner. The relatively small size of the boards led to some complaints from excluded local authorities and interests not represented such as education. There were also criticisms of the absence of women, picked up by a parliamentary committee, which linked this to the relatively low proportion of jobs created for women. Such complaints were based on a misunderstanding of the power of boards: because there was generally more money than suitable projects (in Merseyside at least), the question of allocating resources between areas or types of occupation rarely arose – to that extent, it did not matter much what interests were represented or what the 'balance of power' on the board was.

Arguably, however, composition may sometimes have affected what projects were regarded as suitable. At the start, for example, employer and union representatives showed some anti-intellectual inclinations in their rejection of survey work and certain types of community service, but this did not last when they learnt more about such activities and/or realised that there was little scope to pick and choose. Employers in certain unrepresented sectors felt that representation might have given them a veto over projects they considered competitive, notably the building industry.

The representation of unions was a more serious matter. When UCATT (building workers) came onto the boards, its attitude to JCP changed markedly for the better. This was clearly the result of the involvement of its regional officer in the programme and the growing sympathy he felt and transmitted to his officials. NALGO was not represented, and this may have explained some failures to develop projects within local government offices. Although approval of the relevant unions became a requirement before the board would even consider an application, more direct involvement on their part would have been desirable; and given the limitations of size in the committees, thought might have been given to other ways of associating them. While union representatives on the boards looked at projects to ensure that they did not conflict with their members' interests and proper rates were paid, the main contribution of the boards tended to be on a personal basis. Their representative character could nevertheless be useful as members gave access to networks of expertise in the early days before JCP officials established their own contacts. Above all, the boards served to legitimate the programme. This required the appointment of very senior people, however, who already had too many commitments. More project visits (essential to get a 'feel' of how the programme was working and an invaluable form of public relations) could probably have been obtained from a less distinguished cast at some sacrifice of symbolic value.

The real function of the boards and their chairmen was another matter. They were originally promised wide responsibility to promote JCP, to make plans for their areas, and to approve or reject individual projects. The first of these functions, essentially public relations, did not involve many problems as no question of powers arose. Making plans did not mean very much either because JCP had to react to what sponsors offered, so that there was little point in planning the allocation of resources between areas, age groups and types of activity, for example. As guidelines from the centre grew more numerous, the scope for other decisions of principle tended to diminish. There was thus less and less discussion of general criteria of acceptability (e.g. on a permissible element of private profit; the circumstances in which someone might be employed for more than a year; training requirements; the ratio of adult supervisors to juveniles). In the end, it was a case of making judgements on marginal applications, usually where the community benefit or the worthwhile quality of the work itself seemed doubtful. In this, boards were very rarely over-ridden.

The role of the chairmen was more difficult to define. When chairmen were first appointed, area managers were as new to the work as they, and office structures did not yet exist. While most chairmen had a good knowledge of their area as well as extensive local contacts, the JCP officials came to the programmes with a more specialised background in the Employment Service, but with fewer contacts. For a short time, therefore, the chairmen tended to make the running, not only in promoting JCP but in discussion with potential sponsors. It soon became clear, however, that neither they nor the boards could easily exercise anything like an executive function.

The chairmen, apart from being unpaid, had no place in the official hierarchy, indeed no office to work from within JCP. Lines of communication flowed from centre to area manager and from sponsors to the JCP office. There was really no way in which a chairman (much less a board member) could follow the day-to-day business and thus keep a finger on the pulse of what was going on. Even for non-executive chairmen and boards this is bound to cause serious problems. Some found time to visit sponsors or inspect projects, but this was patchy and proved even more so as the number of projects increased (not to mention the large area over which they spread). They lacked the direct knowledge of how the programme was working which would have come from some involvement in management. Some chairmen did more, but their involvement was not built into the system and, as the organisation grew and procedures became routinised, it became increasingly difficult. There was a price to pay, moreover, as sponsors contacting chairmen became confused between formal and informal channels of communication, and as local staff came to resent what they saw as outsider intrusion into their preserve. Boards had no authority over staff and could therefore not control the way staff handled business. Just as serious, they had little contact with London, except for occasional national meetings of local chairmen with MSC. Board members sometimes felt, therefore, that they were talking in a vacuum, isolated from the real world of administration, and that their views did not always get through to London. Information flow the other way was equally difficult, as guidelines, queries on particular applications and general information about developments in central unit were addressed to the area manager.

All this raises the question whether non-executive boards with non-executive chairmen can ever be effective. Even if they have some powers of decision-making, their discussion is bound to remain abstract, lacking information as well as direct experience, and their authority is bound to be weak if they cannot give directions to staff on how policies are to be implemented (i.e. how the office is to be run). Having said that, the chairmen and the boards doubtless played a useful role apart from legitimising the programme. They introduced expertise, local knowledge and contacts. In the early days they also had some impact on the way JCP developed, but after a while the scope for such pioneering diminished.

As more and more ground rules were laid down, however, it was still useful to have the occasional non-official assessment of projects – boards acting as 'juries' to make commonsense judgements where rules were of little help. (Officials, for their part, sometimes preferred to shelter behind their boards in dealing with rejected applicants.)

Although area managers were told informally to 'work to their boards', the notice remained ambiguous: JCP staff were career civil servants operating in a hierarchy running to London; chairmen and boards were clearly outsiders. A distinction might have been made between policy-setting and decision-making by boards (within the central guidelines) on the one hand, and responsibility of the area manager for implementation (deployment of staff and the organisation of office routines) on the other. Such a distinction is quite unrealistic, however. The way JCP was promoted, who advised sponsors and how, and whether they got sympathetic treatment, for example, were as closely related to policy as criteria for the approval of projects. Officials, after all, were the gatekeepers who could choke off applicants or advise them in ways that the applicants believed to be authoritative. The manner in which projects were monitored once under way also had a considerable impact, as did the balance struck in the use of limited personnel between advice to sponsors (of which there was never enough) and audit. In these and many other aspects office management was not just a technical matter but a fundamental influence on the way the programme developed. Control over administration, in other words, is just as important as control over policy, and local boards had almost no influence on this score.

One may also ask whether meaningful decentralisation of decision-making is possible without a reversal of administrative hierarchies. The presence of a strong local official, as senior as any at the centre, might have made a difference, giving something more like administrative, if not 'political', decentralisation. Local staff, however, were drawn from officials in the Employment Services, most having worked before in Jobcentres. They were headed by a Senior Executive Officer, assisted by a few HEOs and EOs (some promoted from clerical grade). There was no member of the (old) administrative class, i.e. no graduate entrant to the civil service. Status apart, therefore, a point can be made about their limited background (e.g. no experience of youth and community work or further education). They found some difficulty in adjusting to the different values of those with whom they now came into contact – at first hostile, although a number swung the other way and accepted almost uncritically what sponsors told them about the worth of the work they were doing. A few graduates might have been useful, partly because they are likely to have a broader – if more superficial – knowledge, partly because they might have been expected to assimilate more easily (and then judge more critically) the problems of the many diverse fields in which JCP operated. A spell as area manager, moreover, would have been valuable experience for a young administrator from London which is so often accused of being out of touch with provincial life.

Effective local impact could also be a matter of the area manager's status. There was something paradoxical in the fact that generally lower ranking, and certainly less widely experienced, officials were left to pioneer the programme on the ground, to negotiate with sponsors, argue with unions, persuade local government, and so on, while senior and perhaps more sophisticated (certainly wider-experienced) officials at the centre spent their time checking on paper what local officials did and making policy guidelines in a reactive fashion on the basis of this paperwork. JCP, because new, would have offered an excellent opportunity to reverse this trend and it was a pity that it was missed.

Though local officials did remarkably well in getting JCP off the ground and showed increasing initiative, another criticism was their limited expertise. Their small number (reflecting MSC determination to keep administrative costs down to a few per cent of the budget) made it hard to bring in officials with other backgrounds, as did career considerations. In assessing projects, a wider range of experience would nevertheless have been desirable. Moreover, if JCP was to do more than vet applications and monitor operations, this wider background becomes doubly important. It was difficult enough for the JCP office to play a positive role in coordinating training and further education facilities, for example, given the structural factors mentioned earlier. The presence of some staff with experience in these fields (drawn from the Training and Careers Services, education, local government) might have helped in establishing closer links and thus a better framework within which projects could operate. JCP should have been established at the start as an inter-service agency, even an inter-ministry agency, rather than just another division of MSC. But that would have raised other problems.

If staffing tended to reinforce vertical fragmentation of services, another problem was the weakness of technical capacities. This was particularly noticeable in the assessment of building projects. Moreover, some voluntary organisation sponsors, planning to rehabilitate a derelict building as a community centre for example, needed expert advice about labour and material requirements, and the like. The Merseyside office was allowed to employ one specialist adviser, an unemployed former manager of a building firm, on a temporary basis, and he proved a valuable asset. Youth leaders, community workers and teachers would have been equally useful, helping to 'educate' other officials by interacting with them. Indeed, the whole programme would have been immensely strengthened by a unit of specialists who could have produced project packages and prepared the ground for potential sponsors. They could have been recruited on a temporary basis from unemployed people with relevant qualifications. The civil service unions prevented any form of job creation of this sort within the administration: an unforeseen paradox. All these factors on the side of implementation affected the shape of the programme.

While MSC provided a framework for job creation (guidelines and funding), the real implementation of the programme lay with the sponsors. In principle, there was much to be said for this idea – it reduced bureaucracy, keeping JCP offices small and administrative overheads down; it harnessed the energies of others more experienced in running projects than MSC officials; it allowed for flexibility as the shape of the programme could react to local conditions and sponsors' initiatives. In all this, it reflected a tradition of government 'at arm's length', with central government intervention at two removes (MSC and sponsors). Yet in this lay a weakness. It depended on the assumption that local authorities and voluntary organisations would come forward with sufficient suitable schemes to meet the needs of JCP. Whether this is a reliable way of mounting a programme is another matter. One may end with its character being shaped by the interests of sponsors rather than the interests of the unemployed clientele for whom it is intended.

In practice, there were difficulties in attracting sponsors. Local authorities were sometimes short of money for additional costs, particularly in areas where JCP was most needed; despite commitment by councils and chief officers, the middle-level staff who would have to operate the schemes were sometimes reluctant to add to their own work load; sometimes they had union problems. Voluntary organisations, for their part, had a natural inclination to offer projécts that would promote their own goals rather than start from the problems of the unemployed. The distribution of jobs, therefore, turned out rather different in terms of location, age and types of work from those a policy-maker might have laid down if he had started with an assessment of categories in need. As direct management of projects by MSC is hard to visualise administratively (and would certainly break down under the weight of its own bureaucracy if tried), the sponsor system was inevitable. As MSC could not direct local authorities or voluntary organisations, the only way it might have shaped the programme more effectively would have been by offering greater inducement to sponsors proposing more desirable projects (e.g. their entire costs), and this was not feasible financially.

The sponsorship principle caused other problems. Many voluntary bodies were clearly incapable of managing a labour force, with consequent loss of morale among employees; often they had equal difficulty in keeping financial records. This was most marked with small organisations and *ad hoc* groups. Having encouraged sponsors to come forward, JCP failed to provide them with the expert help they required. A central pool of specialists to advise such organisations, even to serve within them, would have done much to improve operations. The determination of MSC to keep its own bureaucracy small was a double-edged weapon in this respect. The result was that sponsors tended to be left to their own devices once a project was approved. Many got into difficulties, some through incompetence, others through dishonesty. As awareness of this grew, JCP staff resources were shifted more and more towards monitoring, though given their limited expertise this tended to concentrate on auditing accounts and time-sheets, rather than attempts to assess output in terms of either community benefit or benefit to youngsters employed. It was sad that well-meaning groups, encouraged by MSC to sponsor projects, subsequently found themselves in trouble because they were unable to cope with the administrative load. Having willed the end, JCP should have done more to provide the means. This was particularly true in certain areas – the now notorious Toxteth, for example. It was extremely hard to find reliable sponsors there: the professionally competent do not live there and coloured youngsters would not work for them if they did. To develop self-help in such areas one must perhaps write off some incompetence, even a little dishonesty, without too much fuss, as part of the learning process. As this was not acceptable for political as well as administrative reasons, JCP was bound to be weaker in areas where it was most needed.

Conclusion
This account has not been concerned with the economic or social merits of JCP, but with its implementation. The story illustrates some of the themes of this book. The first is that policy-makers go astray if they seek remedies to a problem facing government – in this case juvenile unemployment – without considering methods of implementation at the same time. This is so obvious that one assumes every policy-maker knows it, yet JCP illustrates the temptation to regard machinery questions as secondary. Of course, the response-to-crisis origins of the programme explain – and justify – its speedy adoption. It cannot, however, entirely justify the way in which the planners based their programme on demand-side considerations (the needs of youth) without an equal assessment of the supply-side of the equation (the delivery potential). Much of the programme's delivery system lay outside central government/MSC control, in local government and the voluntary sector. The policy-makers seem to have assumed – a strange optimism – that sponsors would come forward in sufficient numbers and that they would come forward with projects in line with the policy-makers' aims rather than their own. The policy of JCP was shaped in practice by the sponsors who came forward to implement the programme almost as much as by MSC and, to some extent, though not too seriously perhaps, the original intentions were distorted in the process (the balance of age groups, for example, and the emphasis on community service rather than work more closely related to future employment). This is a particular problem when governments do not want to take on the implementation of policies themselves. We see much the same thing in regional development policies based on incentives to employers which there is no guarantee they will take up. The obvious lesson is that if one wills the end, one must also will the

means. JCP relied on the goodwill of sponsors – an element of uncertainty from the start. Despite that, it must be said that greater energies were harnessed than one might have expected and that, in face of a multitude of difficulties, sponsors did surprisingly well.

A similar point can be made about the extent to which the fulfilment of the original hopes was affected by existing administrative structures. While new offices were set up for JCP, much depended on the collaboration of other public services, and it seems clear, in hindsight at least, that the division of responsibility described in this chapter made aspects of the original policy somewhat unrealistic. The absence of a Ministry for Youth and the splitting of responsibility for education and employment made it impossible to deliver (in the short run at least) a package combining work projects and training places – just as that division still bedevils the debate about 'education for work' and 'education for life'. Even within MSC, the functional separation of placement services from JCP meant that the programme was not always able to provide opportunities for those most in need and for whom it was presumably intended. While one cannot reorganise the entire administrative system for each new policy and, indeed, different policies may require contradictory administrative structures, this is another example of the need to consider delivery systems as an integral part of policy-making.

The lessons of this chapter go further. Even if policy-makers design an appropriate delivery system, it is unlikely that this will exhaust the impact of implementation on policy. Implementation affects the evolution of policy as well as its feasibility. This is the more likely when, as in the case of JCP, the policy-makers do not control the entire delivery system. We are back at the sponsors and their values, sometimes hidden, sometimes openly stated. JCP is an illustration of policy adjusted in the process of implementation by compromise and exchange between organisations. The programme had to accommodate itself to other elements in the system.

Chapter 1 suggests that the appropriate approach to implementation is one that takes full account of complexity, change and unpredictability; it should leave margins for creativity, new ideas and contributions from outside. The skeletal policy outlines at the start of JCP and original statements by MSC about the positive role of area boards appeared to leave room for creative flexibility. We have seen, however, that decentralisation had strict limits within the administrative system, partly because of the political responsibility of the minister to Parliament, partly because of the hierarchic organisation of MSC staff. The result was an inbuilt tendency to formalisation through centralised rules which throttled some of the spirit that was apparently intended.

The original outlines of policy were very general. This, again, was partly a result of the speed with which the programme was launched, and the absence of the sort of debate that usually precedes new policies; but it also reflected a British preference for discretionary administration compared to the administrative law countries of continental Europe. Policy was therefore given substance through practice. Practice was often translated into guidelines, but to an extent policy remained practice. While this allows the system to adapt, it may leave clients at a disadvantage because they cannot refer to published rules. The point to be made here, however, is also emphasised in the final chapter – the extent to which implementation shapes policy through the values of those who implement it. We have referred to the attitude of board members and local JCP officials to what, for example, constituted worthwhile work and community benefit. We have also noted, however, the extent to which these values changed over time as a result of their interaction with the environment, so that a permanent learning process affected policy interpretation.

Policies are, in fact, bound to be general in character and tend to be incomprehensible except by reference to practice. Even if translated into rules, there is a limit to how specific they can be. One can try to codify for most eventualities, of course, but we know from the work of our law courts the extent to which even quite detailed legislation depends on judicial interpretation of phrases and their application to individual cases. A major purpose of this chapter has been to show how very little real meaning phrases like 'community benefit' and 'worthwhile work' have in themselves. Even phrases like 'temporary employment', 'training' and 'profit' are ambiguous. A large part of policy is made in the decision on cases and turns out to be case law, even if codification in the form of guidelines follows. That is obvious. So is the fact that the interpretation of aims, the fleshing-out of policy statements, is not an activity carried out by philosophers divorced from their environment. Those who make policy through implementation not only have values of their own, as noted above; they are also part of the administrative system, so that the machinery of implementation also has a decisive influence on the evolution of policy. To take only the most glaring example, the original aims of JCP would have been translated quite differently if that programme had been implemented within the framework of the Department of Education.

The point that policies often have ambiguous objectives and that stated objectives may not be the real (or sole real) ones was made in Chapter 1. This, too, is relevant to JCP. Its critics said often enough that it was a political gesture to satisfy the annual conferences of TUC and the Labour Party at a time when unemployment was reaching the then unthinkable million mark, or that it was a cosmetic to mask unemployment statistics. In the world of politics all policies have such multiple objectives, but the motives of the policy-makers need not detract from the worth of the policies themselves. Given the difficulties of the time, the urgency of the need, and the absence of better prepared plans, it is hard to think that anything much more effective than JCP could have been launched. For a crisis measure, barely planned and experimental in character, it achieved more than one has come to expect of British government these days.

Looking back on the two years of the programme, one can criticise the original policy and the methods of implementation. The student of public administration can indicate weaknesses in the machinery adopted. To a large extent, as we have seen, these were inherent in the existing system of government, but other ways of doing things might have been possible. We have referred, for example, to the failure to integrate area chairmen in the organisation, the relative isolation of the boards, the limited background and relatively low status of local officials, the lack of coordination between functional services, and the emphasis on audit at the cost of positive help to sponsors. Chapter 1 rightly refers to the pervasive scepticism in Whitehall about the ability of academics to contribute in any significant way to the solution of problems in contemporary government. The discipline of public administration is not yet sufficiently regarded by those responsible for implementation.

Note

During the life of JCP the author of this chapter was chairman of the Merseyside board. The focus, to that extent, is on Merseyside's experience. While in part an 'insider's' view, it is also, as the chapter shows, an 'outsider's'. The views expressed here are those of the author alone.

Bibliographical note

While some research reports have been produced on the effectiveness of JCP projects (and many more on YOP), these do not really deal with administrative questions. The post-JCP period has seen a flood of publications dealing with the policies of YOP and alternative strategies for youth, but little of this related to the JCP experiment. The literature is therefore limited. For background, see Janet Lewis 1978, *Labour market administration in the United Kingdom*, IIM Papers, International Institute of Management, Berlin; Jaqi Nixon 1980, *Policies for the 16–19 year olds: an overview*, CSC Working Paper 10, Civil Service College; David J. Howells 1980, 'The Manpower Services

Commission: the first five years', *Public administration*, Autumn; Michael Hill 1980, 'Unemployment and government manpower policy', in B. Showler and A. Sinfield (eds), *The workless state*, Oxford, Martin Robertson; Santosh Mukherjee 1974, *There's work to be done*, London, HMSO. On JCP, see *Job creation: the first year*, MSC 1976, and annual reports of MSC; House of Commons 1977, 7th report of the Expenditure Committee, session 1976–77: *The Job Creation Programme*, Report and Minutes of Evidence, London, HMSO.

5 Education
Back to basics in the USA and Britain
Gaynor Cohen

The first and longest part of this chapter is devoted to certain programmes introduced in California in the 1970s by the State Department of Education (SDE) in order to improve the quality of the education offered in schools. It begins by reviewing briefly the nature of the American education system, with special reference to California, and certain trends that were taking place within it. The improvement programmes are then described, and the role of the State Superintendent of Public Instruction (SSPI), who heads the SDE, is considered in some detail. An examination of the impact of the programmes shows that, whatever the motivation for them, a major effect of their implementation was to increase considerably the involvement of the SDE in the affairs of local school districts. The second part of the chapter deals with the developments in Britain (more precisely England) centred on what was known at the time as the 'Great Debate' on education launched in 1976. The final part seeks to identify the major similarities and differences in the two situations. It should be noted however that, whereas the first part reports the findings of research carried out by the author in California, the analysis of the British experience is based solely on published sources.

There has been a traditional emphasis on local autonomy in British education, as was shown in Chapter 2. The same is true of the USA (Male 1974). In the terminology of the organisation theorists, education can be described as a 'loosely-coupled system' (Weick 1974) with competing centres of power. This has a considerable effect on the nature of the improvement programmes as policies, and on the nature of the implementation process.

At the same time, education plays a key role in maintaining social values, and many important propositions about it are difficult to substantiate in terms of factual evidence. For all these reasons it is a natural field for the use of symbolic language, which appeals to social values and, by meaning different things to different people, has the capacity to condense different perspectives into one unifying experience (Edelman 1971, 1974). The SSPI exploited to the full the possibilities of symbolic language in order to gain support. This also had a major significance for the policies and their implementation, as we shall see.

The Californian education system

Since the late 1950s there have been attempts by the federal government in the USA to influence the education provided in schools, and in the 1960s federal aid to school districts was greatly expanded (Atkin 1980). Federal grants were seen as a means of achieving national objectives, such as aiding disadvantaged children through 'categorical programmes' (that is, programmes which offer additional resources to specific categories of children). Greater federal involvement has been accompanied by increased state involvement. The Elementary and Secondary Education Act 1965 made it a condition of receiving federal grants under a variety of categorical programmes that local projects should be approved by the relevant state agency. A proportion of the funds went towards strengthening the state agencies for that purpose. Moreover a number of state courts declared their state's school finance system unconstitutional and encouraged SDEs to level up the expenditure of those school districts which had a relatively poor tax base in terms of property tax. The pace of reform has been slow but 'political leaders in many states felt they faced litigation unless there was reform' (Kirst 1981).

One consistent theme in the USA has been that education should be protected from party politics. Indeed, both the general public and professionals have been reluctant to recognise the political aspects of it at all (Karabel and Halsey 1977). In California the SSPI is directly elected on a state-wide, non-partisan ballot. In contrast, the state governor's role in education is limited to appointing the members of the State Board of Education, a supervisory body which lacks influence (Wirt and Kirst 1975), although it does have the power to veto proposals by the SSPI. It is the SSPI, as head of the SDE, who acts as an advocate for education with the media and the legislature, and is well placed to bring about innovations.

The California legislature has a 40-member Senate elected for a four-year term and an 80-member Assembly elected for two years. Their powers are nearly identical and either House can introduce any Bill. As far as education is concerned, the Senate members staunchly support local control, and have consistently opposed any measure which might increase the power of the SDE at the expense of the school districts. Assembly members on the other hand have supported categorical programmes which strengthen the influence of the SDE.

At local level school districts are independent of other agencies and of local government, and have elected boards of lay members and their own professional and administrative staff. The actual powers of school districts have varied from state to state: in California, for a number of reasons, they have been relatively weak.

One explanation for an influential SDE is that some states 'have been more aggressive than others and even more aggressive than federal government in advancing the interests of the disadvantaged through categorical programmes' (Kirst 1972). California was particularly vigorous in implementing the federal Title 1 program under the 1965 Act and has developed its own categorical programmes. Moreover, in 1971 its supreme court was the first court to rule, in the Serrano *vs.* Priest case, that expenditure per pupil by school districts must be equalised. In fact subsequent action was slow and was overtaken by the passage of Proposition 13 in 1978 (see Chapter 6).

Greater federal and state involvement coincided with growing public dissatisfaction with American education. Costly programmes which have not been successful in substantially raising the achievement levels of disadvantaged children (Cohen 1970) have increased public animosity towards federal interference, not to mention the bitter battles over court-ordered desegregation which have transformed the nature of many school districts. None the less, the image of schools as ladders for upward mobility is still a powerful one and 'major interest groups will avoid formal positions which can be interpreted as being "against public education"' (Kirst and Catterall 1980). The blame has been placed on the reformers, and on 'social engineering'.

The improvement programmes
In 1973 the California State Board of Education adopted as a categorical programme the Early Childhood Education Program (ECE). It had been conceived by a task force of child development experts appointed by Wilson Riles shortly after his election as SSPI in 1970. Schools were encouraged to compete for state grants on the basis of improvement plans designed by and for the individual school. The school district was responsible for publicising the programme and the improvement plans were submitted through it. The district was also required to devise a district master-plan for eventual assessment by the SDE.

The objectives of the ECE were to improve the quality of education through improving basic skills, to introduce change into the organisation of schools, and to encourage community involvement. The grant could be used for buying materials, or for hiring teaching aides, specialists or resource teachers. Each ECE school had to set up a school site council (SSC) made up of the principal, parents and teachers. This had the function of assessing the needs and priorities of the school and deciding how the money should be spent. Monitoring of the programme and inspections of ECE schools were carried out by SDE staff.

The School Improvement Program (SIP) extended the same basic concept to secondary schools. Once again, it resulted from a report by an independent working group appointed by Riles to devise an idealistic programme: 'I told them to dream. I told them to think, not of what could be, but of what ought to be.' It was presented as a programme which, as well as improving the quality of education, increased parental and community control at the expense of the traditional coalition between the local school board and school district administrators. School board members, predominantly upper-class conservatives, influenced by their administrators and supported by middle-class parents, had tended to inhibit innovation in education (Jennings *et al.* 1974).

There were other reasons for bypassing school districts. It is the districts which bargain with the increasingly powerful teachers' unions; money controlled by the districts was therefore at risk of dissipation into increased teachers' salaries. There was also the risk that it would be dissipated in increased administrative staffs; these had greatly increased at district level and, as will be shown in Chapter 6, attracted public hostility. The goals for an individual school's SIP programme were therefore to be set, not at district level or at state level, but at school site level.

The SIP represents a bottom-up approach to policy-making:

> School improvement is not a 'program' in the conventional education sense. . . . It does not require schools to provide certain predetermined services. Instead it allows each participating school community to determine for itself, through its site council, what it needs to improve and how to go about doing it. Thus, school improvement . . . is more of a process than a program. (California SDE 1979)

Parents and teachers in individual schools were the key agents in the process. It was seen as necessary for those who would be involved in implementing the policy to play a part in designing it. This approach also fits the notion that the most effective method of bringing about change in an educational organisation is from within:

> The SIP does not impose any outside change agent on a local district. Instead it allows individual schools to determine for themselves what improvements are desired. . . . The best way to improve teacher effectiveness is to engage the entire staff of a school in self-directed development activities, locally designed to meet local problems, as called for under the SIP. (ibid.)

It should be noted that the original intention was to bypass school districts entirely. Opposition from the association of school boards and district administrators resulted in some modifications. The school districts were given responsibility for informing schools about the SIP, for establishing a timetable for phasing schools into the programme, and for developing a district master-plan. They also held the power to approve or reject an SSC's plan. The SDE prescribed what the plan should cover, and direct communication channels were established between the SSC and the SDE, to which it was accountable for the grant provided.

A major difference between the SIP and Title 1 of the federal Act of 1965 on which it was modelled, is that the latter is targeted exclusively at disadvantaged children and their schools. The SIP, although specifying that half the schools in the programme should be those with educationally disadvantaged (that is, low-achieving) children, made it possible for the other half to be schools with a high proportion of middle-class, high-achieving children. Critics have argued that it is therefore bound to further the interests of the middle class, because it is only middle-class parents who have enough leisure, and are sufficiently articulate and informed to participate in SSCs. On the other hand the ECE experience showed that many non-middle-class parents were encouraged to participate. Moreover, it can be argued that the involvement of middle-class parents is likely to enhance the programme's overall effectiveness, because they can apply more effective pressure on a school principal to take advantage of the SIP and can ensure that, within the SSC, the principal and teachers do not overrule or manipulate parents. The SDE wanted each school to have sufficient money to convince parents that their involvement in decision-making in the SSC could be worth while:

> The stimulation is primarily in the form of state planning and implementation grants to participating schools. Planning grants are worth thirty dollars per pupil in average daily attendance for each school involved in the program. Implementation grants vary with grade level. 148 dollars per pupil in kindergarten through grade 3, 90 dollars per grade 4–8 pupils and 65 dollars per pupil in grades 9–12. The money involved for each school is substantial (ibid.)

The role of the politician
The personalities of the main individual actors must affect the policy process. Wilson Riles, the SSPI and instigator of the improvement programmes, had been a teacher and his early experience in a 'community school', where 'parents were free to come and involve themselves in their children's education', influenced his subsequent

attitudes. To him 'local control' meant control by parents, teachers and the community, rather than by school board members and school district officials. His experience with Title 1 also influenced him and provided a model in that he had been director of that programme within the California SDE and retained a great interest in it.

Although he is not identified with a political party, the SSPI has to run an election campaign and win popular support in the same way as any other state politician. Riles was the first black to obtain such an office in the USA. He gained it on his personal and professional qualities rather than his ethnic origin (blacks form only 7 per cent of the population of California). As he put it: 'I want to be seen as an educator who happens to be black and not as a black educator.' He had to steer clear of contentious issues such as school desegregration on which blacks and whites were likely to be divided. In his campaign he performed the balancing act of condemning the lack of progress towards integrated education in California on the one hand, while opposing state-mandated desegregation ('bussing') as the solution on the other.

In office Riles (who was still SSPI in 1982 when this chapter was written) has continued to maintain a skilful balance. In July 1976, following the decision by the California Supreme Court in the case of Crawford *vs.* the Board of Education of the City of Los Angeles that all school districts should take reasonable steps to desegregate schools regardless of the cause of segregation, the SDE was forced to issue a directive to school districts. Its terms however were open to a variety of interpretations and there were no stated penalties for non-compliance. It should be noted that the improvement programmes depended upon a relatively stable school population, and bussing would have been a threat to their success.

At the same time Riles manages to retain support from blacks by his continued involvement in the Title 1 program (which is closely associated with blacks) and by his encouragement of affirmative action in hiring teachers and SDE staff from minority groups. He is a well-known public figure in California with a reputation for skilful handling of the media, to which he devotes considerable time and effort. He is seen as a mediator, someone who supports a consensus approach, someone whose interests are universal rather than partisan: 'Riles is for all kids.' A former rival commented 'Wilson has done a good job . . . he really cares about kids' (Bather 1981).

The task of building and maintaining public support is particularly difficult given the volatile political and social environment of California. Even though blacks make up only a small minority of the total state population, they are significant in the large urban school districts such as Los Angeles and Oakland, and their support is therefore vital for policies like the improvement programmes. These had the overall appearance of being remedial, but were also presented in a way that appealed heavily to a public disillusioned with the social engineering represented by such programmes and its effects on schools. The dominant messages were 'quality education' and 'back to basics'. Naturally these messages appealed to parents. But as only 25 per cent of the California electorate are parents of children in public sector schools it was also vital that they should appeal more widely. Riles achieved this by the use of highly symbolic language which sustained the cherished American concept of schools as effective channels for self-improvement, social mobility and economic success. The notion of community control also appealed to the 'anti-expert' mood of the California public. In using such language, he was seeking to maintain broadly-based support for the education system as a whole, as well as to elicit support for specific programmes.

The impact of the programmes

Because the objectives of the improvement programmes were expressed in very general terms (in the case of the SIP, for example, to 'ensure a quality education for all children'), and because they left the detailed content to be filled in at the level of the individual school, it is difficult to evaluate what they have achieved. There is the further complicating factor that the SIP, particularly, was overtaken by Proposition 13, which (as shown in Chapter 6) produced a crisis in the financing of education in California and brought about some overall deterioration in its quality. However there is rather more information available about the effects of the ECE.

An evaluation carried out in 1975–6 did not find evidence that the ECE had improved performance, or made the majority of parents more at ease with schools. However the proportion of parents helping in the classroom or involved in school activities was higher in ECE schools, as were measures of parent influence in choosing classroom goals, selecting school staff and evaluating school programmes (Baker *et al.* 1976). A study by the Stanford Center for Research and Development in Teaching also suggested that ECE schools had closer relationships with their communities than non-ECE schools; but that the programme had introduced organisational changes into the schools which had created conflict between parents, teachers and principals. There is also evidence that there is less coordination in ECE schools.

These findings make it unlikely that the SIP, in its turn, will be shown to have improved basic skills or the academic performance of children. Yet, from these findings and my own observations, I would argue that the SIP has had important effects on the organisation of the participating schools. The evidence of increased conflict in ECE schools is a reflection of the pace of changes within those schools, and a measure of the success of the programmes in exposing schools, teachers and especially principals to lay scrutiny and pressure. Moreover some teachers supported the SIP because it improved their position within the school in relation to that of the principal or school district officials. Involvement in the SIP has offered parents a degree of real, rather than token, control over schools (Cohen 1979), and it enjoys their support. It has had the effect of drawing together parents from different social classes into an educational support network, and establishing a new system of collaborative relationships between individual schools, school districts and the SDE.

However, there has been strong criticism of the programmes from some quarters, particularly from the Education Committee of the California Senate in the course of 1979. Starting from the assumption that the SIP, like the ECE, would have no demonstrable effect on performance, they argued that the major objective had been a covert one – to increase the amount of control by the SDE and SSPI over the educational system in the state. These critics generally supported state aid for school districts, but argued that it ought to be unrestricted in order to preserve local control. They claimed that the SIP had been used for the self-aggrandisement of the SSPI and to create an independent power base for him at state level (Bather 1981).

In fact, this criticism reflected in large part the successful steps taken by the SSPI, following the passage of Proposition 13, to secure the necessary pressure for the continuing funding of education. This centred on the formation of a group known as the Friends of Public Education to lobby for the relevant Bill. The resources of the SDE were used for that purpose, and full advantage was taken of the channels of communication established as a result of the improvement programmes. The SSPI's chief assistants contacted active members of SSCs throughout the state and set them the task of developing support networks in their own areas. However the Friends of Public Education also included the traditional pro-education groups within the state, both lay and professional, with the aim that they should take a unanimous stand on this issue. It goes without saying that such groups have otherwise had widely varying views on the right structure for the education system and the role of the state. In that education is now 'in competition with the asphalt spreaders', as one school board member put it, the need for such lobbying is likely to be a continuing one. Certainly, education has become much more politicised, but that is an outcome of Proposition 13, rather than a result of the improvement programmes.

However the improvement programmes, and especially the SIP, have had a major impact on the education system in California. This impact is primarily on relationships, both within individual schools and across the overall system. Effects on child performance have not been demonstrated, at least not yet. The crisis precipitated by the extrinsic factor of Proposition 13 probably made it inevitable that the state would assume the predominant role, rather than as previously a minor role, in the financing of education. However, it was still an open question how much genuine influence the state would have at local level, and it was that influence which the SIP served to increase. It is not unreasonable to suppose that an unexpressed objective of the SIP was to increase the power of the SDE and SSPI. But paradoxically it also made possible a considerable, and much increased, degree of participation in decision-making at the level of the individual school. Moreover this feature of the programme, and the high degree of flexibility that it made possible, helped to overcome the problem of simultaneously satisfying the expectations of the very different social groups whose support had been enlisted. The detailed content of the policy could be tailored to the circumstances of the individual school. Conflicts between different groups were likely to be less significant at school level than at state level, or even at district level, because the population involved would be more homogeneous. Finally, it can be pointed out that the SIP could only serve to provide a power base for the SSPI, if that was indeed a covert objective, if people were first persuaded to become involved in it and were then satisfied that it represented a viable and worthwhile programme.

The 'Great Debate' in England
In England, likewise, successive governments have gone some way towards attempting to change the balance of the 'partnership' between the Department of Education and Science (DES), local education authorities (LEAs) and the teaching profession in what has been interpreted as a move towards a greater role for national government (Ranson 1980). The Education Act 1944 created a division of powers and responsibilities, and a web of interdependent relationships, within which it proved difficult to identify a 'controlling voice' (Bogdanor 1979). The post-war period saw a gradual shift in the balance of power in favour of the LEAs, largely because the Local Government Act 1958 abolished the separate grant for education, and ended 'the close scrutiny by the Department of LEA recurrent expenditure' (Ranson 1980: 7). The 1960s witnessed also the heyday of professional power: 'a good deal of what was officially local authority responsibility devolved upon individual schools and head teachers' (Broadfoot 1980: 58),

allowing them a great deal of autonomy and control over the curriculum. The Plowden Report 1967 urged still greater discretion for teachers and schools. However, there were also trends such as the introduction of new maths and science syllabuses and the establishment of teachers' centres which represented increased central influence.

From the early 1970s relationships came under strain because of changes in the social, economic and political environment, which were somewhat different from those in California. Cuts in public expenditure brought demands for greater accountability in education and an increasing emphasis on its utilitarian function. Because of Britain's poor industrial performance, national interests were defined in terms of the need for a skilled labour force. Desire for change in the pattern of relationships within the education system was heightened by the economic depression, and by growing public disillusionment with the achievements of the system.

The trend towards social engineering manifest in programmes such as Educational Priority Areas, although much weaker than in the USA, likewise failed to offer convincing results. British education, disrupted by the reorganisation of secondary schools, was accused of failing to maintain high standards. Schools, their curricula and their teachers came under attack from the authors of the Black Papers. Much of the criticism had a political motivation. The first of the Black Papers said: 'The most serious danger facing Britain is the threat to the *quality* of education at all levels. The motive force behind this threat is the ideology of egalitarianism' (Cox and Dyson 1969). In fact, there was little evidence that standards had fallen. There are in any case major problems in measurement: 'There are no universal standards; there are only people's perceptions of standards' (Silver and Silver 1977). However the suggestion that standards had fallen was sufficient to weaken public trust in the education system. The Bullock Report on language teaching (DES 1975) questions 'this concept of standards', but did little to allay anxieties about levels of literacy.

Politicians from both main political parties responded to such anxieties. Conservatives used the fear of falling standards as a weapon with which to attack comprehensive schools. On the Labour side Shirley Williams, as Secretary of State for Education, together with James Callaghan as Prime Minister, were accused of making the Black Paper stance respectable and stealing the Conservatives' thunder by launching in 1976 a series of well-publicised debates in various parts of the country and arguing for greater parental and community involvement in schools.

The theme of the 'Great Debate' was the need to maintain standards and make education more relevant to the needs of the economy.

Undoubtedly a shift in the balance of relationships between DES, LEAs and teachers was also envisaged, although this was rarely made explicit. The Great Debate was seen as an attempt to win support from teachers and LEAs for the concept of a core curriculum closely monitored by DES. The monitoring would be provided by a strengthened national inspectorate and by LEA advisory services, but Mrs Williams was eager to allay fears of state control over classroom practice.

At the same time a committee chaired by Tom Taylor was reviewing the arrangements for the management and government of maintained primary and secondary schools in England and Wales. It had been set up in 1975 at a time when accountability was a particularly topical issue as a result of a dispute at William Tyndale Junior School in Islington, London. There was nothing in the terms of reference of the Taylor Committee about relationships between central and local government; nevertheless the fact that one of the Committee's major concerns was 'assigning responsibility for the school curriculum' (DES/WO 1977: 47), and that its deliberations were taking place concurrently with the Great Debate, meant that these issues became fused in public discussion (Owen 1978).

The final report of the Taylor Committee sought to make teachers more accountable to governing bodies for individual schools, which would be made up of parents, teachers, the head teacher and community representatives; and to give these bodies a role in monitoring the curriculum. The report provoked criticism from the profession, which labelled it 'a busybody's charter'.

Callaghan and Williams were accused of selectivity and special pleading in some of their contributions to the debate. Findings which demonstrated the effectiveness of formal as opposed to informal teaching methods were used 'in order to launch a blanket attack on progressive education, as sections of the media did' (Sockett 1980: 7). One of Mrs Williams' main arguments for a more uniform curriculum in schools was that it would benefit children who had to change schools frequently because their parents were geographically mobile. Yet only later, as an afterthought, did DES ring round to see if there was any research to support the idea that changing schools impedes children's progress (Devlin 1977).

The 1977 Green Paper which was the immediate outcome of the Great Debate (Cmnd 6869 1977) retained the theme that education should be made more relevant to the needs of the economy, but was criticised at the time for having lost the momentum of the drive towards more central control. 'There is too much of an urge on the part of the government to face both ways to encourage much hope of radical educational reform' (Butt 1977). Yet the Green Paper did propose that LEAs should have the responsibility of monitoring educational standards in schools. The implication was that 'central government decides how and on what basis the quality of schools will be judged and, in so doing, identifies curricular priorities' (Broadfoot 1980: 63). The Green Paper was followed by Circular 14/77, which requested all LEAs to report on the curricula of their schools, and all but one of the 105 LEAs finally responded. In November 1979 the government published the results of this survey in an attempt 'to give a lead in the process of reaching a national consensus on a desirable framework for the curriculum' (DES 1979). In 1980 it published its own recommendations in *A framework for the school curriculum* (DES/WO 1980) and the following year saw further papers on the subject from the government and the Schools Council (DES/WO 1981; Schools Council 1981).

The initial reaction had been that the Great Debate had failed, as witnessed in such headlines as 'Neither great nor a debate' (Wilby 1977) and 'Whatever happened to the Great Education Debate?' (Butt 1977). Certainly it did not immediately lead to a DES-sponsored programme to improve and control the curriculum, but there has been a clear long-term trend of increased central government involvement in that field. In evidence to the Education, Science and Arts Select Committee (HC 116–11 1981/2: 77) DES states that although

> direct involvement of central government in the development of the school curriculum has been relatively limited . . . [evidence from surveys of schools' practice in respect of the curriculum suggested] that for both practical and educational reasons, a re-examination of the assumptions underlying the present secondary school curriculum was timely. . . . The Government concluded that the time had come to seek a measure of national agreement on the basic principles underlying the school curriculum. . . . In taking the lead in the process of establishing national consensus, the government has not sought to change the distribution of statutory responsibilities for the curriculum.

This attempted reassurance did not relieve the fears of the National Union of Teachers, which told the Select Committee (46–7):

> The emphasis on defining a curriculum related to national needs is misconceived. . . . It would shift power and influence to central government and the Whitehall bureaucracy, which has neither the knowledge nor the experience to exercise such responsibility.

The objective of achieving greater national consistency in curriculum content is still as evident today as in the 1970s, but the manner in which it is to be achieved has changed. The Great Debate appeared to be a dramatic appeal for public support, an attempt to use parents, employers and the general public to bring pressure on LEAs and teachers. Subsequent initiatives made use of more conventional approaches such as DES circulars, performance assessment techniques and departmental publications (Schools Council 1981; DES 1980) which aim to gain support from within the education service rather than from the general public.

Comparisons between England and California

Comparisons between countries are notoriously difficult, but in view of the obvious points of similarity between the Great Debate and the SIP in California, it is worth while to try to make them. The basic parallel is that a policy was expressed in symbolic, ambiguous terms at a time of growing public discontent with the education system. The speech by James Callaghan at Ruskin College, Oxford in October 1976 has become a landmark in discussions of educational policy. He tried to capitalise on public anxiety at supposedly falling standards in order to gain support for central government intervention in securing an educational system more relevant to the world of work. He has since been criticised for a naive and simplistic analysis of the issues and for making education the scapegoat for Britain's poor economic performance (Sockett 1980: 7).

The very concept of a Great Debate was politically symbolic, and was magnified by the media. The debate – described in one article as 'the great road show' – sought to establish the legitimacy of increased central control by showing that the public, in the shape of parents and employers, wanted it (*The Economist* 1977: 26). The DES statement on the debate claimed that its primary intention was to test opinion at the regional grass roots and 'to listen to people from whom we do not normally hear' (Wilby 1977). Shirley Williams was admirably suited to a campaign of this sort: like the SSPI in California, she had a great deal of popular appeal and was able to convince people of her sympathy with all the various interests involved: 'Who better, now that public opinion has forced the government to note at last the concern of ordinary people about the state of public education in Britain, to take on the task of what is called a national debate on the subject' (Butt 1977).

However, in England the Great Debate did not succeed in harnessing public support to a specific programme. In California the SSPI generated support for the SIP which cut across social class, ethnic and lay/professional divisions. In the Great Debate, because of the way the regional meetings were arranged and structured, the views of the general public scarcely surfaced. The arguments reflected only the views of national interest groups and the teaching profession, and thus merely reiterated entrenched positions: 'It does not occur to civil servants that there is any way of consulting except through institutions and pressure groups' (Wilby 1977).

There were other significant differences. The effectiveness of symbolic language in building widespread support was undermined in the Great Debate by going into too much detail at too early a stage. The analyses which were offered of the problems were complex: simplicity, an important feature of political symbolism was lost. A specific measure, the core curriculum, was advocated before the different groups were convinced that it was either necessary or feasible, and the discussion became tangled in the problems and potential conflicts of implementing it. It should also be emphasised that, whereas the SIP was an inherently flexible policy in which objectives were set at the local level in response to local circumstances, the core curriculum, and the linked concept of common assessment procedures were obviously an attempt (despite the reassurances offered by DES) to achieve a measure of standardisation across the entire education system. By their nature, therefore, they became embroiled in conflict at a stage and at a level at which the SIP was able to avoid conflict. As one critic subsequently put it, 'Far from teachers being responsible for the definition of educational goals, these are now increasingly being defined at the greatest possible distance from the chalk-face among the professional administrators of Whitehall and the professional test-constructors' (Broadfoot 1980: 64).

It has also been shown how the SIP changed the power structure within the educational system by building up its own network of support at the local level; school-based groups of parents and teachers provided a powerful antidote to the school boards and district administrators. The Taylor Report represented a similar attempt. Its proposals included reform of governing bodies to ensure that they included not only local councillors but teachers, parents and community representatives. It suggested that the local community should monitor educational progress and gave 'Shirley Williams a heaven-sent opportunity to develop the job of putting into practice the curricular reforms she so badly needs' (Price 1977). The hostile response to the report by the teaching profession reflected their anxiety that their power might be weakened by opening up classroom practice and school organisation to lay scrutiny, and their suspicion that the link between the Great Debate and the proposals of the Taylor Committee was not accidental. The Education Act 1980, which followed the change of government, accepted only some of the recommendations of the Taylor Committee. It has not altered the powers of school governors, but has made governing bodies much more broadly based (Jackson 1981) and may have long-term effects.

Of course, many other factors have to be considered in comparing the

SIP with the Great Debate: the greater involvement of the teachers' unions in the policy process in Britain, differences in the political culture of the two countries, a lay presence in the form of teachers' aides in the American classroom. Some people might argue that these differences were more fundamental than differences in the handling of the issue in England and California. Another significant factor may have been the transfer of Shirley Williams to a different government post.

Nevertheless, the most significant feature of this case study is that it deals with the implementation of policies which were advocated and expressed in language which was vague and general, and had a high symbolic content. This reflects the value-based nature of education as a field of policy, and its intimate connection with the perpetuation of social values and structures. The values are not necessarily identical in each country. In the USA the notion of quality in education is more intertwined with an idealised concept of local (lay) control. Although from one aspect the improvement programmes in California were in conflict with that concept, the SDE could also appeal to it in generating and sustaining support for the programmes, at the expense of a discredited and increasingly powerless intermediate tier of single-purpose bodies whose functions may not have been well understood and valued by the general public.

In a sense policy was formulated in California through the implementation process: detailed goals were left to be set at grass-roots level by parents and teachers. This was not simply political ingenuity, but was the outcome of a view about the ways in which organisational change can best be brought about. The programme was allowed to evolve, through adaptation and negotiation, in the light of the circumstances in each school. It successfully overcame the basic difficulty of converting a vaguely worded policy, appealing to many conflicting interests, into practical measures.

References

Atkin, M. 1980, *The government in the classroom* (9th Sir John Adams Lecture), University of London Institute of Education

Baker, E. *et al.* 1976, *Evaluation of the California early childhood education program*, Los Angeles, UCLA Center for the Study of Evaluation

Bather, S. 1981, 'Wilson Riles: he's come a long way', *Sacramento Bee*, 21 June

Bogdanor, V. 1979, 'Power and participation', *Oxford review of education*, vol. 5, no. 2

Broadfoot, P. 1980, 'Assessment, curriculum and control in the changing pattern of centre–local relations', *Local government studies*, vol. 6, no. 6, pp. 57–68

Butt, R. 1977, 'Whatever happened to the Great Education Debate?', *The Times*, 28 April

California State Department of Education 1979, *California schools beyond Serrano: a report on Assembly Bill 65 of 1979*, Sacramento

Cmnd 6869 1977, *Education in schools: a consultative document*, London, HMSO

Cohen, D.K. 1970, 'Politics and research', *Review of educational research*, April, pp. 313–39

Cohen, G. 1979, 'Symbiotic relations: male decision-makers–female support groups in Britain and the United States', *Women's studies*, vol. 2, pp. 391–406

Cox, C.B. and Dyson, A.E. (eds) 1969 and 1971, *The Black Papers on education*, 1 and 11, Davis Poynter

DES 1975, *A language for life* (report of a committee chaired by Sir Alan Bullock), London, HMSO

DES 1979, *Local authority arrangements for the curriculum*, London, HMSO

DES 1980, *A view of the curriculum*, HMI Matters for Discussion Series, no. 11, London, HMSO

DES/WO 1977, *A new partnership for our schools* (report of a committee chaired by Mr Tom Taylor), London, HMSO

DES/WO 1980, *A framework for the school curriculum*, London, HMSO

DES/WO 1981, *The school curriculum*, London, HMSO

Devlin, T. 1977, 'How four ministers found their way through the blackboard jungle', *The Times*, 31 May

The Economist, 1977, 'The great road show', 10 May

Edelman, M. 1971, *Politics as symbolic action*, Chicago, Markham (Institute for Research on Poverty Monograph Series)

Edelman, M. 1974, *The symbolic uses of politics* (6th edn), Urbana, University of Illinois Press

HC 1981/2, Second Report from the Education, Science and Arts Committee, *The secondary school curriculum and examinations*, London, HMSO

Jackson, P.M. 1981, 'Education: evolutionary change in a harsh climate', in Jackson, P.M. (ed.), *Government policy initiatives 1979–80: some case studies in public administration*, London, Royal Institute of Public Administration

Jennings, M.K., Ziegler, H. and Peak, W. 1974, *School district governance in America*, North Scituate (Mass.), Duxbury

Karabel, J. and Halsey, A.H. (eds) 1977, *Power and ideology in education*, New York, Oxford University Press

Kirst, M.W. 1972, *Delivery systems for federal aid to disadvantaged* children: problems and prospects, Stanford University Occasional Papers in the Economics and Politics of Education 72–2

Kirst, M.W. 1981, *The state role in educational policy innovation*, Policy Paper no. 81–C1, Stanford, Institute for Research on Educational Finance and Governance

Kirst, M.W. and Catterall, J. 1980, 'Voucher politics: the anatomy of failure', *Newsletter of the Stanford Institute for Research on Educational Finance and Governance*

Male, G.A. 1974, *The struggle for power*, Beverly Hills, Sage

Owen, J. 1978, 'A new partnership for our schools', *Oxford review of education*, vol. 4, no. 1

Price, C. 1977, 'A voice for parents', *New Statesman*, 23 September

Ranson, S. 1980, 'Changing relationships between centre and locality in education', *Local government studies*, vol. 6, no. 6, pp. 3–23

Schools Council 1981, *The practical curriculum*, Working Paper no. 7, London, Methuen

Silver, P. and Silver, H. 1977, 'The political quest for educational standards', *New Society*, vol. 39, no. 751, pp. 382–4

Sockett, H. 1980, *Accountability in English educational systems*, Sevenoaks, Hodder & Stoughton

Weick, K.E. 1974, 'Educational organisations as loosely-coupled systems', *Administrative science quarterly*, vol. 21, pp. 1–18

Wilby, P. 1977, 'Neither great nor a debate', *New Statesman*, 18 February

Wirt, F.M. and Kirst, M.W. 1975, *Political and social foundations of education* (revised edn), Berkeley, McCutchan

6 Cutting Public Expenditure
Proposition 13 in California
Gaynor Cohen

This chapter examines how taxation, and hence public expenditure, was cut dramatically in California as a result of a referendum on 6 June 1978 on what was known as 'Proposition 13'. This represented what Chapter 1 distinguished as a quantum cut, rather than a decremental cut, in public expenditure. Unusually, and uniquely among the cases considered in this book, the vote in the referendum represented the adoption of a specific policy, not by any organ of government, but by the electorate as a whole. Other policies may have figured in the election manifesto of a winning party, and to that extent can be regarded as policies which had been endorsed by the electorate; however, in the case of Proposition 13, adoption of the policy by the electorate took a much more direct and precise form. Proposition 13 became part of the constitution of California, and it had particular and immediate implications for fiscal administration, and hence effects across a wide range of government activity.

Although Proposition 13 specified which taxes had to be cut, and by how much, it did not say anything about which services were to be cut. This latter feature can be regarded as characteristic of retrenchment policies, and hence of the policy process generally in the field of public expenditure. The central problem in this field is making the translation from a broad aggregate (whether this is total expenditure, total reduction in expenditure, or total increase) to appropriate figures for individual services and/or localities. In fact, the nature of the tax cuts required by Proposition 13 did have certain implications for where the cuts in services would fall, but the evidence is that these implications were not intended by those who supported it.

Moreover, because Proposition 13 had an unusual status as a policy, the process of implementation was also unusual in its nature. Those who had adopted the policy (the electorate) had no direct responsibility for, or power over, its implementation. After outlining briefly the circumstances which led to Proposition 13, therefore, this chapter discusses the campaign leading up to the referendum as evidence about the expectations of the electorate. It then describes what actually occurred after the proposition was approved. It pays particular attention to the effects on education, on the basis of a detailed study carried out in one school district which appears to have been typical. In particular, it discusses whether enforced reductions in the expenditure there led to increased efficiency, or the opposite. It then relates this case study to Chapter 5 by summarising briefly the interaction between the implementation of Proposition 13 and the contemporary 'back to basics' policy in California education.

The background

California is the most popular state in the USA and has attracted immigrants since the days of the gold-rush in the last century. The desirability of this 'golden state', and the land speculation accompanying the rapidly rising prices of the 1970s, have created some of the fastest growing residential property values in the nation. Homes in the Los Angeles area that cost $50 000 in 1974 could sell for well over $110 000 in 1981. Combined with this was an efficient property tax system that required reassessment every three years, or at the time of sale. In addition to property tax, California had a high and progressive income tax and a 6 per cent sales tax which was one of the highest in the nation. Government expenditure in California has, over recent years, grown by 17 per cent annually, while government employment has increased by 10 per cent per year.

Behind this overall growth lay pressure for growth in particular services, of which education can be taken as an example. Throughout the late 1960s and early 1970s there was a network of groups advocating growth in educational programmes. They were pro-public schools (i.e., public sector schools) and believed that a larger input to education would have a direct benefit in student outcomes. A former president of the California State Board of Education contrasted the skill with which such special interest groups seized the attention of state legislators with the ineffectiveness of 'the silent majority' who supported tax cuts in getting their views represented:

> I have met with taxpayer groups for about four minutes in the past four years. We hear overwhelmingly from people who want to spend more. They are organised lobbies, and over time they tend to level up public spending. The diffuse interest of the public in restraining spending does not function effectively through the normal state/local political system. The special interests are organised around specific programs. The anti-spending groups are not organised except in a general, diffuse way. (Kirst 1980)

The same was no doubt true of other public services.

Thus there was latent support for measures to limit taxation and public expenditure, and the problem was to mobilise that support. The system of popular initiatives and referenda introduced into the California constitution in 1911 provided a mechanism for that purpose. This had been an attempt at 'direct democracy': placing power in the hands of the people, rather than with their representatives, or with the political lobbyists of the time, who had been associated with gross abuses; but it fell far short of the goal. Instead of bypassing interest groups, it has often been used by them.

Political life in California has become very complex. Organised interest groups, even more than in other states, play a very significant part in political life. They are influential in shaping public opinion and in swaying the legislature. Their variety is endless, and ranges over economic interest groups, unions, minority associations, voluntary women's associations and professional groups. More than 600 such groups in California employ registered professional lobbyists, and use a variety of techniques: campaign contributions to sympathetic candidates, testimony for or against Bills being considered by committees, informal contacts, information and statistical data on pending legislation, newspaper advertising, letters to legislators in support of Bills, protest marches, demonstrations and favourable publicity for sympathetic legislators. While such groups are valuable as channels of communication between government and the public, their danger lies – as the above list of techniques indicates – in the advantage which the more affluent groups have over others.

As more than 300 000 signatures (defined as 5 per cent of the votes cast in the previous election for governor) are necessary to place any proposition on the ballot, many contend that this can be effected only by wealthy groups. It is also argued that proposition measures are far too complex for most citizens to understand, so that the electorate generally is vulnerable to manipulation. The main group behind Proposition 13 was the United Organization of Taxpayers, headed by Howard A. Jarvis, and assisted by a political consulting firm which specialised in fund-raising through mail campaigns.

Yet the resources available to Jarvis's group do not wholly explain Proposition 13's success. For 15 years prior to 1978 Jarvis had waged an unsuccessful battle for property tax reduction. In 1973, when Governor Reagan sponsored an amendment to limit state spending and tie it to growth of the state economy and personal income, he lost by a 50 per cent margin. Despite the fact that since that time California, like most other industrial societies, has witnessed growing public discontent with the escalating growth of public expenditure, a further move by Jarvis in 1980 to limit the state rate of personal income tax was decisively rejected by the electorate. In fact, before Proposition 13, no major fiscal reform measures had been passed at any government level in California. Instead, as government spending programmes and the size of the public sector increased, public faith in the efficacy of government policy waned. 'Waste in government' was a key theme in the presentation of Proposition 13.

Another key factor was the unpopularity of the property tax at which Proposition 13 was primarily directed. The property tax is the system of revenue for local governments in the USA (counties, cities, school districts and other special districts). It has been claimed that its unpopularity rests on the fact that it is highly visible as it is paid once or twice a year and also often unjust in that, because it is based on an assessment of the current market value of property, 'the level of the tax has no necessary relationship to the taxpayer's current ability to pay' (Danziger 1980).

The campaign

In Chapter 5 I pointed out that symbolic language may be used to fuse disparate sections of the public and bring them into line in support of a particular policy, especially in fields which are politically sensitive. Symbolic language may also mask the fact that those proposing a particular policy may not in fact have the solution to the relevant problems and may not be able to specify in advance its probable consequences.

To succeed, Proposition 13 had to achieve the support of a majority of those voting. It was therefore presented in a simplistic fashion as a measure which was against 'big government' and 'remote government', and which would cut out the 'waste in government', as the majority of the population were likely to sympathise with these objectives. They were promised greater control over their own lives, and more efficient and effective government. This approach generated substantial support even from public employees who might have opposed Proposition 13's aim of cutting bureaucracy.

Public hostility towards the growth of expenditure on social programmes was focused on welfare and day care. A political scientist's assessment of factors affecting inter-county differences in support for Proposition 13 showed no relationship between the degree of support and the size of the county, the fraction of the county's population enrolled in public schools, or the income of the average citizen taken as a measure of ability to pay taxes (Brody 1978). What he did find was that one of the major unifying themes behind support for Proposition 13 was a negative attitude towards welfare. Opinion polls support this view: most voters wanted to do no more than stabilise spending on other government activities, but wanted to cut welfare spending. Yet, as Brody shows, this anti-welfare sentiment was not related to a county's per capita expenditures on AFDC (Aid to Families With Dependent Children). Counties with low expenditures differed little in their support for Proposition 13 from counties with high expenditures. The anti-welfare attitudes were part of the myth of the evils of government. Such attitudes contributed to the success of Proposition 13 despite the fact that it was unlikely to have a major effect on welfare spending, which is largely financed from federal and state taxes.

In contrast, most Californians who supported Proposition 13 did not think that it would diminish the quality of local schools. According to a post-Proposition 13 opinion poll conducted by the Field Institute for the Education Commission of States, 44.6 per cent of respondents claimed that the initiative would have little effect, while 9.7 per cent felt that it might even have a positive effect. Undoubtedly those who held the latter view felt that Proposition 13 would merely 'cut the fat' out of school budgets and promote a healthier education service. Again, according to this poll, 51.2 per cent felt that public schools in California were doing a good job, and ranked only ninth in the list of services in which voters would most like to see financial cuts made. There was also a general feeling expressed that local school districts should retain control of education: 55.8 per cent of respondents felt that more state control would be detrimental to schools, which compares with 26.2 per cent who were in favour of increased state control. The main dissatisfaction with the education service related to the increase in the number of administrators, which was not seen as having any benefit through increased efficiency in management.

Public schools, followed closely by health and medical services, sanitation and highways, were the services which respondents wanted to keep either at the current level or even at increased levels of service provision. Leading the list of candidates for cutbacks was the welfare category, followed by child day care, recreation and parks. The campaign for Proposition 13 had been successful in reassuring the public both that popular services would retain their quality despite a 40 per cent reduction in their budget, and that unpopular services would be severely curtailed. The symbolic and generalised language used undoubtedly served an important function in bringing together diverse elements of the California electorate. This political style also suited the colourful personality of Jarvis, the campaign leader.

In contrast, the 'No on 13' coalition, the main opposition group, was more divided in its views and adopted a more closely reasoned approach in its campaign. The coalition was formed after the Jarvis initiative qualified for the ballot. The membership represented almost a *Who's*

Who of California, and included the main unions, business groups, education interest groups, 'good government groups', such as Common Cause and League of Women Voters, and politicians such as the Speaker of the Assembly (Leo McCarthy), the Los Angeles Mayor (Tom Bradley), and the State Superintendent of Public Instruction (Wilson Riles). The main problem they faced was their diverse positions on the alternative measure, Proposition 8, which would have reduced property taxes by half the amount proposed by the Jarvis initiative. Not all members endorsed Proposition 8, and a separate 'Yes on 8' committee was formed at a late stage. The 'No on 13' campaign was also organised by a political consulting firm, Winner and Wagner; their preferred tactic was rationality rather than scaremongering. They did not, for example, exploit Jarvis's political background or play up the windfall to business. They also downplayed the disruption likely to follow in education. Their main messages were 'It costs too much and will result in drastic reductions of services', 'Renters will not benefit' or 'A better alternative exists in proposition 8'. This approach did not capture the attention of the voters.

The 'Yes on 13' campaign had support from conservative taxpayer groups and real estate interest groups, but also from a large grass-roots element which was against high taxation and government spending. It was endorsed by several prominent Republicans and economists, notably Milton Friedman. The group gained considerable public support through constant media exposure, and this contributed substantially to its success. The dominant media messages were anti-government, anti-welfare, anti-politician and anti-tax. These were presented in a highly symbolic way and were easy for the public to understand.

Proposition 13 became national news in the last three weeks of the campaign. The issue was presented as 'the California taxpayers' revolt'. Local television shows gave Jarvis free air time until, in the last two weeks, he was seen debating daily with different officials on the virtues of Proposition 13. The media presentation of Proposition 13 was simplistic, and there was very little detailed discussion about what the repercussions would be on services or the structure of government.

Finally, Governor Jerry Brown, who was standing for re-election, played some part in the campaign's success. After opposing Proposition 13 initially – criticising it as defrauding the electorate – he changed his position two weeks before the referendum. Although he continued to oppose Proposition 13 officially he assured voters that he could 'live with it' if the measures were to be passed. Following the primary election in the California gubernatorial race, Brown went to work to implement Proposition 13 as though he had proposed it initially and earned for himself the nickname of 'Jerry Jarvis'. He was criticised as a political opportunist, although he claimed that he was merely doing his job in carrying out the mandate of the people. The result was that Brown won the election and polls show that voters identified Brown, who had initially opposed the measure, more closely with the tax revolt than the Republican candidate, who had supported it.

Ironically an important factor which is said to have influenced the California electorate was not a decline in the state's economic resources, but the existence of a large revenue surplus in state government. Governor Brown was forced to admit that the surplus, which he had declared in March as $3.6 billion, was in fact over $5 billion. The figure grew larger as the campaign progressed. The knowledge that this large surplus revenue existed reassured the public that the state government could counter any possible adverse effects arising from a cut in property taxes.

Impact of Proposition 13

Proposition 13 limited property taxes to 1 per cent of the market value of property. It rolled back the assessed value of real property for tax purposes (25 per cent of market value) to the 1975/6 level. Inflation could be reflected by not more than 2 per cent annually of assessed values. Increases in state taxes must have the approval of two-thirds of both Houses of the legislature, and increases in any local taxes other than property taxes would be permissible only with the approval of two-thirds of those voting. In 1979 there was a reinforcing effect from Proposition 4 (nicknamed 'Spirit of 13'), which limited state and local expenditure from all tax sources.

In its first fiscal year, 1978/9, Proposition 13 cut local revenues by about $7 billion, representing over half of what property tax receipts would have been, and nearly a quarter of what local government revenue from all sources would have been. School districts were the largest losers. Their $3.5 billion loss represented over 50 per cent of their property tax receipts and nearly 30 per cent of their revenues from all sources. Although the main source of resentment about the property tax was among owner-occupiers, it was ironically business which received the largest share of Proposition 13's benefits. Out of the $7 billion cut in the first fiscal year 24 per cent went to owner-occupiers, 12 per cent to owners of rented property, and 28 per cent to owners of commercial property. There was a shift of 36 per cent from local governments to state and federal governments. The impact of Proposition 13 on the quality of local services was not as great as predicted by some of the measure's opponents, because the state government provided more than $4 billion a year from the state surplus to bail out local governments. Nevertheless the cuts, and the uncertainty about future finances, led to a gradual reduction in the numbers employed by local governments in the form of hiring freezes, redundancies and voluntary retirement.

The poorest section of the Californian public was worst hit by Proposition 13. Resource constraints forced local governments to impose charges for services formerly provided free such as libraries, zoos, tennis courts, museums, and even services such as refuse collection. Undoubtedly such charges had the greatest impact on the poorer sections of the community. In welfare, the most unpopular service, costs remained high (*California Journal* 1979). There are several major programmes for the poor: AFDC, already mentioned, and paid for from federal, state and county sources; SSI/SSP (Supplementary Security Income/State Supplemental Payment), paid for from federal and state governments; the Social Services Program, under Title 20 of the Social Security Act, covered by federal, state and county funds; and Medi-Cal, which provides medical assistance for the financially disadvantaged.

Counties administer welfare programmes but generally have no control over the eligibility criteria or the levels of grants. They are also accountable to federal and state laws and regulations. The effect of Proposition 13 was to ensure that counties were more dependent than ever before on state and federal funding. Before that more than one-third of county property tax money went to welfare-related programmes: an estimated $1.5 billion out of $3.15 billion. After Proposition 13 welfare expenditure was an even greater drain on a decreased property tax base and the state therefore stepped in and bought out the county share of the costs of major welfare programmes. For the programmes are mandatory and, if counties cannot continue to maintain them, responsibility cannot be abandoned but must be taken over by the state.

The administrative costs of welfare programmes are high. A more efficient assessment system would need even more money spent on administration. Simplifying procedures may result in more people qualifying for benefits. In an effort to simplify Medi-Cal, the state set substantially less restrictive requirements for the medically needy (MN) and the medically indigent (MI) categories. Previously MI applicants had to apply monthly at the local welfare office, while MN candidates applied every three months. The new procedure allowed recipients to fill out eligibility determination forms only once a year; and such forms could be posted rather than handed in at county offices. The result was that case loads and programme costs grew, and counties returned to a system of more frequent reporting.

Another issue is whether the state should assume even more of welfare costs. Two programmes were not bought out by the state: the county's share of the federal Title 20 Social Services Program and the General Relief (GR) Program. For the latter, the tendency has been for most counties to keep eligibility criteria limited and grant levels low. Welfare rights advocates argued that the system was inequitable as people received aid based not on need, but on their county of residence. This view was supported by a California Supreme Court ruling in 1977 that San Francisco's standard of aid was 'arbitrary and capricious'. If the state were to assume responsibility for the GR Program then undoubtedly grant levels and the total would rise.

A third major financial issue is the cost of Medi-Cal, one of the fastest growing programmes in the state. Both counties and welfare advocates might press for recipients of GR to qualify automatically for Medi-Cal and this would push the cost of the latter programme still higher. In fact the GR population is but a small part of the population provided with free health care through county hospitals and clinics. Counties provide health care services to thousands who do not qualify for Medi-Cal and who have little or no other health insurance, including illegal aliens and the working poor. If the state takes over the GR program, then the issue of who pays for indigent health care will still have to be faced.

Child day care, like welfare, was another unpopular service unaffected by Proposition 13 as the publicly-funded child care and development programmes are paid for either with federal or state money. But Proposition 13 had a significant impact on a wide range of organised recreational activities provided after school hours by local government. These services, organised by libraries, public schools, recreation departments, museums or private agencies such as scouts, have for years been viewed as valuable unofficial child care alternatives for working parents. Proposition 13 forced local governments to reduce significantly their cultural and recreational service. Most districts have cancelled summer school activities, even though during the summer there are virtually no other child care facilities available. Parks, libraries and recreation have also experienced drastic cuts in funds. However, the main impact on the child population was through the effect on the education service.

Effects on education
Paradoxically, and contrary to the impression given during the campaign, Proposition 13 had a far greater impact on the education service, which voters had expressed a desire to protect, than on an unpopular service such as welfare. Nevertheless the supporters of Proposition 13 might have believed that this impact would, on balance,

be favourable to education. The symbolism of cutback management in the USA has stressed the need, in the name of efficiency, to 'cut out the waste' in education. The system has expanded through the addition of tiers of administrators at school district level. The popular reaction is that these additional staff are unnecessary and do not carry out any essential function. 'Cutting the fat' out of the education bureaucracy would, according to the popular view, serve to improve the quality of schooling, as in the slogan 'leaner means fitter'. It has been argued that 'If crisis is the mother of invention, one might expect to see many American school districts facing retrenchment pressures engaging in interesting innovations in pursuit of greater efficiency of operation' (Boyd 1979). One basis for this argument is that the USA 'still has a highly decentralised system of educational governance in comparison with many other countries', and the probability of innovation is said to be enhanced by a greater degree of decentralisation of control over schools.

Against that, we may set the alternative prediction that the staff involved, and particularly the administrators, would react defensively, adopting various devices to minimise the effect of cuts on their own departments or organisations (Heclo and Wildavsky 1974). The bureaucratic core would remain unscathed, putting up good grounds for its own existence but responding more readily to the need for more distant sacrificial offerings such as 'the bureaucrats bureaucrats do not like – the planners and research staff' (Glennerster 1980: 374; cf. Niskanen 1971). Similar defensiveness would be displayed by other staff faced with the possibility of redundancies. The overall effect would be that, far from strengthening the organisation and testing its capacity for innovation, 'less is achieved by the same staff' (Glennerster 1980: 377).

What actually happened in one large school district, that serving most of the major city of San José? Broadly speaking, Proposition 13 led to more centralised control and greater standardisation rather than innovation. This was contrary to the intertwining of the notion of quality in American education with an idealised concept of local control. One important factor was that a substantial proportion of school programmes were mandatory. Moreover federal grants for categorical programmes were an addition to state and local funds and at times of resource constraints local school districts might be tempted to apply for these additional funds even though they corresponded to federal rather than local priorities (Jones 1981).

The limitations on local discretion are illustrated by the response to a questionnaire from the San José school board asking for parents' preferences about where the cuts should be made. A series of public meetings was held to discuss the issue. The overwhelming majority of parents wanted to cut back on administrators and on programmes such as bilingual education. The school board however was unable to respond to either of these demands. In the first place programmes such as bilingual education were mandated by federal or state government, which then provided a proportion of the necessary funds. Local discretion covered only a limited number of programmes such as adult education, library services and sports, which were the first victims of expenditure cuts even though they might also be those programmes which met the distinct needs of that school district.

The school board also failed to comply with the popular demand for a drastic reduction in the number of administrators. In fact it was the number of classroom teachers which was reduced. In that it is the administrators and not the teachers within a school district who have the decision-making power, this is not surprising. But there were several other factors at work. There were burdensome administrative tasks which it was difficult or impossible to reduce. Much of the great expansion in educational administration since the mid-1960s had been to cope with the widespread use of education by both state and federal governments to solve social problems through such programmes as bilingual education, compensatory education and 'special' education. State and federal legislation on subjects like equal employment opportunities and supreme court decisions over such complex and controversial issues as desegregation all became the responsibility of school administrators. Over the past 15 years, many school administrators had spent a considerable part of their time learning new roles. The majority of these responsibilities persisted after Proposition 13 had been passed.

At the same time it is plausible that 'retrenchment conditions increase the need for administration at precisely the time when everyone tends to expect administrative costs to be reduced' (Boyd 1979). Moreover, the style of operation encouraged by a prolonged period of expansion was ill-suited to the careful planning techniques demanded by this new phase. In fact, planning for cutbacks has not been well served by the research and planning measures previously adopted in education. For although many school districts do have sophisticated data collection and planning techniques, the significance of education as a central institution in American social life means that it is very difficult to define what efficiency actually means: 'The problem is usually phrased in terms of "*maintaining* educational quality" not improving educational productivity, and this, I think, is symptomatic of what is probably the largest obstacle to innovation: the lack of a well-understood production function in education' (Boyd 1979: 5). The symbolic content of education commits decision-makers in that field to maintaining the symbols of perceived quality, thus reducing even further any school district's ability to introduce innovative change. Political considerations again affect the way in which decisions are made, with the result that educationalists' standard response to the need to retrench may simply be to reduce the scale of operations or resort to minor adjustments in order to minimise the costs of change both for the professionals themselves and for the public.

The general conclusion from San José is a pessimistic one, and it seems to have been typical of events in California generally. Although it is difficult to assess the quality of the service provided, there is no reason to believe that it improved, and some circumstantial evidence points in the opposite direction. Even with quantum cuts in expenditure, the general strategy adopted was to defend the base and retain existing programmes. To a large extent, this strategy was dictated by legal requirements and other commitments, which overrode the expressed wishes of those for whom the service was provided.

Moreover the different groups within the education service were forced together into a defensive coalition to protect education expenditure at state level, as described in Chapter 5: this discouraged free debate on other educational issues, and thus also discouraged innovation. A case study of the implementation of one policy is bound to be a simplification of reality, because in practice it is accompanied by, and interacts with, the implementation of other policies. At the same time as the California education system was experiencing the repercussions of Proposition 13, it was also implementing the 'back to basics' policy described in Chapter 5. Although these were two distinct policies, there was an overlap both in their effects and in the symbolic terms in which they were expressed and justified: the phrase 'back to basics' can carry an implication of cutting out inessentials which is consistent with a general wish to cut public expenditure and would appeal to many of the same people. Nevertheless the 'back to basics' policy was adopted independently by the State Department of Education for reasons which stemmed almost entirely from within the educational system.

The effects of the two policies on the California education system are more difficult to disentangle. Both fostered a process of centralisation, with the initiative moving from the school district to the state level. Indeed, Proposition 13 created a massive opportunity for the State Department of Education to increase its influence by increasing its role in funding. At the same time as an offset to increased centralisation, the 'back to basics' policy gave an increased role to the individual school and to parents. The financial threat to education was a powerful incentive to increased parental involvement. Moreover such involvement was deliberately fostered by the State Department of Education in the cause of defending education's share of the reduced total of public expenditure. But the concept of parental, and more generally community, involvement contained in the 'back to basics' policy went well beyond simply providing the base for a pressure group at state level. In that sense, there is a tension between structural developments within Californian education and recent changes in the methods of funding it.

How the policy process operated

Because of the unusual nature of the case, Proposition 13 and its implementation allow us to discern certain features of the policy process with particular clarity. Proposition 13 was the result of an initiative from outside government and the legislature. It was apparently brief, precise and straightforward. However, to succeed it had to obtain the support of the majority of voters. Its supporters and opponents formed temporary and disparate coalitions to fight this one issue. There were also other coalitions campaigning on related, but alternative propositions which went to referendum at the same time. To that extent, we can see unusually clearly where the lines of support and opposition were drawn in this case.

Because of the disparate nature of the coalitions, however, Proposition 13 carried a wide range of meanings for those who supported it. The major element in its appeal was no doubt its simplicity and its precision about the limitations placed on taxes. However, it said nothing about such important issues as the distribution of the benefits, the consequential transfers of funds, and the effects on public services. It was therefore sufficiently ambiguous in its implications to carry different meanings for different groups, and that is why it was possible to form a winning coalition. To be adopted, every policy has to be sufficiently attractive to a sufficient number of people, but the whole process is writ large when a single issue has to be decided by popular vote, and it is writ still larger when the electorate is a very large one, and the campaign takes place through the mass media and is conducted by sophisticated public relations firms.

The success of Proposition 13 can be regarded as a popular reaction against 'governmental overload' (a concept mentioned in Chapter 1) and the accompanying feelings of alienation on the part of the voters. The great increase in fragmentation and complexity in American government has led, despite some trend towards decentralisation, to a remoteness from political life for the majority of the public who cannot cope with or understand current political issues. 'One of the many things that become harder to predict in an atomized politics is what the consequences of one's actions will be. . . . There comes to be even less connection than there once was between what the voters, even the majority of voters, want and what they get' (King 1978: 392). King puts the success of Proposition 13 down to the fact that the issue at stake was not just high property taxes, but a remote, complex government which was increasingly hard to understand and which had got beyond the voters' control. A leading line in Jarvis's campaign was the need for the people of California 'to gain control of the government again'. Proposition 13 was 'a form of generalized emotional release as well as a response to specific grievance for many voters' (King 1978: 393).

It is hardly surprising therefore that this particular policy was simple, indeed simplistic, in some respects, and ambiguous in others. These ambiguities and over-simplifications were exposed at the implementation stage. They were exposed all the more vividly because, in the nature of this particular case, those who had formulated and enacted the policy had no involvement in its implementation. Naturally the state officials and legislators who were responsible for implementing it took into account, in doing so, what they saw to be the general wishes of the electorate. Nevertheless there was only minimal feedback, and no opportunity to amend or develop the policy itself in order to overcome problems encountered during implementation and ensure that the end result reflected original intentions. In other words, the policy was prevented from evolving.

As we have seen, the end result was in marked conflict with the expectations held by supporters of the policy. Clearly, in California the most unpopular service was welfare, yet its funding pattern protected it from drastic cutback. Proposition 13 did not have the drastic effects on the economy which its opponents had predicted and it did offer tax relief to residential property owners, but in total individual taxpayers derived far less benefit than business (*The Economist* 1980). Some voters had been hoping for less remote government, but undoubtedly local governments have lost influence and there has been increased centralisation. The impact on education proved to be particularly severe: within the education service it proved difficult to 'cut administrators' because the latter were more capable than others of defending their own interests. Even more significant was the centralisation and politicisation of the service. Greater centralisation can actually increase the level of administration expenditure, while politicisation operates against the notion of a leaner and more innovative education service.

Unintended consequences like these are likely to be more marked if a proposed policy marks a sharp break with previous practice, or needs to mobilise diffuse public support through the use of symbolic language. This rather suggests that, where there is an attempt to make quantum cuts, a strategy of calculated risks, the gap between 'what the voters . . . want and what they get' may become larger rather than smaller. On one level, Proposition 13 succeeded in introducing dramatic fiscal constraints. On the other hand, a policy of this sort has a multiplicity of effects which it would be difficult for any political system to control.

Postscript

Recent evidence suggests that the California education service is still experiencing the negative impact of Proposition 13 (Pollard 1982; Fallon 1983; Kirst and Guthrie 1983). First, schools are suffering a financial crisis: the 1982/3 legislature (and schools are now highly dependent upon the state for financial support) gave schools no increased funding above the level of the previous year. In effect this means a substantial decrease in purchasing power.

The corollary of increased state-funding has been an increase in state control. Community colleges have been particularly vulnerable. The 1982/3 legislature reduced state-funding for personal development courses, including physical education and fine arts courses. The indications are that the state will be even more closely involved in priority setting in the 1983/4 budget year. The repercussions of Proposition 13 are so diffuse and multifaceted that they could not have been envisaged by supporters of the original initiative.

A marked deterioration in the quality of education may be an effect of increased financial pressures. The quality of teaching and teachers' salaries have dropped, the level of school achievement scores for high school students has fallen, and students spend less time at school studying less relevant subjects.

There is a general mood of discontent with public education in California which has not been countered by a strong pro-education group in the legislature. Former supporters of education in the legislature are reluctant to associate themselves with a service which is now generally perceived as deteriorating. Erosion of public confidence in public schools has meant an increase in the popularity of private schooling.

References

Boyd, W. 1979, 'Retrenchment in American education: the politics of efficiency', paper presented at the American Educational Research Association annual meeting, San Francisco, April

Brody, R. 1978, 'Who voted for proposition 13?', unpublished paper, Department of Political Science, Stanford University

California journal 1979, *Tax revolt digest*, Sacramento

Danziger, J.N. 1980, 'California's Proposition 13 and the fiscal limitation's movement in the United States', *Political studies*, vol. 27, no. 4, pp. 599–612

The Economist 1980, 'American survey', 5 January, pp. 15–23

Fallon, M. 1983, 'Community colleges' challenge: setting priorities for survival', *California journal*, March, pp. 129–31

Glennerster, H. 1980, 'Prime cuts: public expenditure and social services planning in a hostile environment', *Policy and politics*, vol. 8, no. 4, pp. 367–82

Heclo, H. and Wildavsky, A. 1974, *The private government of public money*, London, Macmillan

Jones, C. 1981, 'Cutting taxes in California', *Parliamentary affairs*, vol. xxxiv, no. 1

King, A. 1978, *The new American political system*, Washington DC, American Enterprise Institute for Public Policy Research

Kirst, M.W. 1980, 'The new political conflict in state education finance', *Taxation and spending*, vol. 3, pp. 46–53

Kirst, M.W. and Guthrie, J.W. 1983, 'Declining teacher quality', *California journal*, October, pp. 141–4

Niskanen, W. 1971, *Bureaucracy and representative government*, Chicago, Aldine Atherton

Pollard, V. 1982, 'California's classroom crisis', *California journal*, October, pp. 357–59

7 Industrial Strategy 1975–1979
The strategy that never was?
J.L. Metcalfe

Glendower: I can call spirits from the vasty deep.
Hotspur: Why, so can I, or so can any man;
            But will they come when you do call for them?

(Shakespeare, *Henry IV Part I*)

In November 1975 the Labour government launched a tripartite Industrial Strategy. It was intended to improve industrial performance and raise the rate of economic growth by getting to grips with long-term weaknesses of British industry. In its aims and initial diagnosis of problems, Industrial Strategy resembled earlier unsuccessful attempts to institute indicative planning. What differentiated Industrial Strategy from its predecessors was the means it adopted rather than the ends. It was much less technocratic than indicative planning and much more concerned to build support and commitment from the bottom up, by drawing management and unions into partnership with government. The hope was that a new spirit of co-operation could be summoned up through joint participation in existing Economic Development Committees (EDCs) and the newly-formed Sector Working Parties (SWPs). These tripartite groups were formed under the aegis of the National Economic Development Council (NEDC) and supported by the National Economic Development Office (NEDO). 'Neddy' provided a link between micro- and macro-level decision-making.

With the benefit of hindsight, centring Industrial Strategy on Neddy may appear a triumph of hope over experience. After all, Neddy had been involved in all previous planning exercises mounted by successive Conservative and Labour governments since the creation of NEDC in 1961. Each attempt had ended in failure. It was widely recognised that one factor contributing to failure was that too much top-level effort went into securing superficial commitments to broad policies and too little into assessing the feasibility of implementation: the path to economic decline is paved with declarations of intent.

Industrial Strategy sought to avoid this error through a bottom-up approach which gave greater weight to the nuts and bolts of implementation at company and sectoral level. Precisely how this realism was to be injected was not wholly clear and Industrial Strategy was viewed with more than a little scepticism. In part this was directed at Industrial Strategy *per se*, but often it encompassed the whole concept of Neddy and tripartism (Budd 1978; Grant 1980). It would be idle to pretend that Neddy was above criticism or that it could resolve fundamental questions about implementation. However, criticisms of Neddy are often based on misconceptions about its role and status. Constitutionally, Neddy is not part of government. It is an independent organisation based on voluntary participation. It has neither the statutory authority nor the resources to undertake implementation itself. As a non-executive body, it operates through persuasion rather than power.

If effectiveness is equated with direct executive action, Neddy is bound to be judged ineffective. But this evaluation ignores what it accomplishes indirectly by strengthening the network of relations among organisations at the government–industry interface. Neddy's distinctive role is developmental rather than executive. Its effectiveness should be judged by its success in cementing the precarious partnership between government, management and unions. Implementation of industrial policy is an inter-organisational process. No organisation or set of organisations can control or direct the whole process. Whereas policy implementation in some fields is in the hands of a single organised hierarchy, in the industrial policy field this is not so. Successful implementation depends on designing organisational roles to dovetail with one another rather than perpetuating adversarial conflicts (Metcalfe 1981a). It is because its effectiveness depends on producing results at one or two removes that Neddy is best regarded as a network organisation (Berry *et al.* 1974).

In order to see how far Industrial Strategy came to grips with the real problems of implementation as an inter-organisational process it is essential to consider several interrelated questions. Was there in fact a coherent strategy, or was the phrase high-sounding but empty rhetoric? If there was a strategy what was required to implement it? What approach to implementation was actually adopted? Did the capacity to implement exist? If not, what was done to create it?

This chapter is not a post-mortem, it is intended to draw out lessons about implementation relevant to the future conduct of industrial policy. The lessons are thrown into relief by first discussing the new features of the contemporary industrial policy context, then examining the events leading to the adoption of a tripartite approach, and finally analysing the requirements for implementing Industrial Strategy.

The industrial policy context: aspirations and capabilities
In the industrial policy context the gap between political aspiration and economic capability has widened considerably over the past decade. Even the poor growth record of the British economy in the 1950s and 1960s appears as a golden age of economic advance by comparison with recent experience of high inflation, high and rising unemployment, stagnation, and falling output. It is important to see that this change is common to the political economy of all advanced industrial societies. British problems are more acute but not unique.

There is a sharp contrast with the post-war period when Keynesian demand management seemed sufficient to cope with most foreseeable problems. Keynesian theory gave governments confidence that in principle, if not always in practice, they could manage – even fine-tune – their economies by choosing appropriate combinations of fiscal and monetary policies. The macro-management of demand stabilised the economic environment and allowed micro-level market forces to operate. Keynesian demand management also had the important political advantage that crucial macro-economic variables were under the control of government.

Through the post-war period, discrepancies between actual economic performance and the forecasts of demand management models were attributed to technical shortcomings, errors of judgement, or political irrationality. Failures did not undermine belief in the efficacy of demand management. But, since the breakdown of the international monetary system based on fixed exchange rates, the oil crises and the unexpected and unexplained occurrence of stagflation, the concept of demand management has been under severe attack. Governments no longer feel in control of events as economic managers lose confidence in their ability to deal with emergent problems.

The macro-management of supply
This sharp change in the industrial policy context has led some to conclude that demand management has failed and Keynesian policies should be discarded. This chapter proposes an alternative diagnosis with major implications for the conduct of industrial policy and hence for the evaluation of Industrial Strategy. Demand management is still necessary, but no longer sufficient. The complexity and interdependence of advanced industrial economies requires complementary processes for the macro-management of supply as well as demand management. In short, Keynes was not wrong, but in focusing on macro-problems on the demand-side and ignoring the supply-side, he was only half right (Metcalfe 1977, 1979, 1981b).

The missing element in current theories of economic management is an understanding of the need for the macro-management of supply. The lack of a capability for supply management in this sense was a major practical obstacle to the implementation of Industrial Strategy. Current macro-economic theories, monetarist as well as Keynesian, assume an asymmetry between the demand-side where there are macro- and micro-problems and the supply-side where only micro-problems are presumed to arise. The reason why there is now a need for supply management is that a substantial change in the nature and importance of adjustment problems on the supply-side has taken place. Demand management theories assume adjustment processes can operate incrementally through micro-market processes to bring about industrial change. The contention here is that some adjustment problems cannot be resolved in this way. Some adjustment problems require coordinated policies and concerted action at the sectoral and macro-levels.

This opens up a new conceptual domain for macro-economic management. Whereas demand management is concerned with the short-term utilisation of existing productive capacity, supply management is concerned with long-term structural change in productive capacity. Demand management can remedy unemployment by job creation and increased capacity utilisation within the existing industrial structure. It was never designed to deal with large-scale, qualitative shifts in industrial structure and attempts to use it to deal with macro-adjustment problems have proved counter-productive. The distinctive contribution of supply management is to address problems of large-scale structural transformation – industry creation rather than job creation.

Supply management and structural adjustment

Keynesian reliance on demand management led to a neglect of deep-seated structural problems on the supply side. Priority was given to minimising unemployment or averting balance of payments crises and the side-effects of stop–go policies on industry were largely ignored. The restricted time horizon of demand management, encapsulated in Keynes's remark that 'in the long run we are all dead', deflected attention from long-term industrial adjustment problems.

In the last few years, the situation has changed. Events have forced supply-side problems onto the political agenda. Eminent economists such as Klein (1978) have been moved to point out the supply-side implications of demand management. This rearguard action was partly prompted by monetarist criticisms of expansionist Keynesian policies. However, monetarist advocates of supply-side economics have added little to our understanding of the behaviour of the supply-side of the economy. Their main assumption has been that adjustment problems could be satisfactorily solved at the micro-level if market forces were given a freer rein. Indeed, much of the recent debate about industrial policy has followed familiar lines: individualism versus collectivism; market forces versus government intervention. But, this polarisation of views fails to reflect the emerging realities of the contemporary industrial context.

A more appropriate model of the industrial policy process is founded on the assumption that modern economies are pluralistic rather than atomistic or unitary. The supply-side is a complex network of functionally interdependent but formally autonomous organisations. Coordination depends primarily on inter-organisational bargaining. To some extent economic adjustment is achieved incrementally by piecemeal bargaining within an existing industrial structure. But industrial structure is not static, it evolves, and the processes of evolution are not all reducible to marginal changes. The demise of obsolete industries and the development of 'sunrise' industries are punctuated by sudden discontinuous changes. These problems of structural adjustment require careful management to avoid costly and widespread disruption.

As this suggests, the distinctive characteristics and problems of the political economy of pluralism originate in organised complexity (LaPorte 1975). Organised complexity means more than diverse forms of business enterprise operating in an environment dominated by large businesses and oligopolistic market structures. In addition there are trade unions, trade associations, employers' organisations, professional bodies and government departments all with roles to play and interests to pursue.

Industrial turbulence

The network of relations among these organisations creates a disturbed reactive environment of precarious stability. Even at the best of times individual organisations underestimate their dependence on the framework of relationships which is produced by bargaining and negotiation; and pluralistic economies tend to drift rather than plot a definite course. When change is rapid and discontinuous, conventional bargaining to advance particular interests undermines the stability of the industrial environment and creates turbulent conditions. While turbulence is something of a vogue term, it is used here in a precise sense to designate a situation in which organisations are driven to act in ways which are self-defeating from their own standpoint and counter-productive from the standpoint of the efficiency and productivity of the economy as a whole. Major structural change requires investments which only bear fruit in the long term. And only then if others continue to play their part. Lack of confidence in the ability and willingness of others to co-operate in making changes destroys the value of otherwise worthwhile investments and industrial adjustment fails to occur (Emery and Trist 1965; Metcalfe 1974).

Furthermore this self-fulfilling prophecy, in which expectations of failure lead to actions which guarantee failure, establishes a vicious circle. Conflicts spread and escalate instead of being localised and moderated. Groups remote from the initial flare-up become embroiled in increasingly intractable and long drawn-out disputes which embitter relations among those responsible for resolving them. As definitions of the situation become less and less realistic and more and more politicised the prospects of economic development recede further into the future.

Industrial turbulence is an example of one of the classic problems of public policy where individually rational actions produce a collective irrational outcome. Because of lack of insight, mutual mistrust or lack of appropriate institutions, the uncoordinated pursuit of separate interests produces an outcome no one desires and none had intended (Buckley *et al*. 1974). Overcoming these centrifugal forces requires coordinated action at the macro-level to create a new framework to guide organisational activity and regulate inter-organisational conflict. Managing turbulence requires a capacity for supply management at the macro-level. The implementation of the changes needed cannot be done by government alone. It is a process to which both sides of industry must also contribute. Hence supply management imposes significant new demands on government–industry relations which existing institutions are not necessarily equipped to meet.

The background to Industrial Strategy

There is a clear correspondence between the concept of supply management outlined above and the tripartite approach to Industrial Strategy. But it is important to stress that Industrial Strategy was not conceived on this basis. The build-up was much more empirical and in certain respects it was a reaction to circumstances.

Perhaps there is never a good time to try new ventures in industrial politics, but the situation in which Industrial Strategy sought to create common ground was distinctly unpropitious. Economically, the shock of the oil crisis created new problems and increased the urgency of dealing with long-term problems of industrial adjustment. Politically, there was a need to make good the damage due to persistently poor economic performance and years of increasingly bitter adversarial conflict.

Both Conservative and Labour governments had become embroiled in unsuccessful attempts to reform industrial relations. The Conservative government which held office from 1970 to 1974 had a series of confrontations with the trade unions. The Labour government which took office in 1974 had better relations with the unions; but creating the National Enterprise Board and attempting to institute planning agreements with individual companies was almost calculated to alienate employers. After the referendum on entry into the European Community and the replacement of Mr Wedgewood Benn by Mr Varley at the Department of Industry there was a reversal of attitude symbolised by the initiation of Industrial Strategy. The tripartite bottom-up approach to industrial policy-making offered the government a means of rebuilding relationships with both sides of industry and sharing responsibility for managing industrial change.

Industrial Strategy was also attractive to the representatives of industry. From the standpoint of the CBI, Neddy appeared to offer a means of bringing the views of industry more effectively before government. From the TUC point of view tripartism gave an opportunity for greater involvement and participation in industrial policy-making. Thus, there was a congruence of motives but certainly not a consensus or an identity of interests behind the willingness of the three estates of industrial politics to take part in developing a strategy for industry.

However, Industrial Strategy was based on more than a political desire to build bridges and mend fences. For some time beforehand NEDO had been involved in activities which foreshadowed the development of Industrial Strategy. Economic analyses by NEDO economists gave a sharper picture of where there was a need to shift resources out of declining industries and into growing industries (Panić and Rajan 1971). This work underscored the urgency of developing policies to steer the economy in accord with changes in patterns of world trade. It provided a strategic objective, a target – albeit a moving target – against which to gauge the extent and direction of required structural changes.

In parallel with this analytical work, Neddy had been gaining experience in aiding the process of structural adjustment at the sectoral level. The work of the Wool Textiles Economic Development Committee in diagnosing the problems of the wool textile industry and moving on to formulate and implement an industry-wide reorganisation scheme provided a model which other sectors might follow. Importantly, there were in wool textiles institutions and inter-organisational relationships at the industry level which could facilitate diagnosis of industry-wide problems and share responsibility for implementation. Neddy drew on the good working relationships among the organisations at the industry level and facilities for participation by and communications with groups and organisations at the micro-level. In this respect, wool textiles was unusual. Few other industrial sectors possessed a political and organisational infrastructure as well developed as that in wool textiles (Metcalfe and McQuillan 1979). An analysis of implementation requirements would have raised doubts about the feasibility of applying the same approach more widely without a substantial amount of groundwork to create the infrastructure for strategic decision-making.

The role of implementation analysis

It is common but inappropriate to treat implementation as an afterthought, as subordinate and secondary to policy formulation. Often problems of implementation are swept under the carpet to gain a temporary political advantage, only to re-emerge later. Ignoring implementation can lead decision-makers to choose ill-thought-out modifications of existing policies in the name of pragmatism or to oscillate between inaction and blind commitment to new policies. 'There is a tendency to delay a long time the introduction of a new programme because of uncertainties and then suddenly jump in with a large commitment to a prescribed programme with no better knowledge than before when political pressure for doing something becomes too strong' (Nelson *et al.* 1967: 173). Once announced, policies are presented as if implementation is assured.

Neglect of implementation leaves policy advice incomplete, because the feasibility of policy options is not evaluated; consequently, policy statements are apt to remain vague and ambiguous. Early attention to implementation requirements, on the other hand, enables participants to nip in the bud problems that would later foment misunderstanding, conflict and delay.

Concern for implementation is the exception rather than the rule and for that reason alone it is worth quoting a positive example of careful attention to implementation ensuring policy success. The example is Montgomery's El Alamein campaign. Bernard Montgomery was appointed to command the Eighth Army in North Africa in early August 1942. He arrived in Egypt with his strategy for containing the enemy's advance and subsequently defeating them already formulated. But he found an army, demoralised after a series of defeats, with plans for rearguard action to cover its retreat. He acted immediately to prepare for offensive action and to assess the readiness of his troops to implement his plans.

The confidence and clarity with which Montgomery presented his plans made an immediate impact at all levels. Churchill approved them at once and Montgomery went to considerable trouble to ensure that the details were communicated effectively to his troops. As planned, the holding operation of Alam Halfa halted Rommel's advance. This reinforced Montgomery's credibility as a commander who could formulate and implement realistic strategies.

Though this success was welcome, it did not satisfy Churchill. His domestic political position was shaky and he had entered into commitments with the Americans and Russians which depended on early success in North Africa. Churchill was anxious that Alam Halfa should be followed up quickly to consolidate his position. Montgomery refused; not because of policy differences, but because he needed to create the conditions for successful implementation of the agreed policy. Success depended on greater coordination of ground and air forces, and troops needed training in new tactics. These preparations needed time and Montgomery informed Churchill that the Eighth Army would not be ready until the end of October. As a trainer of soldiers as well as a commander, Montgomery knew his troops needed thorough preparation to assure success.

The battle of El Alamein began on the night of 23 October 1942 and raged for twelve days. Its successful outcome was due in no small measure to the trouble Montgomery had taken to see that his troops were capable of implementing his plans. As Karl Deutsch (1966) observed, leaders neglect 'internal intelligence' at their peril: the effectiveness of policies depends on the commitment of those who have to carry them out. 'Even in warfare the first thing a general must know is not the numbers and capabilities and intentions of the enemy, but the numbers, capabilities, and reliability of his own troops' (Deutsch 1966: 159–60).

The politics of implementation: two key issues

Though turbulence does sometimes produce conflicts which are referred to as 'industrial trench warfare', it is not suggested that Industrial Strategy could or should have been conducted like a military campaign. Its purpose was to create a framework for co-operation among interdependent interests to supplant destructive conflict. The Montgomery example is useful because it is a positive example of close attention to implementation requirements which highlight two key issues in the politics of implementation.

The first key issue is managing the relationship between policy implementation and the political environment. There is an inescapable tension between those primarily responsible for policy and those responsible for implementation symbolised in the case of El Alamein by Churchill and Montgomery. Often responsibilities for policy and implementation overlap; the boundaries between the expectations of external publics and the internal needs of implementation are blurred; maintaining a workable balance means coping with ambiguity and conflict. If external political considerations dominate, it is impossible to buffer implementation from the disruptive 'action this day' mentality of electoral politics. If internal administrative considerations dominate, policy-making is apt to become oriented to maintaining the *status quo*. Good judgement is needed to separate the wheat of significant political change from the chaff of passing fads and fashions.

The second key issue in the politics of implementation is the design of an approach to implementation which takes account of the character-istics of the policy problems, available resources and the interests involved. There is no one best way, no single approach works in all circumstances. Implementation analysts should follow the lead of organisation theorists in developing a contingency approach to the design of implementation processes. Berman's (1980) analysis of pro-grammed and adaptive implementation provides a useful beginning. Programmed implementation

> assumes that implementation problems can be made tolerable if not eliminated, by careful and explicit pre-programming of implementation procedures. The other view, which could be called adaptive implementation, holds that policy execution can be improved by procedures that enable initial plans to be adapted to unfolding events and decisions. (Berman 1980: 205–6).

The evolution of Industrial Strategy
In the light of this discussion we can consider how the implementation problems of Industrial Strategy were addressed. The adaptive or bottom-up approach had two potential advantages. First, by focusing on specifics it could moderate unrealistic expectations of rapid results. The process began with SWPs analysing the problems of their industries and producing detailed recommendations. SWPs were charged with examining the prospects of their industries over a five-year period and formulating objectives in terms of increased share of world trade, improvements in export performance and import substi-tution. The implications of these objectives for changes in government policies, company policies and industrial relations were then worked out, along with actions needed to improve performance. Thus the early phases of Industrial Strategy were to be buffered from national political pressure to give those directly involved the chance to formulate feasible policies.

The second potential advantage of the bottom-up approach was to permit those directly involved the chance to design and develop appropriate means of implementation. As observed earlier, given the pluralistic character of the economy, the tripartite approach, the non-executive role of SWPs and the complexity of adjustment problems, it was clear that implementation would be an inter-organisational process. Further, the problems of managing supply precluded a programmed approach. An adaptive approach was needed to allow for unforeseen eventualities and to permit plans to evolve through negotiation over time. But adaptive implementation calls for greater organisational capabilities and resourcefulness as well as greater confidence and mutual trust among the participating organisations.

Starting from a base of existing EDCs, thirty SWPs were formed. Subsequently, the number was increased to forty. Seventeen SWPs were created to cover sectors formerly under the umbrella of the Mechanical Engineering EDC. The priority given to engineering was part of a topical concern with deindustrialisation and the erosion of the UK economy's manufacturing base.

Emphasis on manufacturing industry had negative as well as positive implications. Non-manufacturing industries, such as agriculture and hotels and catering, were excluded from Industrial Strategy even though they had performed better than many manufacturing industries. Moreover, the significance of its well-developed institutional infrastructure for the performance of the agricultural industry was overlooked.

Sectoral investigations supported the initial attempt to maintain a low political profile. The paper presented at the Chequers meeting of NEDC by the Chancellor of the Exchequer and Secretary of State for Industry on 5 November 1975 outlined 'An Approach to Industrial Strategy', not a blueprint. There were no political fireworks and no directives. This tactic was intended to give time to unfreeze negotiating positions and circumvent the ideological disputes about economic planning engrained in British political culture. The involvement of scores of industrialists and trade unionists in a process of inquiry on an equal footing with government did not fit the ideological preconceptions of Left or Right.

The extent to which this low-key approach succeeded in gaining time and space was qualified in three ways. First, the charge of corporatism was made. By selective extrapolation of trends and attribution of guilt by association with planning agreements and the National Enterprise Board, Industrial Strategy was portrayed as a harbinger of an autocratic corporate state (Pahl and Winkler 1974). A substantial amount of contradictory evidence had to be ignored to sustain the corporatist thesis, which directly contradicted the common view that tripartism was quite ineffective and Neddy merely a talking-shop. Second, Industrial Strategy was attacked because it involved 'picking winners'. On the face of it this was a difficult criticism to rebut. Industrial

Strategy was intended to discriminate between industries with good prospects and declining industries. In part this criticism was deflected by NEDO's pointing to substantial scope for improving the efficiency distribution of firms within industries.

Finally, and perhaps most important, the political credibility of Industrial Strategy was damaged by the response of NEDC to the Treasury's medium-term economic forecast presented by the Chancellor, Mr Healey, in August 1976. It contained two scenarios: one based on current policies, foresaw a rise of GDP of 3½ per cent per year to 1980 – this implied increased unemployment; the alternative projected growth of 4½–5½ per cent per year to 1980 with manufacturing output growing at a remarkable 8 per cent. The first scenario was rejected by NEDC as unacceptably low and the more optimistic targets of the second scenario were adopted. Despite the supposed commitment to a bottom-up approach NEDC took this decision without consulting SWPs.

SWPs were asked to work out medium-term projections for their sectors based on these unrealistic macro-assumptions. The credibility of the whole exercise declined still further as a result of the Treasury's reticence about disclosing more realistic medium-term forecasts. The confidence of some SWPs was lost. While some accepted the assumptions, others simply ignored them. But as growth slowed to stagnation, and inflation and unemployment rose, it became clear that even the assumptions of the pessimistic scenario were over-optimistic.

The sequence of events was symptomatic of a real dilemma in handling the relations between different levels of decision-making. If individual SWPs conducted their own analyses they could be combined only if they were based on common assumptions. But if common assumptions were handed down to SWPs from macro-economic forecasts, was this bottom-up strategy formation or merely top-down planning with token involvement?

There was, as one participant described it, an extended theological discussion in NEDC about how to resolve this dilemma. But the problem was badly posed; strategy formation required both top-down and bottom-up processes to ensure internal consistency and build organisational commitment. In addition to the technical problems of aggregation and disaggregation, this multi-level process involved negotiating political solutions to problems of integration. Translating and interpreting feedback from different levels and diverse interests was a complex and unfamiliar task.

It is not surprising in this context that Neddy found difficulty in projecting itself as a catalyst of inter-organisational problem-solving and concerted tripartite action. By contrast, observers of Japanese business and government–industry relations have found substantial cultural support for group problem-solving at all levels. Individuals and organisations seek to align their policies and avoid setting out on collision courses. Group problem-solving does not necessarily ensure better decisions, but it does increase the probability of effective implementation (Pascale 1978a, 1978b; Vogel 1979). In West Germany, Switzerland and Austria the involvement of representative industrial organisations in industrial policy-making also increased the problem-solving capacity of their respective industrial policy systems. Joint action achieved results government alone could not implement (Lehmbruch 1977).

Lack of established institutional support made Industrial Strategy vulnerable to short-term political pressures. SWPs were asked to identify obstacles to immediate expansion. When the belief that growth was just around the corner proved unfounded, a new start had to be made. Although it had the advantage of a government commitment to give a high priority to industrial needs, Industrial Strategy was bound to disappoint expectations of a comprehensive attack on industrial weaknesses. At most, SWPs and EDCs covered 60 per cent of manufacturing industry and even this was achieved only by creating SWPs which took time to become operational.

Implementation: requirements and realities

Man-traps are dangerous only in relation to the limitations on what men can see and value and do. The nature of the trap is a function of the nature of the trapped.

(Vickers 1972: 15)

Even if Industrial Strategy was not well protected from unrealistic political pressures, it is still worth considering how well it used its limited room for manoeuvre. How much effort went into designing a viable approach to implementation? Measured against the requirements of implementation based on the concept of supply management, what was done was disappointing. Three sets of requirements can be inferred from the earlier discussion of structural adjustment, industrial turbulence and supply management. First, implementation of large-scale structural change required substantial institutional capabilities and robust inter-organisational relations. But the existing industrial infrastructure was neither substantial nor robust. Shonfield (1965) had observed the 'weak industrial nexus' of industrial policy-making. Metcalfe and McQuillan (1979) presented detailed empirical data documenting institutional deficiencies. Ironically, relations among government, management and unions were particularly fragmentary in the engineering sectors where Industrial Strategy was supposed to make a major impact. *Thus, there was a marked gap between institutional requirements and existing capabilities.* Successful implementation depended on closing that gap. Neddy, as a network organisation, had experience of the problems of catalysing this kind of organisational development. Even so, bringing institutions up to the required standard across most of industry could not be accomplished quickly.

The second requirement of effective implementation followed from the strategic objective of withdrawing from obsolescent industries and identifying opportunities to create new industries. The adjustment problems associated with managing industrial decline and industry creation are far more complex than adjusting existing activities to changing levels of demand. *Different types of adjustment problem require appropriate handling to maintain momentum for change without provoking counter-productive conflicts.* Conflict is an unvoidable part of large-scale structural change. The need is to devise ways of promoting constructive processes of conflict resolution. Failure to do so is massively costly in itself and leaves a residue of bitterness which hampers subsequent efforts.

The third requirement followed from the first two. *It was essential to be clear at what levels problems should be addressed.* Many problems can be handled only at the micro-level. The introduction of new products and technologies, with consequential changes in manpower needs, management structures and working practices, involves changes within companies and plants. Even at this level intra-organisational changes may depend on redefining relations with the industrial environment to seek new sources of finance, identify new suppliers and open up new markets.

But not all changes are reducible to sequential adjustments at the micro-level. Some changes in the environment involve simultaneous adjustment by the whole network of organisations in an industry. Some changes involve redefinition of relations among industries. Finally, a limited range of issues are so broad in scope that they can only be dealt with at the macro-level. Supply management is necessarily a multi-level process with higher levels creating a framework for more specific decision-making.

These demanding requirements indicated a need for early consideration of implementation and for an adaptive rather than a programmed approach. The problems were not well defined or homogeneous and solutions could not be prescribed in advance. In practice this did not happen. Perceptions of implementation requirements were severely constrained and at first they did not receive a great deal of attention. Perhaps some delay was excusable because management, unions and government had to learn how to work with each other in a tripartite context before addressing implementation problems. But it was not until 1978 that the focus of attention shifted from strategy formulation to implementation. When it did, the three requirements outlined above received only superficial consideration. There was no thorough-going analysis of implementation needs. Excessively simplified assumptions were made about the nature of adjustment problems, the level at which they should be dealt with, and little was done to rectify organisational deficiencies. By default rather than design, reliance was placed on working through existing organisations.

Reliance on existing institutions imposed severe limitations on what was feasible. Implementation became a piecemeal process with the various participants being assigned separate responsibility for particular SWP recommendations rather than combining in the joint resolution of structural problems. At first, largely because lines of communications were better, implementation by government received prominence. Government signalled its commitment to Industrial Strategy by giving the Department of Industry a more active role. Non-industrial departments were also required to give industrial needs higher priority, for example, by giving more attention to industrial training requirements and speeding the processing of planning applications. In some ways it was easier for government to implement specific recommendations. For example, several SWPs asked for the Exports Credits Guarantee Department to adopt policies better attuned to their exporting efforts. Partly as a result of the Electronic Components SWP's work a £70 million micro-electronics industry support programme was announced by the government in July 1978.

Despite these indications of government commitment there could still be problems. One case which provoked public controversy was the independent line pursued by the National Enterprise Board when it launched its INMOS venture in disregard of the work of the Electronic Components SWP. More generally, there was dissatisfaction in industry because of the restrictiveness of macro-economic demand management policies. As the international economic environment deteriorated and the performance of the domestic economy worsened, control over the money supply was tightened and restrictions on public expenditure hit industry. This reduced industrial incentives to invest and meant that the take-up of grants was less than government wanted to see. Demand management policies undermined rather than supported the implementation of Industrial Strategy on the supply side.

It was assumed that the burden of responsibility for implementation would fall on companies and workers at the micro-level. But implementation in industry was slow to get under way. In view of institutional deficiencies this was unsurprising, but instead of confronting the issue of increasing capabilities the implementation problem was narrowly defined as a communications problem. It was a short step from this diagnosis to the conclusion that a communications exercise was needed to get the message down to the micro-level.

The communications exercise

The communications exercise mounted by NEDO in 1978 had government backing, and support from the TUC and CBI. It was intended to sharpen the public image of Industrial Strategy, but its main function was to bridge the gap between the sectoral activities of SWPs and their industrial grass roots. A wide variety of methods of communication was used but the results were disappointing. There were two important weaknesses in the communications exercise as a design for implementation. First, it was based on a programmed rather than an adaptive concept of implementation. The criterion of success was whether specific recommendations of SWPs were adopted at the micro-level. This type of diffusion of innovations process (Schon 1971) works most effectively in relatively stable conditions, where there are already well-defined patterns of communication, influence and opinion leadership. As already indicated, in much of British industry institutional linkages are rather weak.

The second weakness was that it fell into the trap of attempting to decompose complex, systemic problems into a series of micro-problems amenable to separate solutions. In so doing it disregarded the high level of interdependence in a pluralistic economy. Hence, the communications exercise did little to create the environmental conditions on which its ultimate success depended.

Although the communications exercise represented the main thrust, it was not the only element in the implementation of Industrial Strategy. In addition there was widening appreciation at the sectoral level of customer–supplier relationships. An important function of the Neddy machinery was that it provided a context in which general problems affecting the relationships between industrial sectors could be aired and ways of improving them identified. For example, the Footwear SWP, representing a very fragmented industry supplying a very concentrated retail trade, gained an improved understanding of future customer requirements. In order to maintain this level of understanding substantial development of inter-organisational relations at the sectoral level would be needed. Operating in a more integrated industry network the Mining Machinery SWP with participation by the NCB helped direct attention to the development of export markets.

Thus the approach to implementation adopted fell well short of all three of the requirements outlined above, perhaps because, as the Director General of NEDO observed, it was basically empirical and lacked a guiding theoretical rationale (Chandler 1978). The communications exercise was too little, too late and too piecemeal. It was a surrogate for and not a solution to the problems of implementing supply-side structural change. In many ways it perpetuated the old demand-management concept of government and industry having separate roles and responsibilities rather than sharing in an integrated process of managing industrial change.

Conclusions

With the defeat of the Labour government in May 1979 Industrial Strategy formally came to an end even though EDCs and SWPs continued to produce reports and make recommendations. The political impetus had been lost some time earlier as economic and political events distracted attention. It is easy to dismiss it as a failure – as the strategy that never was. Many would go further and share Grant's (1980) view that Industrial Strategy was not only an implementation failure in a narrow sense, but also revealed fundamental weaknesses in Neddy and the concept of tripartism. However, such a conclusion would only be justified if any future tripartite strategy were subject to the same practical and conceptual limitations as Industrial Strategy. This chapter has sought to show that there are other options and to outline the implementation requirements they imply.

On the assumption that the problem of steering large-scale structural change is not about to evaporate it is worth considering the lessons of Industrial Strategy for the political economy of pluralism. Following Scharpf (1978) this can be done by comparing the results of descriptive analyses of actual inter-organisational networks with requirements deduced from a prescriptive theory. The most important general lesson is that structural problems require capacities for the macro-management of supply which far exceed the actual capabilities of governmental, management and union organisations. Effective supply management, as an inter-organisational process, requires sustained co-operation from organisations with a history of mutual antagonism and mistrust. Before new relationships and roles could develop negative attitudes would have to be unlearned. Despite previous experience in facilitating such developments, Neddy did not persuade its constituents to make the organisational investments and strengthen inter-organisational relations.

Failure to deal with this basic weakness meant that implementation was too piecemeal. Reliance on the existing industrial infrastructure severely limited what could be achieved. Implementation was a segregated rather than an integrated process; government departments made certain changes and firms were expected to make others. The communications exercise was based on the assumption that economic adjustment depended primarily on decisions within firms. It largely ignored the fact that organisational interdependence made the success of changes in one firm contingent on what was happening elsewhere in the industrial environment. Not all adjustment problems are little ones. Changes in the behaviour of firms is the end product of more complex adjustment processes.

The more complex, turbulence-generating problems which required concerted action at the sectoral and macro-levels were not well handled. As the El Alamein example showed, successful implementation means taking care that general objectives are consistent and comprehensible to those at the sharp end, as well as adapting detailed plans in response to feedback indicating that initial proposals are unworkable. In contrast, the objectives of Industrial Strategy were unrealistically ambitious and, despite espousal of a bottom-up approach, they were not revised to bring them into the realms of feasibility.

Improvements in customer–supplier relations were an important exception to the general failure to provide an internal intelligence function. Individual customers and suppliers could make little headway in improving their mutual relations. But once the general problems were identified at the industry level, SWPs could act as network organisations to establish a dialogue and to create more effective links across industry boundaries.

Underlying specific criticisms is the general point that implementation was perceived as a programmed process rather than an adaptive, evolutionary process. Of course the burden of developmental responsibilities would have proved too great for the severely limited capabilities of the organisations involved. But a necessary condition for guiding the evolution of the economy is a serious effort to strengthen inter-organisational capabilities. It is unlikely that the choice between small but critical institutional investments and the large costs of continuing industrial turbulence will be understood until the concept of supply management is fully appreciated.

Significant as these deficiencies are, they are not irredeemable. Far from revealing inherent defects in tripartism, this analysis shows that Industrial Strategy did not address some of the major challenges of tripartite policy implementation. To echo Chesterton's observation about Christianity: it is not that tripartism has been tried and found wanting. It has been found difficult and left untried.

References

Berman, P. 1980, 'Thinking about programmed and adaptive implementation: matching strategies to situations', in Helen M. Ingram and Dean E. Mann (eds), *Why policies succeed or fail*, London, Sage

Berry, D.F., Metcalfe, L. and McQuillan, W. 1974, 'Neddy: an organizational metamorphosis', *Journal of management studies*, 11 February, pp. 1–20

Buckley, W., Burns, T.R. and Meeker, L.D. 1974, 'Structural resolutions of collective action problems', *Behavioural science*, 19, pp. 277–97

Budd, A. 1978, *The politics of economic planning*, London, Fontana

Chandler, G. 1978, 'The reindustrialisation of Britain', *CBI review*, Autumn/Winter 1978, pp. 2–8

Deutsch, K.W. 1966, *The nerves of government*, New York, Free Press

Emery, F.E. and Trist, E.L. 1965, 'The causal texture of organizational environments', *Human relations*, 18, 21–32

Grant, W. 1980, *The last Labour government's industrial strategy. Problems of policy implementation through a tripartite framework*, PAC Conference, York

Klein, L.R. 1978, 'The supply side', *The American economic review*, vol. 68, no. 1, pp. 1–7

LaPorte, T.R. (ed.) 1975, *Organized social complexity*, Princeton, N.J., Princeton University Press

Lehmbruch, G. 1977, 'Liberal corporatism and party government', *Comparative political studies*, vol. 10, no. 1, pp. 91–126

Metcalfe, J.L. 1974, 'Systems models, economic models and the causal texture of organizational environments: an approach to macro-organization theory', *Human relations*, 27, pp. 639–63

Metcalfe, J.L. 1977, *The macro management of supply as a frontier problem*, EIASM Conference, 'Frontier problems in Strategic Management', Venice

Metcalfe, J.L. 1978, 'Policy-making in turbulent environments', in Hanf, K. and Scharpf, F.W. (eds), *Interorganizational policy making*, London, Sage Modern Politics Series, vol. 1, pp. 37–55

Metcalfe, J.L. 1979, 'A strategy for economic development', Preprint series, West Berlin, International Institute of Management

Metcalfe, J.L. 1981a, 'Designing precarious partnerships', in Nystrom, P.C. and Starbuck, W.H. (eds), *Handbook of organisational design*, Oxford, Oxford University Press, pp. 503–30

Metcalfe, J.L. 1981b, *Planning for structural change*, Inter-University Centre Conference on 'Planning and democracy', Dubrovnik

Metcalfe, J.L. and McQuillan, W.F. 1979, 'Corporatism or industrial democracy?', *Political studies*, vol. 27, no. 2, pp. 266–82

Nelson, R.R., Peck, M.J. and Kalachek, E.D. 1967, *Technology, economic growth and public policy*, Washington, Brookings Institution

Pahl, R.E. and Winkler, J.T. 1974, 'The coming corporatism', *New society*, 10 October, pp. 72–6

Paniç, M. and Rajan, A. 1971, *Product changes in industrial countries' trade: 1955–68*, NEDO Monograph No. 2, London, HMSO

Pascale, R.T. 1978a, 'Zen and the art of management', *Harvard business review*, March–April, pp. 153–62

Pascale, R.T. 1978b, 'Communication and decision-making across cultures. Japanese and American comparisons', *Administrative science quarterly*, vol. 23, no. 1, pp. 91–110

Scharpf, F.W. 1978, 'Interorganizational policy studies: issues, concepts, perspectives', in Hanf, K. and Scharpf, F.W., (eds) *Interorganizational policy making*, London, Sage Modern Politics Series, vol. 1, pp. 345–70

Schon, D.A. 1971, *Beyond the stable state*, London, Temple Smith

Shonfield, A. 1965, *Modern capitalism*, London, Oxford University Press

Treasury/Department of Industry 1975, *An approach to industrial strategy*, (Cmnd 6315), London, HMSO

Vickers, G.C. 1972, *Freedom in a rocking boat*, Harmondsworth, Penguin

Vogel, E.F. 1979, *Japan as number one*, Cambridge, Mass., Harvard University Press

PART II

8 Implementation across National Boundaries

Helen Wallace

In entering the international arena of policy-making we find many fleeting shadows but little of apparent substance. Consultations among governments abound: since the second world war international organisations have multiplied, dealing with almost every subject of governmental involvement, yet much of international 'policy' remains rhetoric and good intention and such substantive agreements as emerge still depend largely on the willingness of individual governments to implement them. Though many students of international relations have laboured to identify an international system or international society, policies agreed internationally cannot rest on the bedrock of a state or on a broadly stable political and legal framework, or on a pattern of shared expectations. International co-operation lacks the powers, authority, legitimacy and structures on which policy-makers within states rely so heavily to give effect to their policy decisions (Donelan 1978). Inevitably, therefore, the process of agreeing and executing policies through international agreement is often experimental and tentative by comparison with the policy processes discussed earlier in this volume.

In Part II we are dealing with an animal of an unusual and rather primitive species. The literature on the implementation as distinct from the negotiation of international policies is sparse. The case studies which follow are intended to aid our understanding of how international agreements are given substance through implementation within states. The examples are all British and by no means typical of the untidy patchwork of contemporary international co-operation. But they are cases in which either policies new to the participating governments have been executed, or national policies and laws have been significantly altered. The Polaris project (Chapter 11) rested on tightly-knit and highly co-operative collaboration between the American and British governments. Its implementation benefited from the strikingly intimate bilateral relationship between the UK and the

United States. Chapters 9 and 10 examine the implementation in the UK of policies agreed within the European Community (EC), dealing respectively with legal regulation and financial distribution. Of all international organisations the EC has become the most state-like in terms of its political structures and policy processes. Fortuitously, our examples have a perverse connection: brilliant negotiating skills by the British at Nassau may have laid the ground for the effective implementation of the Polaris project, yet the adverse reaction of General de Gaulle to the announcement of the agreement contributed to the breakdown of negotiations for EC membership, as a result of which in the 1970s British officials were to find themselves implementing EC policies which they had played no part in formulating.

Over the last three decades or so governments have found themselves increasingly and intensively addressing through international consultation problems which transcend their individual capabilities. Political, economic and security interdependence have resulted in international co-operation biting deeper and deeper into areas of direct domestic relevance and traditional domestic responsibility. In implementing the Polaris programme British policy-makers had, for example, to accept restrictions on the right to manufacture a wide range of standard equipment in the UK. Within the EC framework programmes *inter alia* to train young workers entering the labour market have been part-funded from the Community exchequer. The subject-matter and contents of our case studies are such that they throw back recognisable echoes of the features identified earlier in this volume as relevant to understanding policy implementation. Those who struggle to make international agreements stick and to secure compliance with international obligations can draw some lessons from the implementation strategies that have been enunciated as relevant within states (Berman 1980). Programmed strategies seem to be possible only in limited cases where close partnership, high interdependence or functional specialisation permit, or where there is a firmly established legal and institutional code. Elsewhere adaptiveness and gradual adjustment emerge as the predominant modes, dependent on the characteristic features of international negotiation.

International co-operation: policies without process
Yet clearly the context of international co-operation is qualitatively different from policy-making within states. First and foremost the persisting sovereignty of states means that powers rest largely with national governments and the implementation of international agreements is primarily dependent on national agencies (though by no means always confined to central governments). Powers are horizontally and

unevenly dispersed amongst the participants and thus a top-down strategy of implementation is hardly an option, except in so far as one state is so dependent on or so vulnerable to another that its internal policy machinery can be subordinated. Policy-making at the international level is not embedded in stable structures. Even though the international system has become highly organised its structures are largely those of 'concertation' (a process of gradually concerting or aligning views by mutual persuasion) and consensus rather than of authority and majority rule. Where a government anticipates problems in implementing a proposal under international negotiation, it will rarely give its consent. The rules of the international game are themselves subject to continual challenge and redefinition. To some extent they are conditional, leaving individual governments in practice the opportunity to opt out of implementing agreements which are unpalatable, irksome or practically difficult.

International co-operation is characterised by heterogeneity. The participants are diverse culturally, politically and economically; thus their expectations of what is desirable or possible as the end product of agreement differ markedly, as may their interpretations of their commitments to implement. While international policy co-operation is often highly charged and conflictual, politics takes a different form from that within states. Agreement depends on negotiation, which in turn generally requires compromise to enable different approaches, objectives, ideologies, values and administrative practices to co-exist within the framework of a decision to collaborate or collectively to pursue compatible national policies (Winham 1977, 1979). Though bargaining and compromise often characterise the policy process within states, internationally there is far less chance of coherence of policy at the formulation phase and consequently more chance of divergent and contradictory patterns of implementation. Here it must be noted that a rough analogy can be made with policy-making in federal and confederal systems of government with the intrinsic frictions and differences of perspective which these generally embrace.

The pace at which international co-operation moves is characteristically slow. Agreements have to be built up painstakingly through protracted negotiation. The time lags between the initial definition of the problem and eventual policy output are often such that implementation takes place in an environment significantly different from that originally envisaged. The scope for adaptation is limited since renegotiation is often impracticable or risks prejudicing the earlier agreement. The ratifying governments may faithfully comply with the eventual agreement, but the context and issues may have moved on. Yet a decision not to comply may undermine the fragile structures and

understandings through which policy was formulated. Mechanisms for feedback may be imperfect or non-existent given the number of levels involved and given the co-existence of different yardsticks for evaluating and responding to policy outputs. Information about compliance or non-compliance is at best imperfect, at worst absent; few governments can resist portraying their record of implementation in the most favourable terms possible, and some may happily report entirely erroneous information.

These inchoate features of international co-operation illuminate the difficulties of identifying an international policy *process* or its parameters. We are on more certain ground when we focus on the increasing importance of a dimension external to the state for policy-making within the state. Yet to reduce international co-operation to a bundle of exogenous factors which impinge from time to time on the domestic policy process is to risk understating and thereby misunderstanding the linkages between governmental actions and international negotiations. Governments engage in international co-operation on specific policy issues sometimes because they wish to change what other governments do, sometimes because they want to derive benefits for their own domestic policies, sometimes in the hope of moulding the international environment in a particular way, and often as a defensive reaction to international developments which they neither control nor fully understand (Keohane and Nye 1977). Yet having once embarked on such a voyage governments are quite likely themselves to have to make adjustments in their own policies and the way in which they operate. At a minimum therefore international co-operation constitutes a highly decentralised process of interaction and mutual adjustment which is sometimes given concrete form through the implementation of internationally derived obligations. The fluidity and conditional character of the process may often (though not always) rule out as inappropriate prescriptions designed to promote rigorous strategies of implementation, but equally it generates influences, uncertainties and change within states and often in terms of precise problems of implementation.

The carrots and sticks of compliance
In spite of its diffuse character international co-operation has come to acquire carrots and sticks of its own through which pressures are generated to induce good behaviour by governments (Young 1979). Four in particular are relevant to our case studies: the importance of self-interest; the role of the law; the reliance on negotiation by consensus; and the encapsulation of co-operation within relatively closed groupings of policy-makers. These constitute the preconditions

of implementation which enable international agreements to be translated into actual outputs. Policy-making is shared between the international and national levels, while policy execution is in practice primarily concentrated at the national level or even sub-national level. Implementation throughout this chapter is assumed to encompass not merely the adoption of international agreement within domestic law but frequently also an active process of making it operationally effective.

Calculations of self-interest may and often do dispose both individuals and organisational collectivities to comply with general norms of behaviour and to carry out their own activities in conformity with the parallel practices of others, even in the absence of precise rules and agencies of enforcement. As Oran Young has persuasively argued, this may be as true of behaviour in international relations as of individuals queueing for buses. Thus Dudley Coates suggests in Chapter 9 that much of the 'success' of the harmonisation of food standards across national boundaries should be attributed to the belief by both governments and food producers and processors that it is in their own interest and technologically necessary to operate to comparable and compatible standards. Self-regulation is particularly important in areas where industrial and commercial activities span national boundaries or where deviance from norms is likely to cause confusion, damage or intolerable retaliation – air transport arrangements, controls over marine pollution and the increasing conformity of practice in countering the hijacking of aeroplanes are examples. Formal agreements often follow rather than precede implementing practice.

International law plays a crucial role in structuring the behaviour and attitudes of national policy-makers. Without delving into the questions of the relative status and scope of international and national law, a prevalent feature of international co-operation is its reliance on formalising policy agreements in treaties, conventions and written agreements. Thereby commitments become in a sense entrenched in national law and national administrative practice. Again, as Young (1979) points out, this has the double merit of striking a contract between the signatory governments based on a mutual exchange and helping to ensure that national legislators and policy implementers absorb it in their regular commitments and standard operating procedures. Specifically in the UK constitutional doctrines of ministerial responsibility and legal practice make it highly probable that internationally agreed law will be scrupulously implemented. The law then looks both backwards and forwards: backwards by consolidating a pre-existing consensus, and forwards by structuring subsequent behaviour. How effectively this sticks will obviously, however, often depend on the political and cultural norms of the signatory governments as well as on their specific interests. The painful and painstaking efforts in the United Nations Conference on the Law of the Sea (UNCLOS) to adopt an international treaty that would govern future behaviour by all states have at least for the moment foundered because some governments, notably the American, have decided that the final text commits them to more than they are prepared to deliver on deep-sea mining. In contrast the bilateral Nassau Agreement between the UK and the USA was exploited on both sides of the Atlantic to secure at the same time compliance by the other government and adjustment within each administration.

Almost all international policy co-operation proceeds by negotiations based on consensus. The costs of this are clearly evident in the time it takes to reach agreement, the vulnerability to blocking by even one government, and the risk that the outcome will be an untidy amalgam of different national preferences, satisfying none. But the benefits for implementation can be considerable. First, the consensus method should mean that governments generally consent only if they are prepared to fulfil their consequential obligations. Of course there are cases of deviance and deviousness and more commonly of different interpretations of what the obligations entail. Secondly, the protracted and iterative character of negotiation may often result in a gradual adaptation and alignment of national policies between the opening of discussions and the eventual agreement. Individual governments interact, influencing the attitudes and behaviour of each other through a process of concertation. Sometimes the result is only a marginal and barely perceptible change, but on occasion – as, for example, the move within the UNCLOS context to 200-mile exclusive economic zones – major alterations in and convergence of national policies emerge before the negotiations are concluded. The time bought by negotiation may also permit individual governments to mould domestic opinion to accept eventual changes in policy, although awkward domestic difficulties may equally emerge which, if not accommodated by negotiation, will subsequently inhibit thorough or effective implementation (Puchala 1975). Thus questions of policy formulation and implementation are often rolled together in the process of negotiation by consensus – an approach consistent with the evolutionary model set out in Chapter 1. A process of policy formation in which minority positions could be directly overruled but in which the rules of the game and enforcement mechanisms remained sketchy would serve only to raise more intense problems of implementation.

International policies are generally agreed amongst relatively small teams representing the participating governments. This is not to deny the importance of other influences which bear down on international co-operation from interest groups, parties, parliaments and more rarely public opinion, but to assert the particular importance of the ministers and officials who are directly engaged in negotiation. Compromise and consensus require flexibility and a balance of advantage and disadvantage, but skilful bargaining also depends on not showing your hand at the wrong moment. These factors breed a tendency within all governments towards exclusivity in who is involved and who is consulted over the final outline agreement. From the perspective of implementation this can produce both helpful and awkward results. If a relatively closed group can capture control of *both* the national input into negotiation *and* the implementation of agreements this can serve to make the whole process smooth and tightly-knit with a linear progression towards effective implementation. The international dimension and requirements of confidentiality (whether simply for negotiating or because of subject-matter such as defence and security issues) may combine to take a particular issue out of the domestic political arena. On the other hand, a small group of negotiators may come back to their government with an agreement which cannot in the event carry the necessary domestic consent for thorough implementation to be achieved. The risks of non-compliance for this reason are particularly great on issues of high political salience and controversy, or where implementation involves a chain of different agencies and levels of government, or where agreements need active parliamentary endorsement (a recurrent problem in the USA). Difficulties of these kinds can then in turn undermine confidence in the frail structures and processes of international co-operation.

The European Community as a special case

The founders of the EC always intended that their experiment would create not so much an international organisation as a new form of government. While the EC certainly has not yet and may never constitute the West European federation to which its most passionate enthusiasts have looked, it is nevertheless more state-like than any other arena for international policy co-operation (Wallace *et al.* 1983). The EC has a legal constitution in the form of its treaties and the powers to legislate backed by the Court of Justice, a quasi-Supreme Court. It has formal and developed institutions with fairly well-defined rules of the game within which business is conducted. At the apex stand the Commission, with specific governmental functions of policy formulation and implementation, and the Council of Ministers representing the member states, without the consent of which policies cannot be agreed or executed. As both a goad and a stumbling-block the European Parliament has the capability to exercise some influence over the Commission and the Council, but equally the parliaments of the constituent states can and do constrain how far or how quickly the Council and Commission can move towards agreement. While the context and the period are different, the underlying structures and politics of bargaining in the EC bear some striking resemblances to the early years following the federation of the United States.

The member states of the EC exhibit both marked similarities and certain crucial divergences. Compared with the membership of most other international organisations or alliances their economies and political systems are both broadly similar and highly interdependent. Consequently it has been possible to work from some common values and towards some common objectives against a background of relative mutual familiarity, shared knowledge and similar administrative and legal practice. Of course there have always been diversities of language, culture, economic preferences, administrative methods, political emphasis and priorities and so on, all of which tend to be magnified by the intense and often conflictual bargaining process of Brussels. However, there is sufficient congruence and compatibility to sustain not only policy agreements but specifically defined commitments to, and practices of, implementation.

Another key feature of the EC lies in the scope and substance of its policy repertoire. The Community treaties and subsequent legislation cover a broad and increasing range of external and internal policies from trade to safety standards, from agriculture to employment. EC policy-makers deal with both the macro- and the micro-levels of policy formulation and implementation, sometimes by policies which are thoroughly common – agriculture and the customs union – and often by setting the framework at the Community level and leaving the precise implementation to the member states. But in almost all the areas with which the EC deals policy agreements embrace both the intended outcomes and the precise rules of implementation subject to monitoring by the Commission and with interventions as and when appropriate by the Court of Justice and the Court of Auditors.

Significantly, in both ambition and reality the EC has entered territory which we generally recognise as touching on the core functions of government. In particular it has always been heavily engaged in the politics of regulation – setting common rules, standards and practices across a vast range of subjects – and, indeed, its structures and methods are perhaps peculiarly well adapted to this (Pinder 1968). But increasingly the EC has also become a forum for tackling issues of distribution, partly because EC legislation and economic interdependence amongst the member states impact differentially on different regions and groups, and partly because the EC has its own powers of revenue raising and spending in the form of an independent budget (Wallace 1980).

Thus within the EC we can identify the broad shape of a fairly sophisticated policy system and within it a distinctive policy process. Of course bargaining is often hard, consensus difficult to reach, and the individual member states cling to their traditional policies and practices (as still occurs within established federations where powers and authority are also dispersed and each member tends to guard jealously its own territory). To some extent the rules of the Community game remain contested and the legitimacy of the EC to act is heavily circumscribed. However policy-making in the EC can rest on tolerably certain expectations of compliance and operates both at the rhetorical level and in the concrete expressions of policy.

The relative sophistication and precision of policy implementation in the EC is buttressed by the operation of factors present in a more primitive form in the broader international arena. Self-interest constitutes a strong motive for all the participating governments: geographical proximity combined with economic, political and security interdependence means that individual governments find it difficult to insulate themselves from the actions of their partners. An impulsion towards compatible practices by governments is generated by the economic, political and technological transactions across frontiers and reinforced by the extent to which economic groupings and interest groups operate transnationally in Western Europe. The legal system of the EC is particularly well developed and arguably more integrated than its political system (Weiler 1981). Even though there are occasional and well-publicised examples of deliberate non-compliance, their rarity is striking. Implementation is often untidy, uneven and slow, but such failures are frequent in all federal systems and by no means unknown in unitary systems (Pressman and Wildavsky 1973; Sharkansky 1981). The combination of negotiation by consensus with tight rules to entrench agreements results in significant adaptation of national practices and an acceptance that commitments cannot be readily ignored. Occasionally, notably in the annual budgetary cycle, decisions are taken with compliant dissenting minorities.

In practice much EC legislation is implemented away from the glare of publicity and political controversy not by Community but by national agencies. Once agreed it carries the imprimatur and legitimacy of the individual member government, or sometimes is absorbed in the regular operations of a regional or local authority. The corollary is that the record of implementation must be assessed primarily as a function of the performance of individual governments, though with the important qualification that the Commission – and on financial questions the Court of Auditors – can and does intervene as a supervisor and monitor of Community legislation to a greater degree and with more detail than in other international arenas.

When only two can play

In recent times international co-operation has become increasingly multilateral within regions, large groupings (so-called North, South, East and West) and globally. Amongst the western industrialised countries the character of bilateral co-operation has shifted to focus on two distinct activities: consultations on policy issues addressed in multilateral fora and rather specific projects of direct and immediate relevance to the two partners (Keohane and Nye 1977). Our concern here is with the latter, where a particular project or programme is managed bilaterally, either because a broader international framework is inappropriate or because only two governments have the relevant capability and common interest. By and large, therefore, bilateral projects emerge because there are strong incentives for both sides of the partnership to make them effective, even though the contributions and commitments offered by each may differ and their specific interests may be distinct. The particular agreement to collaborate will tend to rest on the negotiation of a 'contract' in which the obligations for each side can be relatively clearly identified. Reciprocity, equivalence of advantage, and exclusiveness are important elements both in such formal agreements as are laid down and in the informal understandings which underpin them. The performance of the partners is generally more accessible to both scrutiny and counter-influence than in the broader international arena. The relationships of individual policy-makers on each side may serve as the cement which holds together the detailed management of the project and there is limited scope for diffusing responsibility for any failure to implement thoroughly (Neustadt 1970).

Bilateral collaboration has built-in advantages because of its narrowness of scope and precision of subject. The 'success' of the operation is likely to depend to a large extent on the intrinsic merits of the particular project – factors such as its technical qualities, its economic costs, its commercial viability, its detailed deployment and so on, criteria on which the Anglo-French project to build Concorde significantly underperformed. However, other factors inevitably impinge. The confidence and trust with which governments work together are much influenced by judgements of whether previous joint projects have achieved their objectives and of whether officials on both sides can effectively and efficiently co-operate. Both the objectives and the practices of the partners need to be compatible and supported by a willingness to yield ground and to adapt to the requirements of the other party to the contract. Self-interest provides the key to success. Often a legal contract is struck to provide guarantees of good behaviour, sometimes to the point of including terms for compensation in the event of rupture, a major factor in preventing the British Labour government from abandoning the Concorde project in 1964. Where negotiations produce highly specific trade-offs between the two partners compliance and detailed implementation become mutually interdependent. Moreover the more specialised the subject the more likely it is that both negotiation and implementation will depend on the same (or closely connected) groups within the two governments.

Chapter 11 provides a detailed illustration of one such bilateral project in which the Polaris programme was jointly implemented in the USA and UK remarkably smoothly. But its very success perhaps only serves to reinforce the point that effective implementation depends on a conjunction of interests, rigorous definition of objectives, agreement on means and adaptiveness – factors without which even two partners may fail to achieve harmony.

Factors within national boundaries

Just as different models have been developed to explain the policy process within states, so analysts of international relations and foreign policy have produced counterpart models to explain how the represent-atives of states and their domestic clients approach international policies. Graham Allison's classic study drew our attention to the difference in policy-making between the 'rational actor' model and the 'bureaucratic politics' model (1971). Suffice it here to note that the implementation phase almost invariably takes governments (at least within democracies) into the complexities of domestic political and policy processes. None of our examples readily supports the view that the rational pursuit of national interests on its own is likely to ensure effective implementation of international agreements. In the final analysis implementation depends on what happens within each country, if we leave on one side those cases in which policy is thwarted by an extraneous event or the action of a government or governments not party to the agreement.

Inevitably adversarial elements impinge when *we* are required to execute in our country agreements which *they* have tailored to the needs of their country, a theme familiar from studies of policy implementation within the USA (Wallace 1982). Both bureaucratically and politically negative factors come into play which may undermine the success of the project, programme or policy. As already noted, the people actually responsible for implementation often work at the regional or local level; and even if they are in central government they may not have directly negotiated the agreement. Negotiators tend to be educated and to an extent *socialised* by their often lengthy engagement in bargaining, at least to the extent of becoming fairly familiar with the problems and preoccupations of their partners. But the further down the policy-making chain implementation travels, the less we can take for granted knowledge of and sympathy for the needs of partners.

The more decentralised the administration in a particular field the greater the likelihood of misunderstanding and misapplication, unless the policy consists of fairly straightforward rules and procedures. Thus regulatory policies once agreed hold out greater promise of effective execution than distributional policies which are more likely to require further negotiation and persuasion within countries as part of the process of implementation (Lowi 1970). Yet even regulatory policies present difficulties in that they often require people to alter or adapt standard operating procedures which from a worm's eye view may appear fairly satisfactory. Moreover the compromise of negotiation often produces in the common interest an outcome which was not actually what any government wanted – a least-worst option which often involves irritating and apparently unnecessary changes away from established routines (Stein 1982). It is common for national implementers to be sceptical as to whether partner governments will actually comply with the international agreement. Non-compliance by other governments is often regarded as simply bad behaviour, while the home government's reasons for delay or resistance are amenable to justification. Similarly, openness to inspection or monitoring from outside is often resisted as an unwelcome intrusion.

The implementers of policy thus mainly view their responsibilities in a national and traditional context. Often they will cling to autarchic policies and practices with little awareness of the broader canvas, the vulnerabilities created by international interdependence, and the need to maintain the trust of other governments in order to preserve an international policy 'regime' (Keohane 1982).

However exceptions to these generalisations can be identified: specific bilateral projects; issue areas where the international dimension is overwhelmingly important; and sectors which are relatively self-contained. In specific bilateral projects it is likely that policy implementers and policy formulators will be either the same or closely-related groups. Often the project will require intimate collaboration amongst both administrators and technical specialists and operational criteria and practices will be jointly defined and applied. The rationale for co-operation with another government is generally fairly clear to all or most of those engaged in implementation. Thus coherence and cohesion have a good chance of emerging, provided that the initial objectives have been carefully specified and the relevant agencies competently managed. For similar reasons, in those issue areas where the international dimension looms consistently large (for example, trade policy), those responsible for implementing internationally agreed policies are typically regularly engaged in negotiations and have recurrent contacts with other governments. Their knowledge of and responsiveness to actions by other governments is considerable and there are long-established habits of working within the framework of international agreements. Compliance and scrupulous implementation may not necessarily occur, but non-compliance or ragged implementation will frequently be a deliberate act of policy rather than the casualty of ignorance or misunderstanding (though of course this will be less true of those governments or agencies in which administrative practices are lax or management is poor).

In those sectors where the issues can be kept relatively self-contained and functionally distinct, different factors apply. International commitments often help national policy-makers – including implementers – to pursue their own policy objectives. Habits of international co-operation are often not only ingrained but can become an important resource in domestic bargaining, through the emergence of horizontal policy networks which cut across national boundaries. Typically in functionally discrete areas relations between administrators and specialists are close, policy is often developed in a participative style, and awareness of what happens on the ground is generally high. Thus the implementation dimension is often well integrated into policy formulation with relative consistency of aims and interpretation amongst the relevant agencies from each participating government. The corollary may, however, be that the international policy, like its domestic counterpart, is 'captured' by the subject specialists and victim to the vested interests which benefit from policy outcomes – the Common Agricultural Policy of the EC is a powerful illustration.

Conclusion

In implementing policies across national boundaries the shift from rhetoric to substance is plagued with obstacles. It is perhaps remarkable in itself that so much of national policy implementation has become constrained by international co-operation and negotiation rather than that so little is tangible and systematically implemented. Indeed 'success' often lies in the gradual and often painful learning process through which national practices and attitudes are marginally adjusted to take account of external influences. The chances of achieving more concrete results capable of more precise evaluation are limited so far to relatively few categories of policy where specific needs, functional compatibility and high levels of interdependence provide the momentum for translating objectives into outputs.

Internationally negotiated policies thus cannot become embedded in national practice through a stable or predictable process of translation. Governments still endeavour to filter information, to exercise control and to interpret in their own interest, with the consequence that effective or appropriate implementation means different things in different countries. The proponents of an international policy, notably the officials of international organisations and most strikingly the Commission of the EC, will often seek as tight and as programmed a strategy as they can secure in the hope of leaving as little leeway as possible for discretion and slippage to national implementers (Berman 1980). Yet to be realistic they have to recognise that their cherished policies need to be skewed and to some extent distorted to carry along different governments with diverse requirements and often contrary interests. This suggests that adaptiveness is often the only sensible strategy to pursue.

But whose strategy? The absence of a clear political framework means that implementation is intrinsically an interactive process based on give-and-take and on trial-and-error. It is rarely amenable to the rigour and purposiveness which can sometimes characterise the policy process within states, with the few exceptions we have noted above. Its experimental and diverse characteristics do not enable us yet to offer with any certainty a model of an international policy process from which a paradigm of implementation could be extracted. The untidy patchwork of negotiations, concertation and often partial compliance which characterise international policy co-operation only takes on recurrent patterns in the case of the EC and some other cases of high interdependence or close functional co-operation. Even here the patterns remain irregular. To describe implementing policies across national boundaries as evolutionary is appropriate in the Darwinian sense that a different species of the policy process may be emerging in response to changes in the policy environment. But we have yet to see whether it will be fit enough to survive and co-exist with the more sturdy and resilient species – the nation state.

References

Allison, G. 1971, *Essence of decision: explaining the Cuban missile crisis*, Boston, Little Brown

Berman, P. 1980, 'Thinking about programmed and adaptive implementation. Matching strategies to situations', in H.M. Ingram and D.E. Hann (eds), *Why policies succeed or fail*, London, Sage

Donelan, M. (ed.) 1978, *The reason of states*, London, Allen & Unwin

Keohane, R. 1982, 'The demand for international regimes', *International organisation*, vol. 36, no. 2, Spring, pp. 325–55

Keohane, R. and Nye, J. 1977, *Power and interdependence: world politics in transition*, Boston, Little, Brown

Lowi, T. 1970, 'Decision making vs. policy making: towards an antidote for technocracy', *Public administration review*, May/June, pp. 314–25

Neustadt, R. 1970, *Alliance politics*, New York, Columbia University Press

Pinder, J. 1968, 'Positive and negative integration: some problems of economic union in the EEC', *World today*, vol. 24, pp. 88–110

Pressman, J.L. and Wildavsky, A. 1973, *Implementation: how great expectations in Washington are dashed in Oakland*, Berkeley, University of California Press

Puchala, D. 1975, 'Domestic politics and regional harmonisation in the European Communities', *World politics*, vol. 27, no. 4, July, pp. 496–520

Sharkansky, I. 1981, 'Intergovernmental relations', in Paul C. Nystrom and William H. Starbuck (eds), *Handbook of organisational design*, Oxford, Oxford University Press

Stein, A. 1982, 'Co-ordination and collaboration: regimes in an anarchic world', *International organisation*, vol. 36, no. 2, Spring, pp. 299–324

Wallace, H. 1980, *Budgetary politics: the finances of the European Communities*, London, Allen & Unwin

Wallace, H., Wallace, W. and Webb, C. (eds) 1983, *Policy-making in the European Community*, Chichester, John Wiley (2nd edn)

Wallace, W. 1982, 'Europe as a confederation: The Community and the nation state', *Journal of Common Market studies*, vol. xxi, nos 1 and 2, September/December, pp. 57–68

Weiler, J. 1981, *Supranationalism revisited – retrospective and prospective*, European University Institute, Working Paper No. 2, Florence

Winham, G. 1977, 'Negotiation as a management process', *World politics*, vol. 30, no. 1, October, pp, 87–114

Winham, G. 1979, 'Practitioners' views of international negotiation', *World politics*, vol. 32, no. 1, October, pp. 111–34

Young, O. 1979, *Compliance and public authority*, Baltimore, Johns Hopkins Press

9 Food Law
Brussels, Whitehall and Town Hall
Dudley Coates

This chapter deals with food standards, a field in which much policy is now made at a supranational level in the European Community (EC), but is implemented at the national and local level. It begins by summarising briefly the development of policies on food standards within the UK, the present allocation of responsibilities and the way in which the policy process has operated. It then shows how this policy system was affected when the UK joined the EC in 1973, and examines the relationship between Community membership and the technology and structure of the food industry. It discusses the way in which policies are incorporated in law, and the role of the legal provisions in the overall process of implementation. The process is illustrated by examining two contrasted Community directives and concludes by considering, in the light of these examples, the nature of the policy process in the field of food standards, with particular reference to implementation.

In this book we treat implementation as an evolutionary process – a process in which an initial policy statement or objective is put into practice with the result that any weaknesses are identified and reported back to the policy-maker so that the policy-maker can correct the policy, arrange for the implementation of the corrected policy, and so on. In many areas of policy this process takes place repetitively over such a long period that it becomes routine. The political and social environment has its impact on the policy; the volume of resources available may fluctuate over time; the demand, particularly for a service, may also vary, perhaps dramatically. But a set of underlying assumptions – notably that the problem is one with which government should seek to deal and that the basic policy being operated is appropriate to that problem – remains unquestioned by the great majority of those who take an interest in it. This chapter seeks to assess the value of the general approach adopted in this book in the study of a policy area where the process has become so routinised that it rarely surfaces on the political stage. It also considers – unlike other chapters and, indeed, much discussion of the policy process – a regulatory policy whose resource implications are relatively modest.

Modern British food standards

The essential problem which all food standards policies address is the need to outlaw impure and unwholesome food (MAFF 1976). Legislation against impure food can be traced back to 1226, but modern food law derives essentially from the Food and Drugs Act 1875. This set out for the first time the general principle which is still the basis of British food and drugs legislation: 'No person shall sell . . . any article of food . . . which is not of the nature, substance or quality demanded by [the] purchaser.' From the beginning, the central tension in the policy-making process has been between the food producers and those who sought to protect food consumers (Paulus 1974). Laws which seek to alter some social or economic practice must be enforced if they are to be effective. But over and above the direct cost of enforcement, there are resource implications for those affected by it. The dislike of factory owners for the Victorian Factory Acts, for example, was motivated by economic reality. Similar attacks were mounted against the earliest food laws. No one likes to be told how to run his business, especially when he is being told to run it in a more costly way. But over time attitudes change. People get used to new ways, protest ceases, enforcement becomes less costly and the resource implications of the policy, which often went unstated even initially, become less and less obvious. But the resource costs are not always forgotten, as the recent attempt to quantify the cost of food standards legislation to producers of food against the benefits consumers obtain shows (Ashworth 1980).

The present basic legislation is the Food and Drugs Act 1955 (though drugs are now governed by the Medicines Act 1968) and the parallel but separate legislation for Scotland (1956) and Northern Ireland (1958). The Act lays down a number of general offences in relation to food, including prohibitions on adulteration (section 1); on the sale of food not of the nature, substance or quality demanded (section 2); on the 'false or misleading description of food' (sections 6 and 7); and on the sale of unfit food (section 8). It gives the relevant minister (in England, the Minister of Agriculture, Fisheries and Food, usually acting jointly with the Secretary of State for Social Services) extensive powers to make detailed regulations on various aspects of food composition, hygiene, labelling and safety. And it entrusts enforcement to 'food and drugs authorities' (county councils and London borough councils in respect of most matters, but district councils in respect of food hygiene, and port health authorities in respect of imports). On the face of it, this is a very confusing system. Other central government departments are involved as well as the Ministry of Agriculture, Fisheries and Food (MAFF) and the Department of Health and Social Security (DHSS) who share the limelight. The Northern Ireland and Scottish Offices make parallel regulations under their separate legislation. The Welsh Office is usually involved, as both a health and an agriculture department, since most regulations cover England and Wales together. The Department of Trade and the Office of Fair Trading have interests too because they share responsibility for non-food consumer protection and there is overlap, for example, over weights and measures rules.

Yet however complex, this system is said by most of those involved to work quite well. The division between hygiene matters – where DHSS take the lead nationally and the Environmental Health Officers (EHOs) employed by district councils operate locally – and other matters where MAFF's Standards Division operates nationally and the county councils' Trading Standards Officers act locally – is widely understood and accepted by those involved, if not by the public whose benefit the legislation seeks to serve. Points of overlap and conflict certainly exist and the system does mean that those involved in making food law rarely gain practical experience of its enforcement; but such difficulties do not seem to disrupt the main implementation process.

The policy process is relatively easy to describe and is probably not atypical of the processes at work in many policy areas with low political salience. The concept of a policy community has been described by several authors, notably Heclo and Wildavsky (1974) and Richardson and Jordan (1979). Food law is no exception to the general picture they paint in which a fairly closely defined set of more or less organised interest groups are routinely involved in the policy process. Whether discussion and consultation take place at ministerial level or with officials varies from subject to subject, time to time and interest group to interest group. Direct contact on food standards is mainly with officials. The Food and Drugs Act, like much modern legislation, requires that ministers consult those who appear to have an interest in the subject before making regulations. This requirement applies both to regulations which are made nationally and to those which may be made to implement EC obligations. And the obligation is fulfilled both in letter and in spirit by frequent contacts between officials and those groups who show an interest in a given subject. Consultation is certainly not confined to the statutory minimum. The head of MAFF Standards Division has said:

> We consult on any proposal those organisations which seem to be representative of the subject or the interests under discussion. It is a subjective judgment on every occasion but we work on the basis that we

would sooner over-consult than under-consult because you cannot from our position judge the importance on occasions of a particular proposal to a particular group of people. (HL 1980/1)

The international dimension

Membership of the EC in 1973 did not challenge the basics of the Food and Drugs Act, but it did add a major new dimension to the policy process and to the task of the policy-maker and implementer. Food standards are now the subject of legislation at the Community level, which in turn has to be reflected in UK law. The Treaty establishing the European Community has a fundamental objective of ensuring that goods move freely within the boundaries of the Community. In the Community's early years, the major stress was on the removal of customs duties between member states. But from the beginning it was recognised that there were other barriers, and machinery was also devised, in the words of the official English text of Article 100 of the Treaty, 'for the approximation of such provisions laid down by law, regulation or administrative action in Member States as directly affect the establishment or functioning of the common market.' Amongst the early candidates identified for such approximation were national rules governing the composition and description of food. At the point of UK entry to the EC around a dozen draft food standards directives were under active discussion, but only three had gone through the whole process necessary for them to become binding directives (Commission EC 1972); details of the many more subsequently adopted can be found in Institute of Trading Standards Administration (ITSA) (1980a). There are labelling and composition rules made as a direct by-product of the Common Agricultural Policy – notably the complex system for designating and labelling wine – but these are not considered in detail in this study.

The central assumption underlying the Community directives is that differences in national legal and administrative rules about matters such as the composition, description and labelling of food impede the movement of food products across frontiers and create unequal conditions of competition. On the broader international scale, the Codex Alimentarius Commission, set up jointly by the Food and Agricultural Organisation and the World Health Organisation (both United Nations agencies), has also been engaged for many years in the production of common basic food standards, and many of the Community directives are based on Codex recommendations. This activity reflects the fact that government regulatory action frequently has the result, whether intended or unintended, of inhibiting trade, though the practical effect varies from case to case, and it is rarely clear how much food standards alone inhibit trade. But even if any trade inhibition is unintentional, it is often difficult to eliminate rules which have the effect of protecting national industries.

Both in the UK and internationally the food industry is relatively concentrated. But many multinational food companies do not trade much across national frontiers, often because they have plants in each country, but also because there are differences in national tastes, as well as in national regulations. Some companies are, in practice, rather conservative in their product ranges and their willingness to seek new markets. And when a new export market can only be developed in competition with another subsidiary of the same multinational, a degree of conservatism is hardly surprising. But, for whatever reason food industry comments on food standards often seek to preserve existing practices rather than to search out new opportunities. The food industry's rapid adoption of new technology and new marketing methods has to a surprising extent been within national frontiers. International integration of production is rare in the food industry, perhaps because of the high bulk and low value even of its more processed products. Nevertheless the UK food manufacturing industry has generally been in favour of remaining in the EC, but more because membership appears to offer continuity of supply for raw materials than for any other reason (Nicholls 1979).

Enforcement of food law
Community law rarely specifies how it is to be enforced. Member states are simply required to enforce it as appropriate in accordance with their national constitutional, organisational and legal systems. But it needs to be borne in mind that in food standards, as elsewhere, differences between national enforcement systems are of considerable significance. The central features of the UK system are that in most cases an offence occurs in the UK only when the goods are put on sale to the consumer; that each individual article of food sold is capable of creating an offence; that the legislation imposes a strict liability on the seller; and that it is enforced by local authorities. British local government reorganisation in 1974 reduced the number of enforcement agencies, but maintained the distinction between county and district functions and the reduction in the number of county authorities was small. Local authority enforcement officers, such as Allen (Commission EC 1980a: 121) are inclined to stress the great importance of their discretion not to prosecute. But statistics on the resources available to trading standards authorities show up differences which, according to another Trading Standards Officer, are 'too large to be regarded as variations accounted for by local demand' (Manley 1981).

Differences between national systems for enforcing food law were discussed in detail at a symposium in 1978 on the enforcement of food law (Commission EC 1980a). A devolved system, like the British, can be seen as entirely logical given enforcement at the point of retail sale. But in most other member states of the Community, enforcement is much more centralised. France has three national services enforcing various aspects of food law and in Germany it is the eleven *Länder*, not the local authorities within them, which implement food law. Only in Denmark, Ireland and the Netherlands do local authorities have any significant role and in each of those a central government enforcement service retains a significant role. Enforcement typically takes place in the factory on the basis of a statistically validated sampling process to ensure its cost-effectiveness.

It is not easy to point to direct effects of these differences in enforcement patterns on the development of food standards policies. But in the related field of weights and measures legislation the impact has been considerable in that the Community has now adopted the 'average weight' system which reflects the continental enforcement system. The adoption of this system stimulated action to encourage co-operation between local authorities in enforcing many aspects of consumer protection law. A National Metrological Coordinating Unit has been set up by statute to enable local authorities to liaise over enforcement of the Weights and Measures Act 1979 which has put the new system into effect. In parallel, the local authorities' associations have set up the Local Authorities Coordinating Organisation on Trading Standards (LACOTS). The Coordinating Unit and LACOTS are engaged in liaison, and clearly fall well short of a national enforcement service. Nevertheless their creation reflects a need for coordinated enforcement to meet the demands of EC legislation; to meet the challenge which multinational, high technology food manufacturing imposes on the traditional British system (ITSA 1980b); and to make the enforcement system as cost-effective as possible.

On the whole the pressures on the food law policy process deriving from Community membership worked in the same direction as those deriving from the impact of technological and economic forces on the food industry. That industry continued during the 1970s to become even more concentrated. At the retail level, the importance of the large supermarket and hypermarket chains continued to grow. The shift by consumers from fresh, unprocessed foods to manufactured and precooked foods may be abating somewhat but seems unlikely to reverse: 'instant mash' and the many other products of modern food technology are here to stay. Whilst it seems improbable that the shift to the average weight system would have taken place without the stimulus of

Community membership, other adaptations in the consumer protection enforcement system might have occurred in any case in response to technological and cost-effectiveness pressures.

Law as a policy instrument

By definition regulatory policies use law as their main instrument. There is no significant use in food standards of the more flexible code of practice approach which is used in addition to or instead of regulations in areas such as agricultural chemicals and farm animal welfare. Law is neutral, binding everyone equally, but its practical impact depends on its enforcement. Like most law, food standards legislation depends for its effectiveness primarily on the assumption that few people will consciously choose to break it. Providing therefore that its content is sufficiently well known, the need for formal enforcement action – in the shape of warnings or actual prosecutions – may be small. In practice, inspectors often spend more time advising than warning and of some 40 000 complaints about food per year received by enforcement agencies, fewer than 10 per cent lead to prosecutions (Rhodes 1981). But the pattern of enforcement is patchy, partly because of the wide differences mentioned earlier in the resources made available for this work but also because there is no central control over enforcing officers. Though this makes it impossible for someone centrally to decide *not* to prosecute in relation to a particular product, it can inhibit prosecutions in doubtful cases, because an individual enforcing authority may fear the cost of lengthy appeals, even if the probability of final success is high. At the other extreme, local authorities are free to bring a prosecution which others believe to be tendentious. For example, a decision by the Stockton-on-Tees District Council to prosecute a Women's Institute shop for selling jam in contravention of one of the hygiene provisions of the Food and Drugs Act was described in the House of Commons as 'ludicrous' and 'bureaucratic' (HC 1980). But that particular case is also a good – if rather extreme – illustration of the implementation process at work. The discovery, as a result of this case, that such 'shops' were subject to the Act sparked off enormous pressures on MPs and ministers for a change in the law. As a result, the Food and Drugs (Amendment) Bill, introduced by Mr Gerry Neale under the 10-minute rule on 4 November 1980, became law with government support in 1981. Women's Institute jam no longer has to be made in registered premises under the full rigours of hygiene inspection. A weakness – or rather an unintended effect – of the initial policy has been identified, has been brought to the attention of policy-makers, and has been rectified. This example illustrates the role of prosecutions which are as often about clarifying a marginal issue over the scope and effect of the law as about punishing the offender. Over the years, case law has been built up, in this as in other areas, so that all involved need to know not only the content of the statute law but also the key cases. Here, as in many other areas, a standard textbook (now Painter 1980) draws the two sources of law together.

The European legal dimension

Where the law comes from the EC, an additional dimension is added. National governments are required to implement Community obligations and can, if they fail to do so properly, be taken by the EC Commission before the European Court of Justice in Luxembourg. In practice the Commission, which is certainly not generously staffed on food standards, simply tries to ensure that member states have translated the directives into national law. It has no power to make spot-checks on the effectiveness of enforcement and, in practice, if there are no complaints it assumes all is well.

Complainants can in some circumstances take direct legal action which may end up in the European Court of Justice. Though the Court has not adjudicated many food law cases, one it has considered is claimed, particularly by the EC Commission, to be of significance. On 20 February 1979 the Court ruled in Case 120/78, commonly known as the *Cassis de Dijon* case, that *any* product which was legally manufactured and marketed in one member state must in principle be admitted on to the market of another member state. Thus, whilst regulations which impede the marketing of goods can be justified, for example, to ensure the effectiveness of fiscal supervision, the protection of public health, the fairness of commercial transactions and the defence of the consumers, such rules may, the Commission has argued, be applied to imports from other member states 'only if they are necessary to meet essential requirements and have a public interest of which they constitute the main guarantee' (Commission EC 1980b: 13–15 and 1980c).

Underlying such regulatory activity in all fields and at all levels is a fundamental dilemma which this Luxembourg case reopens. Should the law concentrate on general principles, or should it seek to control every detail? In practice, much regulatory action comprises a mixture of the two. The Food and Drugs Act contains a number of general offences, but under it detailed regulations are also made. The issue is less one of opposing alternatives than of where on a continuum one should rest. But on the whole, food manufacturers and retailers, at least in the UK, prefer to have detailed regulations specifying precisely what is and is not permitted. For example, they prefer rules which specify the precise shape, size and format of labels on food rather than rules like 'labelling must not be such as could mislead the purchasers to a material degree.' Though it is sometimes pointed out that such detailed regulations tend to inhibit new developments, the great advantage is that the manufacturer knows where he stands. And where, as in the UK, day-to-day enforcement is not in the hands of the rule-making authority, there is particular advantage for the manufacturer in precise and detailed rules. Representatives of organised consumers and of enforcement authorities tend to prefer statements of general principle, the latter not least because it leaves more scope for the exercise of their professional judgement, a valuable benefit for people who are still establishing themselves as properly professional within the local government service. Most Community directives – not just those on food standards – have tended to be based on the premise that detailed national regulations can only be harmonised by introducing precise and detailed rules throughout the EC. The idea that one might, instead of laying down precise rules, adopt simpler general principles for Community-wide applications is rather new, though it remains possible that judgments of the European Court of Justice may lead the Community somewhat away from the detailed approach. Indeed a trend in that direction can already be seen in the 1978 food labelling Directive.

The jams Directive
The jams Directive maintains the detailed approach. The first formal Commission proposal was made in 1965 and amended in 1967. But, for all practical purposes, the story begins in 1975 when the Commission prepared what amounted to a complete new proposal. As is normal, the discussion started earlier in a Commission working group, where national officials offer advice but do not bind their governments. At this stage the UK officials involved did not consult interested parties, although the Commission had done so. But when the formal Commission proposal arrived, it was sent out by the MAFF to about 100 bodies for comment. Twenty-four bodies replied to this consultation letter, though six of these offered no substantive comment. Indeed this draft Directive was never particularly controversial. It was debated along with the draft labelling Directive in the House of Commons on 21 April 1977 and the responsible minister said of it that it 'would involve some changes to our present law, but would not greatly extend its scope or impose additional burdens on enforcement authorities. Consumers would benefit, so would our jam manufacturers.' He went on to devote most of his speech to the draft labelling Directive.

All the major points which were to emerge in later discussion on the draft were identified in the first round of consultations. As early as

December 1975, the Ministry held a meeting with the Cake and Biscuit Alliance on bakery jam (the special characteristics of which were to be recognised during the negotiations). It was equally clear from the early consultations that only a small number of bodies had a major interest in the proposal. The Food Manufacturers Federation (FMF), represented by its Preserves Section, had a major continuing and active interest in the whole proposal. When the Council working group – the body which largely shapes the final outcome – began a series of monthly meetings in April 1976, the Ministry reported the outcome of each working group meeting by letter to the Chairman of the FMF Preserves Panel and continued to do so until the group finished its work 18 months later. Meetings were held with the FMF, notably in July 1976, July 1977 and November 1977. Other bodies neither received nor sought such detailed reports of the discussions. Enforcement authorities took little interest in the proposals, presumably because they would not affect them until turned later into UK law and would, in any case, change that law little. Similarly, retailers took little interest in these proposals except in the case of the Co-operative Union whose comments also reflected the manufacturing interests of the Co-operative Movement. The Consumers' Association took some interest, particularly by conducting a survey into possible names for the proposed quality jam category (now 'extra' jam) and this led to a meeting with them. But for all practical purposes only the makers of jam took an active interest in the development of the draft Directive, and most of the discussion with them concerned detailed points, there being little consideration of the advantages or disadvantages of having such a Directive.

Brussels Directives have to be converted into national law; in the UK, food standards Directives are invariably implemented by statutory instruments made under the Food and Drugs Act. After the formal adoption of the jams Directive in Brussels, consultations on methods of implementation began. At this stage the local authorities began to take a serious interest. After consulting on the general principles in late 1979, the Ministry issued for consultation on 18 March 1981 to a list of 57 bodies, draft regulations to implement the jams Directive. This consultation exercise is required by the Food and Drugs Act; but there were also substantial issues left unresolved by the Brussels decisions. Thus decisions had to be taken on whether to make use in the UK of various derogations which had been inserted in the Directive under pressure from others, the most important being those permitting low sugar jams and the use of preservatives in them. In the end, after rather more controversy than there had been on the original draft Directive, the Jams and Similar Products Regulations 1981 were made in July 1981. The new rules came into effect during 1982 and new names and labels began to appear during that year.

The labelling Directive

Given the scope of the Commission proposals which envisaged laying down detailed rules on the labelling, presentation and advertising of all foodstuffs and drinks for sale to the ultimate consumer, it is not suprising that some 200 bodies appear on the Ministry's circulation list for papers about them, or that the Ministry found it necessary to apologise for its inability to respond individually to every comment. The letter sent out on 14 May 1976 with the Ministry's commentary on the Commission's formal proposals gives a clear indication of the general approach being taken in the negotiations. The Ministry stressed that it was 'most important that the current proposals [were] studied carefully and that all specific points which might affect [interested parties were] brought to our attention NOW.' They stressed that, though the Ministry would be under a legal obligation to consult on the UK regulations which would be needed to implement this Directive, 'all these regulations will be able to do is to put the requirements of the Directive into UK law.' The Ministry's negotiating stance was clearly shown by their preference 'not to point to existing UK law as justification *in itself* for a particular negotiating position. We must be able to defend any position we adopt with all the possible facts and arguments available to us.'

As matters developed, the Ministry continued to reveal a good deal of its own negotiating hand as well as that of other delegations. Progress reports were issued in September, October and December 1976 with a Community document containing a complete revised text of the Directive being sent out on Christmas Eve 1976. In January 1977, a further commentary document was issued and the practice of reporting on discussions in the Council working group continued, though the pace of the discussions in Brussels prevented a report on every meeting. Almost 50 bodies were also sent copies of records of discussions between the Ministry and representatives of a number of bodies even though 'for purely practical reasons it has been necessary to limit the numbers attending' the consultation meetings. Discussion in the Council working group ended in the spring of 1978 and the matter was referred through the hierarchy of bodies reporting to the Council. The *ad hoc* group of Counsellors and Attachés (which considers food and agriculture harmonisation proposals after the working group has completed its work and before they go on to the senior official body, the Committee of Permanent Representative [COREPER]) completed their work. Since national ministers had been consulted by officials throughout the discussions, the Council of Ministers was able to adopt the Directive without substantive discussion on 18 December 1978. Interested parties were informed of the adoption of the Directive in February 1979 and given a forecast of the probable timetable for making the national regulations.

Within the UK, under the procedures agreed between government and Parliament, the proposals had been considered by the so-called Scrutiny Committees in both Houses of Parliament. The House of Lords Select Committee on the European Communities produced a major report (HL 1975/6). Like the Environment, Public Health and Consumer Protection Committee of the European Parliament (European Parliament 1976) it complained that the Commission consultations had been inadequate. The Lords Committee also argued that the proposals were over-detailed, over-costly and unnecessary. During the House of Commons debate on 21 April 1977, two Conservative members broadly supported the view that the proposals were unnecessary, but the official opposition did not oppose the proposals and indeed the debate took only 62 of the allotted 90 minutes.

The draft labelling Directive raised a number of genuinely controversial issues, most significantly open date marking, the listing of ingredients and the use of certain traditional names. Neither the UK nor other member states had, at the time the draft was prepared, a legal requirement that perishable foods be marked openly with an indication of their shelf-life. For many years, some manufacturers had put coded date marks on food packs, and some of the codes were fairly transparent. In the 1970s there was a significant move towards *open* date marking under which consumers can see which packs have been on the supermarket shelves the longest. On the recommendation of their advisory Food Standards Committee, the UK departments had, in the late 1970s, encouraged the voluntary development of open date marking in the form 'Sell by . . .'. It is probable, given the pressure from organised consumers for legislative action, that the UK government would have made such labels mandatory in the late 1970s or early 1980s. In the event, the Brussels discussions overtook national consideration, but with a subtly different approach.

In Brussels, both the principle that such a 'date of minimum durability' be required and the form and scope of the requirement were controversial. In their very first 1974 draft, the Commission had used the 'sell by' formula; but in the version formally submitted to the Council in 1976, the Commission proposed that the date should appear in the form 'Will keep until . . .'. In late 1976 two member states (Belgium and Denmark) were still formally opposing any such provision, whilst various alternative formulae (in several languages) were under discussion. There was also lively discussion on the precise scope of the requirement which it was argued was superfluous both for very fresh foods (if they could be defined satisfactorily) and for very long-life foods. Space does not permit a full description of the many twists and turns of the debate within the Council working group, but as far as the UK position is concerned, one can note that the 'Sell by . . .' formula, having proved unacceptable to other member states, the negotiators shifted their position to a second choice – the 'Best before . . .' formula – and this, subject to a derogation permitting the use of the 'Use by . . .' formula for highly perishable foods, was finally agreed.

The labelling Directive was described when it was adopted as 'the first real influence on consumer protection to emanate from Brussels' (Churchill 1979). It has been translated to the UK statute book, though not yet (mid-1982) into the laws of all other member states. Its full impact is due to be felt in 1983. But new labels appeared in 1981 and there is every reason to think that, as with most UK food law, all the major manufacturers' products will comply well before the due date. Trading Standards Officers have already been much involved in advice to manufacturers, importers and retailers. Whilst they will no doubt keep a special eye open for offences in early 1983, few would expect a major campaign to be needed to ensure that the new rules are being applied. Indeed with a full two years' warning of the detailed UK regulations and much longer in respect of the main changes due to the Directive, there would be little excuse for any failure to comply.

Implementing food law

There are undoubtedly cases where the policy process runs less smoothly than that described above. EC food standards proposals over the last decade seeking harmonised rules on beer, bread and ice cream have ground into the sands and been dropped, in some cases partly because of objections from the UK. Where there is radical disagreement over the nature of the problem and over proposed means of resolving it, the whole process tends to be slowed or even halted both at the national and the EC level. The Commission's most radical consumer protection proposal – on liability for defective products – has been opposed on the grounds that it would impose heavy costs on retailers in return for marginal benefits to the consumer; discussion on it has lasted a decade and it is still uncertain whether there will ever be agreement. But change can happen. Open date marking had initially been opposed by manufacturing and retail interests throughout the Community. Yet that opposition was outflanked, in the UK largely by the advice which the Ministry of Agriculture received from its advisory body, the Food Standards Committee. And eventually all the member states agreed to introduce it.

In this field, as in others, governments are criticised for incrementalism. A modest incremental step, like the introduction of open date marking for food or the removal of Women's Institute jam from the scope of food hygiene controls, can take place relatively easily, providing that it is not rushed and that there are no deeply entrenched interest groups opposing it. More radical steps are, however, blocked. In an extreme form, this line of criticism treats whole government departments as being themselves entrenched interests; thus MAFF has been accused of defending 'farmers and manufacturers in the production of more profitable food' (Wright 1981). It is undoubtedly true in all areas of human activity that small steps are more easily taken than big ones. It is also true that any policy-maker, be he an official or a minister, is influenced by the pressures effectively brought to bear on him; were he not he would be accused of insensitivity and unresponsiveness. Moreover, pressures against change are often stronger than pressures for it. But the evidence of the cases cited in this chapter suggest that food standards policy-makers actively consult a wide range of bodies and interests and do not accept everything they are told by anyone.

The UK implementation system for food standards appears to fit quite well parts of the basic pattern suggested in this book. At any given time there is an existing body of food standards law representing the existing policy. Pressures to change it emerge whether nationally from consumers or manufacturers, locally from enforcers, or from Brussels. Possible changes are widely canvassed, thoroughly discussed, considered in detail and, if broadly acceptable to all who show an interest, put into effect. If implications of possible changes are missed, the policy-makers can point out that they consulted fully at the formative stage. This continuous process of consultation tends to commit the whole policy community not only to the policy process but also the decisions it brings forth. But it is fair to add in practice that interest in food standards is confined to relatively small parts of certain central government departments and of local authorities and of 20 to 30 interest groups, and even within that group the degree of practical interest shown varies from subject to subject. Not only do almost all members of the policy community have a clear interest in the smooth functioning of the system, but in this mature policy system most of the potential repercussions of any policy shifts are foreseen and taken into account in advance of any statement of the policy. In Dunsire's (1978: 92–4) terms, 'conjectural feedback' is taking place, at least at the national level.

Food standards operate domestically but within an international technological and economic environment. Once the technology for, say, instant mashed potato or frozen cream has been invented in one country it will almost inevitably percolate to other countries either through trade in the relevant products or through the application of the same technology. There seems to be a general acceptance of the need to adapt food law so that it keeps pace with changes both in the technology and in the economic structure of the industry. Food manufacturers and retailers recognise that they cannot afford to be branded publicly as wanting to produce or sell sub-standard or unwholesome products, so they keep up close contact with, and reasoned pressure on, the relevant officials in central government. Conjectural feedback probably ensures that changing technology, the changing structure of the industry and the changing pressures, notably from organised consumers, are taken into account quickly.

The consultative system which had been developed in the process of implementing the earlier UK legislation has been applied, with little adaptation, in the new situation brought about by membership of the EC. A conscious decision was taken to extend the consultative process to cover the preparatory changes of discussions on Brussels directives. Policy-makers receive feedback on both national and EC policy issues from the same people, often at the same time. In practice, little distinction is made between national and EC proposals. It is notable that much more consultation – and hence feedback – takes place within national policy communities. Indeed there hardly is an identifiable policy community at the EC level, more contact at that level being among officials than among interest groups. This probably reflects the fact that the most important stage of the decision-making process in Brussels is the Council working group where the officials of the member states, not those of the Commission, control the process. In practice those national officials seem to be highly skilful at foreseeing pitfalls, defusing awkward issues and generally finding solutions which are acceptable throughout the Community, providing that the initial differences are within manageable dimensions.

Conclusion

The implementation process involves turning policy objectives into action on the ground. Food standards policies have a long history. Much of their content is uncontroversial, almost boring. In that situation it is hardly surprising that an implementation process heavily dependent on a rather small policy community has developed. The policy is almost self-implementing, and even the new European dimension has had little impact on the way the process works. In such cases, it seems that the effectiveness of consultative feedback mechanisms is the central factor which will determine the success of the policy process.

The complexity of the institutional arrangement does not seem to inhibit the process. But it is more doubtful whether the process could operate as smoothly were it not for the absence of effective pressure for radical change, and conversely, the readiness to drop proposals for change which raise real difficulties. The extent to which the technology and the structure of the food industry is international; the preference of most participants in the process for the certainty of detailed rules rather than the flexibility of more general rules; and the skills of the policy-makers at the centre of the policy network both domestically and on the European scene also play a part. Similar factors seem to apply in many other routinised policy areas. Whether such smooth arrangements can, or should, persist against the background of decreasing government resources or of increasing tension between central and local government is beyond the scope of this chapter. But this, like many other routine policy systems, has so far proved remarkably resilient.

References

Ashworth, R. 1980, 'The price of consumer protection', *Local government review*, 5 January, pp. 6–8

Churchill, D. 1979, 'EEC harmonises food labelling', *European Community information*, June, p. 89/12

Commission EC 1972, *Community measures for the alignment of legislation (1958–71)*, Brussels, Bulletin of the European Communities, Supplement 9/72

Commission EC 1980a, *Symposium on enforcement of food law (Rome, 12–15 September 1978)*, Luxembourg, Office for Official Publications of the European Communities

Commission EC 1980b, *Bulletin of the European Communities*, no. 7/8

Commission EC 1980c, *Official Journal of the European Communities*, C 256/2, 3 October

Dunsire, A. 1978, *Control in a bureaucracy: the execution process*, vol. 2, Oxford, Martin Robertson

European Parliament 1976, *Working document 211/76*, Walkhoff Report of 7 July

Heclo, H. and Wildavsky, A. 1974, *The private government of public money*, London, Macmillan

HC 1980, *Official Report*, 4 November, col. 1103

HL 1975/6, *Labelling of Foodstuffs*, 62nd Report of the Select Committee on the European Communities, HL 393, London, HMSO

HL 1980/1, *Flavourings*, Third Report of the Select Committee on the European Communities, HL 38, London, HMSO

Institute of Trading Standards Administration 1980a, *Trading standards legislation: a comparative directory of European Community legislation as enacted in the United Kingdom*, (2nd edn), Benfleet, Essex

Institute of Trading Standards Administration 1980b, 'Consumer protection: a survey of the year 1978/9', in *Municipal Year Book 1980*, p. 59f

MAFF 1976, *Food quality and safety: a century of progress*, London, HMSO

Manley, R. 1981, 'Trading standards', *Local government studies*, March/April, pp. 105–7

Nicholls, J. 1979, 'The UK food industry and the EEC', *National Westminster Bank quarterly review*, August, pp. 10–19

Painter, A.A. (ed.) 1980, *Butterworth's law of food and drugs*, 3 vols, London, Butterworth

Paulus, I. 1974, *The search for pure food: a sociology of legislation in Britain*, London, Martin Robertson (Law in Society Series)

Rhodes, G. 1981, *Inspectorates in British Government*, London, Allen & Unwin (for RIPA)

Richardson, J.J. and Jordan, G. 1979, *Governing under pressure*, London, Martin Robertson

Wright, H. 1981, 'Food without fads', *New Statesman*, 19 September

10 European Funds

How they are spent in the UK
Dudley Coates and *Helen Wallace*

Like the previous chapter, this chapter examines policies formulated at the level of the European Community (EC), but implemented at the national and local level. In a field like food standards, regulatory policies apply uniformly (at least in principle) across the EC and the making and enforcement of laws play a central part in their implementation. The policies discussed in this chapter, in contrast, are distributive and, although they operate within a legal framework, they have as their primary instruments the making of grants from the main funds of the Community. One, the Common Agricultural Policy (CAP), serves a specifically Community policy. The others are not so much common policies as attempts to achieve a degree of compatibility among national policies. Given the diverse circumstances of the member states, 'compatibility' may entail different amounts and kinds of action in each member state. The general practice has been to give money to projects which are already receiving financial support from national governments. Overall these policies involve the raising and spending of significant sums of money. Chapter 1 drew attention to the significance of the 'hard times' in which we live; in such times the value and effectiveness of any public expenditure programme is particularly likely to be questioned (as we saw in the case study from California in Chapter 6). All these factors suggest a much greater degree of tension between the Community and national levels than in a field like food standards, and that is what we find.

This chapter focuses on the expenditure in one member state, the UK, from the three main funds of the Community; the European Agriculture Guidance and Guarantee Fund (EAGGF) with separate guarantee and guidance sections, the European Social Fund (ESF) and the European Regional Development Fund (ERDF). EAGGF (Guidance) and the other two funds are commonly grouped together as the 'structural funds' (see Tables 10.1 and 10.2; and for the rules which govern them, see Bowker [1980]). Community expenditure is financed from 'own

Table 10.1: Community payments by sector, 1973–80

Year Sector	1973 mua[1]	%	1978 MEUA[2]	%	1979 MEUA	%	1980 MEUA	%
1. Administration	239.4	6.0	676.7	5.7	772.9	5.4	820.5	5.0
2. EAGGF Guarantee	3174.2	79.3	9278.6	77.5	10434.5	72.6	11306.2	69.4
(of which on milk products)	1508.3	37.7	3381.6	28.3	4521.4	31.5	4752.0	29.2
3. EAGGF Guidance	123.7	3.1	323.6	2.7	403.4	2.8	601.3	3.7
4. ESF	49.9	1.2	284.8	2.4	595.7	4.1	735.2	4.5
5. ERDF	—	—	254.9	2.1	513.1	3.6	726.7	4.5
6. Research, investment, energy	72.3	1.8	191.7	1.6	253.9	1.8	290.2	1.8
7. Co-operation with developing countries	104.8	2.6	265.2	2.2	405.4	2.8	580.8	3.1
8. Other sectors	3.7	0.1	35.5	0.3	88.3	0.6	77.8	0.5
9. Reimbursement to member states								
(i) 10% of own resources	236.5	5.9	662.1	5.5	726.6	5.1	791.2	4.9
(ii) Supplementary measures for UK and EMS interest rebates	—	—	—	—	173.3	1.2	431.2	2.6
Total	4004.6	100	11973.1	100	14367.1	100	16289.1	100

Notes:
The figures represent payments against appropriations for the financial (calendar) year plus payments against carry-overs from the previous financial year; payments between EC institutions have not been deducted.
[1]mua = million units of account
[2]MEUA = million European Units of Account; the form of the unit changed in 1978.
Source: Court of Auditors 1981a

resources, customs duties, agricultural levies and a precept on the value added tax collected within the member states. The budgetary process is described in Wallace (1980) and a general outline of the EC policy process has been given in Chapter 8. This chapter looks, in turn, at each of the funds, identifying in particular the scope for discretion and the factors which determine actual expenditure in the UK. Finally, it considers the impact of the expenditure and discusses the difficulties of making judgements about its effectiveness.

Assessing the impact of Community expenditure in the UK is especially problematic because of the continuing controversy about the scale of the British contribution to the Community budget. Looked at from a British perspective, the core issue is the extent to which expenditure from particular Community funds contributes to a fair distribution among member states of total Community expenditure. The over-riding objective of successive British governments has been to achieve a more equitable balance of contributions and receipts from the whole Community budget, bearing in mind that the UK ranks amongst the less prosperous member states. While the merits of particular proposals are assessed when it comes to detailed policy formulation and implementation within the UK, much less emphasis has been put on evaluating in broad terms the substantive thrust of EC spending policies, whether current or proposed.

Table 10.2: Payments by sector to the UK in 1980

	Total payments for EC (MEUA)	Gross payment to UK (MEUA)	UK as % of EC
EAGGF Guarantee	11 306	885	7.8
EAGGF Guidance	601	106	17.6
ESF	735	160	21.7
ERDF	727	233	32.1
Reimbursements to member states	1 222	419	34.3
Total	14 592	1803	12.4
Community income from own resources (i.e. excluding miscellaneous revenue and carry-overs)	15 263	3168	20.8

Notes:
Basis as for Table 10.1 (i.e. including payments against carry-overs from 1979 appropriations, but excluding sectors 1, 6, 7, 8).
Average 1980 exchange rate was about 60p = 1 EUA
Source: Court of Auditors 1981a

The traditional view of the Commission often reflected in the rhetoric if not the practice of other member states has reversed these two concerns. Thus, it is argued that one should first decide what policies should be financed collectively, with the distribution of the money among countries regarded as a consequence of such decisions rather than a central issue in making them. Of course, this over-simplifies the debate, not least because most member states, other than West Germany, have never in practice been significant net contributors to the Community budget. Nevertheless, these differing perspectives have impinged on negotiations about money in EC; and they also influence the criteria thought appropriate for the evaluation of Community expenditure programmes.

This chapter does not tackle directly the major issue of the British contribution to the Community budget. But our assessment of the record so far on specific programmes is relevant to that debate. In particular, an understanding of how the existing policies have been implemented is an important contribution to any discussion of what changes could or should be made in the future.

The policy context

Under the Amending Treaties (1970, 1975), the Community's 'budgetary authority' consists of the Council and the European Parliament. The Commission holds the responsibility for formulating expenditure proposals in the form of a draft budget which is then discussed back and forth between the Council and the Parliament. Expenditure on agricultural support is determined by factors (including the weather and the support prices fixed by the Council) over which the Parliament has little influence. Budget appropriations frequently represent little more than informed guesses of the likely costs in the relevant year. The level of the 'structural' funds is open to explicit choice and their classification as 'non-obligatory' expenditure enables the Parliament to make amendments with only minority support in the Council. Their final size is, thus, dependent on political bargaining between the Council and the Parliament. Allocations are subject to frequent adjustments to the cash ceilings at the beginning of the financial year, a factor inimical to their use (as the Commission intends) in order to influence long-term economic developments. In practice this problem is mitigated in part through the distinction between budgetary *payments* for the current year and *commitments* for future years, although it should be noted that in some cases payments are significantly underspent (Court of Auditors 1981a). One consequence is that EC expenditure tends perforce to sustain the previously established policies of individual member states because of the pressure to utilise payment appropriations within the current financial year.

No spending programme can be introduced without a firm base in one of the Treaties, in all our examples the Treaty of Rome (EEC) (1957). This required the Community to develop a common agricultural policy and Article 40 permitted the creation of the EAGGF. Article 123 directly established the ESF, the precise features of which have been set out periodically in regulations. More recent funds, notably the ERDF, have been justified under the catch-all Article 235, as have the 'supplementary measures' agreed to alleviate the British (and more recently the German) budget contribution problem. Whilst the legal framework remains crucial, it is gradually being interpreted more flexibly.

Responsibility for implementing Community policies is divided. Some policies, notably the CAP, are executed primarily by the member states, subject to strict Community rules and in constant contact with the Commission. The execution of the EAGGF (Guidance), ESF and ERDF is divided between the Commission and the member states. In all cases, final payments are disbursed by national agencies using national procedures. But the structural funds, deployed in tandem with parallel national programmes, are frequently executed as a subsidiary part of national programmes. Within the Commission, Directorates General XIX (Budgets) and XX (Financial Control) work with the particular Directorates General responsible for policy content in supervising spending programmes. DG XX has tended to authorise expenditure and to operate an internal audit system in a manner which is like the French system on which it was modelled, and is much criticised for its 'book-keeping mentality'. Its system of financial control is *ex post facto* (Court of Auditors 1981b). When the auditors find something wrong, the expenditure is simply 'disallowed' – that is, the Community reclaims its financial contribution. Often the member states do not reclaim grant from the recipient but carry the cost themselves, and national implementers are increasingly anxious to avoid disallowances. The delay, often of years, between actual expenditure and disallowance decisions causes considerable concern and uncertainty. So far this has been mainly a problem in agriculture though it may well rear its head in other sectors in the future. The perception that the Community financial authorities are often insensitive to the policy context and to the needs of the recipients of EC funds exacerbates the matter.

The Commission's services have an obligation to monitor progress and to scrutinise expenditure. For the EAGGF (Guarantee) elaborate mechanisms exist to handle the necessary collaboration between national and EC authorities. The large sums involved and the relatively complex rules require the financial controls to be adequate to guard against fraud and mis-spending. But the performance of the Commission in administering the smaller – and operationally simpler – structural funds has been limited by two main factors. First, a relatively low priority has so far been given to this function in work and staff allocations. Second, the Commission remains heavily dependent on information and evaluation by national authorities about the policy problems to be addressed, and the appropriate means for solving them. Thus it is extremely difficult for the Commission to ensure that Community policy criteria are respected or to assess the impact of EC spending. The recent creation of the Court of Auditors was designed to strengthen the procedures of financial control over EC expenditure.

Initially the Court's work concentrated on assessing financial regularity and propriety but it is now moving towards the evaluation of effectiveness and 'value for money'.

Financing agriculture

The whole of the large Guarantee Section of EAGGF – and part of the smaller Guidance Section – finances expenditure which flows directly from the CAP. Its dominant feature is a set of support mechanisms aimed at stabilising market prices for the major agricultural products at or near the target prices set annually by the Council of Agriculture Ministers. The support mechanisms vary from product to product; they consist mainly of subsidies (either on domestic products or on exports) and of arrangements under which public bodies (intervention agencies) or private individuals purchase certain goods and store them. The rules governing these arrangements are common throughout the Community and they are backed by a virtually unlimited financial commitment from EAGGF (Guarantee) – itself reflecting the desire for the policy to be both credible and effective. Expenditure on farm price support is notoriously difficult to forecast since it is so dependent on uncertain harvest and market prospects. But in any given harvest and market situation, the cost is determined by the levels of the support prices. If the support prices produce more supply than demand, substantial expenditure (on subsidies or storage or both) is needed to ensure that the resultant surplus does not overhang the market and force the price down. For much of its history, the Council has tended to set support prices, notably for butter and sugar, at levels which produce surpluses. It is too soon to assess the long-term effects of the increasing stress on prudent price policies and the introduction by the Council of 'co-responsibility' and other measures which seek to penalise producers somewhat if production continues to rise (Marsh and Swanney 1980; Pearce 1981).

The framework of CAP rules is laid down in Council Regulations, with Commission Regulations filling in the detail. Occasionally, when an operation is both frequent and routine (such as the fixing of daily import levies for some commodities), the Commission acts alone. But usually it must consult a product 'Management Committee' consisting of officials from the governments of the member states, by formulating a proposal on which the Committee votes using a weighted formula. Commission officials tend to seek the maximum possible support, by adapting their proposal in discussion if necessary; but the rules enable them to go ahead unless there is very substantial opposition.

The implementing agencies in the UK are the Intervention Board for Agricultural Produce (IBAP), a government department created by the

European Communities Act 1972, and HM Customs and Excise. IBAP, headed by a civil servant of Under Secretary rank, has some 500 staff linked for most personnel purposes with the Ministry of Agriculture, Fisheries and Food (MAFF). With the Customs, as collectors of the import levies, IBAP operates the export subsidies and levies and the elaborate system of licences and certificates required under the CAP for most imports and exports (from and to third countries). With help from the agricultural departments and two statutory non-departmental bodies – the Home Crown Cereals Authority and the Meat and Livestock Commission – IBAP operates the various public and private storage arrangements (commonly known as 'intervention'). All EAGGF (Guarantee) funds used in the UK flow through IBAP in the form of monthly advances from the Commission against forecast expenditure. The Commission can provide advances only within the overall budget appropriations and IBAP can make expenditure only within the advances provided. IBAP also handles some UK government funds for the few national schemes it implements, and because the Community does not cover the capital cost of public storage operations.

Whilst in some cases IBAP may find it difficult to implement the detailed EC rules, there is no significant evidence that it has faced major problems. As always where substantial sums are involved, fraud, avoidance and evasion have been found, occasionally in the glare of spectacular publicity. But nowadays the Commission usually acts with reasonable despatch to close identified loop-holes and to meet changing practical circumstances. IBAP's status as a government department permits its direct involvement in Brussels negotiations on detailed arrangements, thus reducing the risk of ineffective linkage in implementation. Whatever its other faults may be, the CAP seems relatively amenable to smooth implementation, partly because of its largely automatic character.

The Guidance Section of EAGGF finances the 'agricultural structures' policy. Though tiny in comparison with the Guarantee Section, some of its schemes illustrate at a micro-level the layers of implementation involved in EC spending. From the early 1960s sums of money were allocated to 'structural policies' intended to complement the price support arrangements. For several years no overall policy was agreed and the available funds were largely spent on 'individual projects' – capital projects with an agricultural bias which were already receiving some national government funding. Only in 1972 was agreement finally reached on several Directives based on the 'Mansholt Plan' of 1968, with the primary objective of encouraging high productivity growth in agriculture and of improving efficiency. Farm sizes and agricultural incomes vary both within and between member states; the measures finally agreed aimed to provide investment to those farms which could be modernised into viable units and earn a return comparable with non-agricultural earnings in the same region. The EAGGF contributes a portion, usually 25 per cent, of national expenditures on capital improvement assistance and some other activities. The 'less favoured areas' Directive (LFAD) of 1975 had its origins in the fear of UK hill farmers that joining the Community would mean the loss of various special aids. The system was extended to cover the whole Community in order to enable farming to continue in the designated areas and thus 'to ensure the maintenance of a minimum population and the preservation of the countryside'. In 1977 agreement was reached on a scheme for capital works assistance intended to increase the efficiency of the marketing and processing of farm produce, a final replacement for the 'individual projects' scheme. Various schemes aimed at discouraging milk production have also received partial support. The Guidance Section as a whole is now heavily oversubscribed (Europe 1982b).

The role of the Commission is relatively weak in administering most of EAGGF (Guidance). Generally, if a farmer qualifies under the rules laid down in the original Directives, EAGGF must contribute the agreed proportion of the member state's expenditure. These schemes are implemented in the UK by the four agriculture departments: MAFF, the Department of Agriculture for Northern Ireland (DANI), the Department of Agriculture and Fisheries for Scotland (DAFS) and the Welsh Office Agriculture Department (WOAD). Most such schemes are, like their counterpart national schemes, automatic in nature; if the application fulfils the criteria, it is approved and in due course payments will be made as qualifying expenditure is incurred by the farmers with the Finance Division of the implementing department claiming from EAGGF the appropriate percentage. In the local offices of the departments those who implement the schemes are aware that it is a Community scheme they are operating if for no other reason than that its rules and criteria are much more demanding than those of parallel national schemes, which usually have weaker criteria and lower grant rates.

The exception to this pattern is the marketing and processing scheme which is project-based, has a finite budget, and a system of loose national quotas. The Commission significantly influences the distribution of the funds, since in the Standing Committee on Agricultural Structures, governed by a 'Management Committee' procedure, only virtually unanimous opposition can block a project which the Commission supports. Like its 'individual project' predecessor, this scheme is implemented in the UK by a unit in MAFF. The terms of the scheme include a rigorous test that the project will guarantee economic benefits for primary agricultural producers and a requirement that the member governments prepare and submit for Community approval sectoral and/or regional 'programmes' identifying areas in which substantial investment on marketing and processing is needed. From 1980, only projects within such programmes benefited from the highest grant rate (25 per cent in most cases) and from 1981 projects outside programmes ceased to be eligible. The implementing unit forwards to the Commission as many valid applications as possible, knowing that many will probably be rejected for lack of funds because the UK continues to receive only 11 or 12 per cent of committed expenditure under the new scheme (as under the old). One unusual feature of the UK implementation of this scheme is a special national grant scheme operating in parallel to it. Community conditions require that a national subsidy of at least 5 per cent is also paid on the project in question. Projects in areas subject to automatic regional development grants, or benefiting from central government assistance in other ways, easily meet this criterion. But few marketing and processing developments outside the UK assisted areas would have qualified, a factor which had inhibited applications under the old scheme. The UK government therefore introduced, when the present scheme came into force, a special scheme providing national grants of up to 8 per cent for projects already approved for Community assistance. This represents an interesting case of an EC inducement producing innovation in national policy.

Improving training and employment opportunities

The ESF is concerned with training and to a lesser extent employment, not social welfare. It was designed to improve geographical and occupational mobility within the Community and its tasks include the amelioration of damaging effects which the common market may have on workers. It assists schemes of training, retraining and resettlement, and to a limited extent job creation, for unemployed workers and those threatened with unemployment. Since its 1971 revision, the ESF's main activities have fallen into two categories. The first concerns certain groups for which Community policies exist – at present former agricultural workers; workers in or leaving the textile and clothing industries; migrant workers; unemployed people under 25; and unemployed women over 25. The second category addresses problems of a persistent or structural nature, currently: regions of high unemployment; training needs associated with technical progress; those affected by restructuring in major undertakings; and the disabled. If a scheme is eligible under both categories, it may receive assistance only under one. The ESF will also, in certain circumstances, partly finance small pilot schemes and studies. The ESF will support schemes run by both public and private bodies, but in both cases the Fund will only match public contributions, up to a maximum of 50 per cent of the eligible costs of the scheme (except in certain areas with very serious problems – including Northern Ireland – which attract a maximum contribution of 55 per cent). Applications for ESF assistance, whether from private or public bodies, must be channelled through member governments – in the UK a section in the head-quarters of the Department of Employment (HL 1980).

Every year the Commission publishes, after consulting the Committee of the ESF, detailed guidelines for the fund for the next three years. Their priorities play a major role in determining the final allocation of expenditure. The decision-making process starts with applications from governments. The staff of the Commission then check these for eligibility under the rules, but rarely reject on these grounds. They then form a view on the priority to which each application can be assigned, if need be seeking further detail from either the government concerned or the individual applicant. Funds are allocated first to applications, or part-applications, which carry a high priority. Only if money remains within the relevant category do projects, or part-projects, assigned lower priorities get any funds at all. Thus the decision on priorities is the key to the allocation process. At the beginning of each budget year the likely distribution of the ESF is inevitably uncertain, since it depends on the scale of applications forwarded by each member government in each priority category. And because the Commission has much influence on these categories *ipso facto* it has a considerable influence upon the eventual financial outcomes.

Commission proposals are presented to the Committee of the ESF, unless the case is 'exceptional and urgent', in which case the Commission may decide without the Committee's view. The Committee, which usually meets two or three times a year, is a tripartite body with six members from each member state – two each from the government, trade unions and industry. Formally, the Committee votes by simple majority on these proposals but in practice a consensus is sought and votes are very rare. Technically, the Committee does not decide but merely offers an opinion to the Commission itself, which then formally commits the funds to the project; actual payments follow as the project is put into practice. On the face of it the involvement of trade unions and employers as well as Commission and national officials might be a source of difficulty and conflict, but it is striking how co-operative a process it has proved to be.

The Commission bends over backwards to insist that the decisions are taken strictly according to the system described above, involving a perfectly neutral determination of priorities and no bias in favour of particular member states other than that which emerges indirectly from the guidelines, such as the priorities for particularly disadvantaged regions or sectors. The Commission has great flexibility in assigning priorities and could formulate its decisions so as to influence the outcome as between member states. It certainly does not do so automatically or systematically, because the proportions of the funds committed to particular member states vary from year to year. But whilst the UK's share has tended not to vary much around the median of about 24 per cent, no assumption that an informal quota system is in operation is made by British officials involved. Also noteworthy is the concern of the Commission to be responsive to persuasively made arguments that particular national schemes merit ESF support.

The majority of the ESF funds coming to the UK tend to be in support of the training activities of the Manpower Services Commission (MSC); in 1980 and 1981, such schemes attracted some two-thirds of the commitment allocations made to the UK. The remaining funds go to parallel schemes in Northern Ireland as well as to local authorities, nationalised industries, private firms and voluntary bodies. Most industrial training schemes fail to qualify either because they are for existing employees or because there is no existing public contribution for the ESF to match. There is some obvious tension within the UK government between the desire to maximise UK receipts from the ESF and the wish not to change tried and tested training systems to meet the lottery of the ESF decision-making system. On the other hand the Overseas Division of the Department of Employment is charged in effect with maximising the returns to the UK from the ESF. To achieve this they need to ensure sufficient applications of good quality in the priority areas. This is not difficult in principle particularly where central government agencies are themselves engaging in eligible activities. But there is a significant element of uncertainty about future funding levels deriving from variations in budgetary appropriations, variations in the total volume of applications made to the Commission, and changes or reinterpretations of the priorities, rules and guidelines. This uncertainty may discourage potential recipients inside or outside central government from adopting schemes to meet ESF criteria. It must be noted that not all the measures eligible for ESF assistance are of equal interest to all member governments. Thus, for example, the British government makes relatively few applications either under the scheme to assist former agricultural workers (because there are few in the UK), or under the scheme to promote by affirmative action training for female workers (because British policy so far has been based on equal not separate access for women). These exceptions apart, the British performance in taking up ESF resources has been impressive, an important point given that the ESF has had a poor record of actual payment as distinct from projected appropriations. Thus the proportions were 49 per cent in 1978, 56 per cent in 1979 and 73 per cent in 1980 for the EC as a whole (Court of Auditors 1981a: 77).

Developing the regions

The key stated objective of the ERDF is 'to correct the principal regional imbalances' (Article 1, Regulation 724/75), but it is clearly confined in practice to financial support for national regional policies. From its creation in 1975 it was seen by UK governments as a major step in shifting the balance of Community policies and spending away from agriculture and towards areas from which the UK could expect to take net receipts reducing or offsetting its net budget contribution – always forecast to be high. The potential impact of the Fund on transfers between member states was a dominant feature of the negotiations to set it up. The result was a decision to lay down rigid national quotas determining how much of the Fund could go to each member state (Wallace *et al.* 1977, ch. 6).

The ERDF supports large (over about £30 000) investments in industrial, handicraft or service activities and infrastructure developments in all areas benefiting from national regional aids. The normal grant rates are 30 per cent for small infrastructure projects and 10–30 per cent for large projects. Only member governments can apply for ERDF assistance, although they can and do apply on behalf of private companies in respect of industrial projects. The Commission checks applications for eligibility within the rules laid down in the Regulation governing the Fund, including a requirement that no more than 70 per cent of the Fund should go to infrastructure projects taking a 3-year period. There is no attempt to assess priorities either within or between member states except in so far as the Fund Regulation states that priority must be given to national priority areas: in the UK, special development and development areas. But the decision on eligibility can itself be controversial. It is taken by the Commission after consulting with the Fund Management Committee which follows the same procedure as agricultural Management Committees. Thus the Commission can, and sometimes does, go ahead even if the majority of the governments oppose it; in this way, a number of UK projects, including one large industrial project and a number of tourist-related infrastructure projects, were approved in late 1979 even though six governments had formally opposed them. But, unless these favourite projects are rejected for ineligibility, governments can in practice determine for which projects they will seek finance. Since they know their quota share and the size of the Fund's resources for the present and, hence, their 'entitlement', they need only submit projects which would cover their entitlement. On the broader issues of policy and large projects the more high-level Regional Policy Committee enables experts from governments to comment in some detail on policy formation and implementation.

A continuing debate has taken place about whether the ERDF should contribute to particular projects in the eligible regions of the member states or alternatively concentrate on supporting agreed programmes for regional development. The Commission has always had a preference for emphasising programmes and thus for influencing through the operations of the ERDF the broad criteria for national regional policies. Some member governments by contrast, notably the British, have preferred to concentrate on discrete and tangible projects. A compromise was written into the Fund Regulation whereby member governments were obliged to present regional development programmes to the Commission, within the context of which individual bids for projects would be evaluated. The Commission proposals current at the time of writing sought to shift the emphasis of expenditure within the quota section of the ERDF to regional programmes. This has been a recurrent source of difficulty for the British government, concerned to avoid new bureaucratic burdens as a consequence (HL 1981). Behind the detailed argument over these proposals lie important differences of perspective and judgement about the character and shape of expenditure on regional development as well as a debate over which policy-makers at which level of government are best placed to make sensible decisions over particular kinds of investment.

At the first renewal of the Fund in 1979 the Commission succeeded in its proposal to experiment with a small non-quota section designed in particular to mitigate regional problems arising from other Community policies and in cross-border areas, and thus to introduce some Community-wide priorities into the application of ERDF funds. Decisions on the actual commitment of funds from the 5 per cent 'non-quota' section would be based on new detailed regulations by the Council. The rules governing non-quota expenditure are more flexible than under the quota section, in particular in that there is no absolute geographical limitation on the areas covered. The Commission's first proposals covered five groups of expenditure: help for tourism and industry in those parts of Italy and France where farmers will suffer from fierce competition when the Community is enlarged; electricity developments in the Mezzogiorno; help in housing and providing new industry in declining steel areas (particularly in the UK, including

Corby then outside the UK assisted areas, though now with development area status; but also in Belgium, and southern Italy); help for five declining shipbuilding areas (all in the UK); and the encouragement of tourism in the Irish border zone. In 1982 the first measures for funding were approved and included steel and shipbuilding measures. Significantly, in the UK this has involved the introduction of a new programme to enable small and medium firms to obtain consultancy services (*Europe* 1982a).

Within the UK, five departments are directly involved in implementing the ERDF – the Northern Irish, Scottish and Welsh Offices and the Departments of the Environment and of Industry. Over the first six years of the ERDF, England received 46½ per cent of the UK share; Scotland, 22½ per cent; Wales, 16 per cent; and Northern Ireland, 15 per cent (HC 1981). This produces a *de facto* sub-division amongst different parts of the UK (Regional Studies Association 1982). Projects funded have varied from the huge Kielder Dam in North-East England – which has received £30 million from the ERDF over several years, as well as large European Investment Bank loans – to a large number of very small industrial and infrastructure projects. The 1979 Regulation specifically provided that ERDF grants could be retained by national authorities in partial repayment for their own disbursements. Thus for industrial projects in the UK the ERDF operates in substitution for the assistance which the concern would otherwise obtain from regional development grant or other UK Industry Act assistance – indeed, if it did not, the Community's separate rules laying down maximum levels of regional grant would often be broken. Whilst the project sponsor may know that his investment is put forward for ERDF support as a component of the contribution from public funds, it makes no financial difference to him. In the early years of the ERDF there was some confusion about when the sponsor should be informed that his project had been submitted for ERDF aid, and the Community Regulation only required that he be told once the Commission had given its approval. Now it is automatic for this information to be communicated at an earlier stage by the British authorities, though it is far from clear that this is the practice throughout the Community (Halstead 1982).

On the infrastructure side the impact can be more direct because for local authorities – and some other public beneficiaries – receipt of an ERDF grant is matched not by an equal cut in the rate support or block grant, but by a cut in the amount which the authority can borrow. Thus a local authority or public utility receives cash and saves borrowing, to the point where at least one local authority, Liverpool District Council, chose in 1979 to lose most of its 'locally determined' loan sanction in order to gain cash-in-hand through the ERDF. More recently, the precise rules governing cash limits for local authorities' capital expenditure have altered, but the effect is the same as regards the ERDF, namely that the ERDF cannot result in increased expenditure though it may permit expenditure to be funded by ERDF grant rather than by loan. However, the extent to which these options are available has been reduced by the tight constraints which now circumscribe local government expenditure from embarking on major investment projects (*Local Government Studies* 1980).

In the UK and more generally in the EC the economic recession and public expenditure constraints have had their effects on the ERDF. Nominally the resources available to the ERDF have increased significantly in cash terms, though inflation has eroded their increase in real value. Originally it was intended that at least half of the Fund's resources should be devoted to industrial projects, though this has been relaxed to enable more to be spent on infrastructure projects and thus maximise utilisation of the ERDF. The British government has sought to maintain a higher proportion of bids for industrial projects (40 per cent) than other member states (30 per cent), but has the option of adjusting the ratio (Regional Studies Association 1982). However, it by no means follows that increases in the total resources of the ERDF will be matched by increases in the eligible bids from the UK or other member states, a serious problem if the EC budget were to shift its expenditure substantially away from agriculture to regional spending. In the past appropriations for payments from the ERDF have often been significantly underspent, though detailed changes in the procedure have considerably improved the rate of utilisation. It is noteworthy that the rate of utilisation of payments often differs from the apportioned shares under the quota section of the Fund, though the UK has been so far impressively effective in absorbing its share. But for the future the picture is much less clear. Much depends on how the detailed EC criteria for eligibility are adapted to changing economic circumstances and on how individual governments draw their own maps of eligible regions (Commission EC 1981; HL 1981, 1982).

Towards an evaluation

What lessons should be drawn from the British record of spending EC money? Experience of implementing the CAP over some ten years has affected the policy environment and attitudes of policy-makers in Britain. Criticisms of the CAP in the UK remain unabated with some arguing for its radical overhaul and others calling for its abolition or replacement. In practice government policy has focused on moderate rather than extreme versions of reform. British policy-makers have adjusted to a changed policy context, with its new modes of operation and different channels for pursuing British interests. This is not to argue, as some critics would suggest, that British officials have sold out to Brussels but rather to comment that the substantial change in the policy framework and its implementing machinery has had repercussions on governmental behaviour. But this does not necessarily imply socialisation to the point of substantially altering their actual behaviour, bound as it is by British doctrines of ministerial responsibility and administrative propriety.

Equally the clients of the CAP – the British farmers – have been engaged in a substantially altered policy framework whilst what they saw as 'their' ministry has become one of ten ministries engaged in determining policy at the EC level. Without losing their desire for close links with British agricultural policy-makers, UK farmers have endeavoured to influence policy through participation in Community fora. Their consequent reorientation has generated different expectations as to the kind of public funding they might prefer or realistically hope to achieve. Indeed for some – the sugar beet and oilseed rape producers are apt examples – the benefits of EC policy are considerably greater than those of the prior British policy. Those who have profited in this way have a keen interest in the continued implementation of the CAP and would be loud voices in any discussion of a different policy. But perhaps the most significant change is that the agricultural lobby has become more visible in the British policy process, to the point where a former NFU President has now become leader of the British Conservatives in the European Parliament. Community price reviews are settled in a glare of media coverage far greater than when the issues were purely domestic.

So striking a permeation of Community influences has not, however, been evident in the other sectors in which EC funds operate. On the contrary the tying of ESF, ERDF and EAGGF (Guidance) finance to British government programming has barely disturbed established relationships and attitudes in the policy process. The programmes are more or less successful in the terms in which they are cast by British policy-makers. One small EAGFF guidance programme has stimulated the adoption of a new British scheme so as to encourage the take-up of Community funds. Some spending under the new non-quota section of the ERDF and ESF support of voluntary bodies may be exceptions, but otherwise it is not possible to identify clearly any actions which result at all directly from the financial flows from the Community exchequer; nor is there significant evidence that employment, regional or agricultural projects have yet been recast as distinct from technically adapted to meet the requirements of eligibility for the ESF, ERDF or

EAGGF. This may be less true for the future as the ESF and ERDF are revised.

But this is not to say that the existence of Community funds has no impact on the policy process. Meeting the technical conditions imposed by Community regulations imposes new work on the British administrator who is obliged to describe projects and produce supporting evidence in terms very different from those used for national purposes. This process is not always viewed with ready understanding by British officials unused to the perceptions and practices of Commission officials or at some stages removed from the intricacies of the Community's operations. Mutual misunderstanding can breed friction. Central government departments have sometimes been the target of criticism from local public and private bodies for providing poor, inadequate or unclear information (Norton 1980).

A different issue arises from discrepancies between British and Community spending priorities. The Commission's priorities within the ESF are influenced by the British government, but purely British priorities would often be different. Yet British receipts depend on the degree to which applications fit the Commission's guidelines. While this may have been simply an irritant in the past it has become much more significant given the current emphasis of the British government on reducing public expenditure. It is conceivable that British policy-makers in assessing the scope for cuts may have to reach a view on whether to sacrifice particular British programmes even though this may reduce the overall British take-up of Community funds. They would no doubt seek to obtain Commission guidelines which reflected national priorities. But decisions, like that to reduce the British assisted areas, will prevent some parts of the UK from benefiting from ERDF, as well as national funds. This may not affect total British receipts; but it may lead to confused debate as British applicants seek the scapegoat responsible for a refusal to fund a particular cherished project.

As for the actual effect of policy programmes financed partially by the structural funds very little solid evidence is available. Receipts go directly to the British exchequer and the clients of the funds (with the exception of ESF allocations for non-governmental bodies and part of the ERDF infrastructure programme) do not actually receive Community cash in hand or engage directly in the policy process. There is no satisfactory way of evaluating a Community component as distinct from the national component since the former is dependent on the latter. Nor can any sensible appraisal be made of the delivery of the Community policies, their cost-effectiveness or their impact on economic development, though some questions have been raised by the Court of Auditors (1981a) in several cases. The policy delivery system remains opaque and the number of administrative layers between the provisions of funds and their deployment militates against thorough and consistent decisions about both the means and the ends of policy. The Community certainly does not possess a panoply of spending programmes comparable to those used by United States federal government to plug the gaps in local provision or to alter local attitudes to priorities and objectives.

The Commission has argued that Community funds should – as the EAGGF Guarantee Section does – do more than simply subsidise national programmes. Community funding should be additional to national efforts so that the total volume of expenditure on priority policies can rise. The rationale for this is partly financial and partly political: financial in that it is something of a nonsense to engage in a convoluted rigmarole of assessing applications and awarding cash if the result within the member states is the *status quo ante* but funded through the Community rather than the national exchequer; and political in that identifiably additional expenditure would link the recipients to the outcomes of EC policy-making. National governments have tended to argue that, since they are already funding all the useful and necessary programmes, any additional spending would merely bring forth projects of marginal value which they would also be forced to support with national money. Even where local authorities and voluntary bodies in the UK have received ESF money directly, this has tended to release their resources for other kinds of spending rather than increase the amount spent on ESF-approved programmes.

British ministers say that the likely receipts from EC funds are taken into account in the forward planning of public expenditure and that total expenditure is thereby enabled to be higher than it would otherwise have been. The Commission publicly accepts this argument; for example, Commissioner Tugendhat said in 1977 that

> Community action should not necessarily be an addition to public activity, spending and taxation. The Community should not seek to duplicate the activities of the nation state, but should rather try to do at the Community level those tasks which are already being, or will have to be undertaken, but which the Community has had a request from the nation state to fulfil. If this is the touchstone, there need be no net increase in public expenditure. Indeed there may even be a net reduction. (European Parliament 1977)

But equally British ministers form a judgement on how far the projected contribution from the UK into the Community's own resources restricts the tax yield which might otherwise be available for domestic expenditure.

A second strand is the argument that the structural funds should be deployed only under rigorously defined Community criteria. This is a particular problem in the Community where the member governments gathered in the Council both pay the piper and call the tune. But the Council reflects the collective view of the member governments, not their individual views. Community criteria determined in the Council range between procedural rules and highly abstract principles. The reliance of the Community on legal formulae for consistent execution means that the fulfilment of procedural requirements tends to be given a higher priority than the economic evaluation of the impact of policy. Indeed many in the Commission would argue that more sophisticated evaluation is not worth while or practicable, unless common policies are agreed. There is a continuous tussle between those in the Commission who tend to press for increasingly stringent conditions and those national governments who – as both implementers and, through the Council, controllers of the policy – try to retain the maximum possible national control.

Another issue is how much room for implementing discretion or flexibility should or can be permitted in so complex a policy process as that of the EC. The CAP system of price support has so far operated with automatic funding of all expenditure which falls within the categories defined in law. Little or no discretion can be applied partly because decisions can be and are subject to challenge through the courts if they seem unwarrantedly discriminatory. The heaviness of the system is to some extent mitigated by the close involvement of the implementers (certainly in the UK) in the policy process at both national and Community levels: the Management Committee procedure under which the rules for CAP implementation are made ensures regular feedback and facilitates adaptation as required. However, quite different circumstances apply to the structural funds. Superficially most EAGGF Guidance money appears equally automatic in that technical eligibility ensures access to funding and thus leaves no discretion to the implementer. Yet under the central Directive on farm development member states have a choice between making capital grants and subsidising interest charges. That choice has a major impact on the shape of national schemes, but still requires conformity with complex directives which cannot easily be changed.

The position on the project-based schemes funded by the ESF, ERDF and in one case under EAGGF guidance, is quite different. The Commission can reject ineligible projects but is often unable to select one eligible project rather than another. In the case of the ERDF the effective locus for exercising selection is unequivocally at the national level as individual governments determine which projects to put forward broadly up to the value of their quota share. But significantly, in the case of the ESF, the Department of Employment tends to pass on all eligible projects, if their sponsors so wish, not least because of the Commission's scope for choosing amongst its priority categories. In such a case the relevant officials both negotiate the policy and are the key 'gatekeepers' in the implementation process. Budgetary considerations retain an over-riding importance and largely explain the high take-up of anticipated UK shares of the funds.

The British government remains strongly committed to preserving and even extending the ERDF and the ESF, but primarily to generate a continuing flow of UK receipts from the Community budget. Whether this is the most promising way of generating such a flow is a different question. Recent developments have pointed in a different direction, as in the 'supplementary measures' agreement of May 1980 and its extension in February 1983, designed to permit expenditure in the UK outside the framework of the existing funds. The latter approach can only be carried a certain way without beginning to imply a different kind of Community. The critics of this development fear that implementation might simply become a matter of technical execution with only superficial Community controls. On the other hand a shift towards a more flexible and selective allocation of Community funding might open the door to, and indeed require, a more active partnership between national and Community authorities.

Conclusion

No single or uniformly applicable judgement can be proffered on the record of spending EC money in the UK. The tentacles of the CAP have spread far and deep, changing the policy environment and the pattern of client–patron relationships. Here we can identify a policy process akin to national analogues with powers, funds and surveillance operating transnationally, backed up by procedures which go far beyond the classical methods of international consensus-building. Within the UK involvement in implementation has engendered a significant process of learning and adaptation, combined with a capacity to execute policy efficiently in spite of its complexity and the number of levels of government concerned. In all of our other examples the EC policy process is more embryonic and in none is there a clear framework of common goals and values. Implementation in the UK has been administratively efficient and compares favourably with the position in some other member states. Technically the formal requirements of implementation have been largely fulfilled. There is some, albeit limited, evidence of EC influences seeping through the filters which continue to separate Community and national officials, but there is no new policy community yet emerging to transcend the boundary between the two. The British record so far should caution us against the expectation that the experience of implementing the structural funds can readily generate qualitative changes sufficient to incorporate national implementation within a new transnational policy process.

References

Amending Treaties 1970, 1975, *Treaties of 1970 and 1975 amending certain budgetary provisions of the Treaties establishing the European Communities* (several publishers, including HMSO)

Bowker 1980, *Action by the European Community through its financial instruments*, Epping, Bowker Publishing Company (no author)

Commission EC 1981, *The Regions of Europe*, first periodic report on the social and economic situation of the regions of the Community, COM(80)816 final, Brussels 7 January

Court of Auditors 1981a, 'Annual report concerning the financial year 1980 accompanied by the replies of the institutions', *Official Journal of the European Communities*, C344, 31 December

Court of Auditors 1981b, 'Study of the financial systems of the European Communities (1981)', *Official Journal of the European Communities*, C342, 31 December

Europe 1982a, 'EEC regional policy', 10/11 May, p. 12

Europe 1982b, 'Agriculture: FEOGA-Guidance cannot finance any large new projects until 1985', 8 July, p. 15

European Parliament 1977, *Official Journal of the European Communities*, 10 May

Halstead, P. 1982, *The development of the European Regional Fund since 1972*, PhD thesis, University of Bath

HC 1981, *Official report*, 15 June, written answers, col. 255

HL 1979/80, Select Committee on the European Communities, *The European Social Fund*, Session 1979–80, 70th Report, 21 October

HL 1981, Select Committee on the European Communities, *Regional policy*, 14th Report, 17 February

HL 1982, Select Committee on the European Communities, *Revision of the European Regional Development Fund*, Session 1981–2, 12th Report, 6 April

Local government studies 1980, Special issue on 'Europe, local government and regional development', vol. 6, no. 4, July/August

Marsh, J.S. and Swanney, P.J. 1980, *Agriculture and the European Community*, London, Allen & Unwin

Norton, A. 1980, 'Relations between the European Community and British local government', *Local government studies*, vol. 6, no. 1, January/February, pp. 5–15

Pearce, J. 1981, *The Common Agricultural Policy* (Chatham House Paper No. 13), Royal Institute of International Affairs, London, Routledge & Kegan Paul

Regional Studies Association 1982, 'Regional development and the EEC', *Built environment*, vol. 7, nos 3–4

Treaty of Rome (EEC) 1957, *Treaty establishing the European Economic Community* (various publishers, including HMSO)

Wallace, H. 1980, *Budgetary politics: the finances of the European Communities*, London, Allen & Unwin

Wallace, H., Wallace, W. and Webb, C. (eds) 1977, *Policy-making in the European Communities*, Chichester, Wiley (1st edn)

11 Defence

US–UK collaboration on Polaris

Masood Hyder

Defence was the first of the major policy areas in Britain to engage in a search for international co-operation and, with the development of seemingly permanent military alliances, it has become a commonplace to look abroad for joint solutions to national security problems. It is not surprising therefore that some of the best case studies of the implementation of policies across national boundaries are to be found in defence, most of them alas unexplored. Among them, the UK Polaris programme provides the outstanding example of the successful transfer of a major weapons system and associated technology. The programme had its origins in the understanding reached at Nassau in December 1962, and completed its developmental stage in July 1969 when the Royal Navy assumed responsibility for deploying the main strategic deterrent force from the Royal Air Force (RAF). It is proposed to look at the formative early period in its development here, concentrating on the process of establishing the basic principles and practices of the 'joint programme', as the Anglo-American collaboration on Polaris came to be known.

Implementation of the Polaris deal depended crucially on working out the most effective and mutually acceptable means of co-operation between the two countries. Some parts of the story are well known, such as the events leading up to Nassau and the negotiating skills deployed by the British side there; something is known too about the subsequent organisational developments, such as the speedy and innovative style of 'project management' adopted by the Admiralty. The initial agreement and the subsequent implementation were underpinned by an extended process of preparation and negotiation, and it is this aspect in which we are primarily interested here. The point may be expressed in general terms as follows: where a policy depends on international agreements it becomes necessary for the national government to monitor and observe developments abroad; to prepare and negotiate suitable agreements; to establish and operate collaborative machinery; to cultivate and maintain informal contacts; and to find ways and means of resolving matters of technical detail. These activities, when examined closely, are neither wholly external in setting and diplomatic in style, nor are they exclusively domestic and administrative in the conventional sense, but straddle these distinctions. Implementation in such boundary areas acquires differences from yet maintains similarities to the processes by which purely domestic policies are carried out. It is proposed to use the Polaris case in order to explore these ambiguities, while keeping in mind its exceptional quality.

The background

The UK government had originally developed its own nuclear strategic force. Increasingly, however, it came to depend on American weapon and missile development. After the cancellation of its Blue Streak programme in April 1960, the two obvious contenders as the main future UK deterrent were both of American manufacture: the Skybolt air-launched ballistic missile, and the Polaris submarine-launched system. Of the two, Polaris was the more sophisticated. It was solid-fuelled and therefore could be fired at short notice; it enabled the nuclear force to be moved out to sea and thus rendered virtually invulnerable to surprise attack; it was safer too in the sense that its invulnerability permitted a delay in retaliatory action. It was the ideal second-strike weapon. But the defence review that took place at this time concluded in favour of Skybolt because its development was further advanced. Skybolt also promised economies as it could be fitted to one of the existing types of V-bombers and so increase the return on that considerable investment. Nevertheless the impression prevailed in contemporary defence circles that Polaris would eventually succeed Skybolt.

The Admiralty had been watching the development of Polaris since 1956 and had taken care to maintain friendly relations with the Special Projects Office (SPO), which managed the US Fleet Ballistic Missile Project. Even in the Admiralty Polaris did not enjoy priority at this stage. However three preparatory acts are worth noting. In October 1958, two years before the decision to opt for Skybolt, a member of the British Naval Staff in Washington was formally assigned to the task of liaison with SPO. Two years later the Admiralty took an even more important step by drawing up organisational plans for a UK Polaris programme. A study conducted by Rear-Admiral Le Fanu concluded that a project management-type of organisation, like the highly successful SPO, would be most appropriate. The Le Fanu Report was followed by a technical mission to the USA in the winter of 1960–1, composed of a number of senior technical personnel who were later to work on the British Polaris Executive. At the time these preparations were regarded as no more than long-range exercises undertaken by a prudent bureaucracy. For, until the US decision to cancel Skybolt in 1962, there seemed little reason to believe that Polaris would succeed Skybolt much before 1970, and the Admiralty wanted to give priority to its carrier and hunter–killer programmes (Pierre 1972).

The Skybolt cancellation therefore came as a shock to the British government, and almost caused a rift in relations with the USA (Neustadt 1970). It also posed something of a threat to the Macmillan government, given the depth of feeling in the Conservative Party about the potential loss of independent nuclear capability. British planning immediately turned its attention to the problem of obtaining Polaris. Time was short. News of the cancellation had been conveyed to the British on 8 November 1962. President Kennedy and Prime Minister Macmillan were scheduled to meet at Nassau in mid-December. In barely five weeks the British government had to prepare its negotiating position in the light of the new developments. After 'protracted and fiercely contested' discussions Macmillan was able to secure Polaris on extremely favourable terms. The US government undertook to provide the missiles, equipment and supporting services 'on a continuing basis'. The British would provide the submarines and the nuclear warheads (Cmnd 1915, 1962). The missiles were sold at the same price as paid by the US Navy and (as later established) the UK paid only 5 per cent extra towards development costs. In a typical understatement Macmillan described the deal as 'not a bad bargain' (Macmillan 1973).

This brief outline fails to convey the distinct advantages attending the birth of the Polaris programme. First, if the UK government had to look abroad for collaborators, the USA was the natural starting-point for its search, given the special relationship between the two governments in defence matters and their experience of co-operation in all aspects of military technology. The 'search environment' scanned by British planners was familiar and friendly. Secondly, Polaris was the best possible choice as a second-generation deterrent system. Between 1960 and 1962 it made very good progress, in contrast to the growing difficulties of Skybolt. Thirdly, the Polaris programme was entrusted to the Admiralty, regarded at the time as an outstandingly competent organisation, with exceptional internal coherence and great political skill (Snyder 1964); its prudent anticipatory staff work also proved invaluable. Fourthly, and perhaps most important of all from the point of view of implementing the programme, there was a clear disposition to find a solution to Britain's problem. Nassau was intended to repair the damage that the Skybolt affair had done to the alliance, and there continued to be political support at the highest level. This maintained the momentum during the detailed negotiations that followed Nassau and led to the Polaris Sales Agreement.

The detailed negotiations

The detailed negotiations about the setting-up of the UK programme involved not only two governments but, as a prior stage, a number of different government departments within the UK. Of all the Whitehall departments the Ministry of Defence (MoD) has enjoyed something of a special relationship with the Foreign Office. They, and their various predecessors, have a long history of successful co-operation in international work; their efforts are supported at home by a well-established committee structure, and by the espousal of complementary views about the relationship between defence and foreign policy (Wallace 1975: 127–9).

Preparatory work on the Polaris Sales Agreement involved close collaboration between them. After Nassau the Foreign Office began to consider, in consultation with the US State Department, what supplementary agreements would be required to define the specific terms of supply and sale; MoD, the Ministry of Aviation (MoA) and the Admiralty proceeded to elucidate the force requirements, the necessary supplies, and the organisation to be set up. In January 1963 a team was sent on a 'deep technical mission' to Washington in order to update and extend the information obtained during the 1960–1 missions. It was headed jointly by Sir Solly Zuckerman (Chief Scientific Adviser, MoD) and Vice-Admiral Varyl Begg (Vice-Chief Naval Staff), and included Sir Robert Cockburn (Chief Scientist, MoA), J.M. Mackay (Deputy Secretary, Admiralty and soon to be chief UK negotiator for the Sales Agreement) and Rear-Admiral Mackenzie (later appointed Chief Polaris Executive). The information gathered provided the basis for the Foreign Office's talks with American officials. By the end of January the State Department sent to London the preliminary draft of an Agreement. The terms of reference and negotiating brief were drawn up after the usual interdepartmental consultations, and the UK negotiating team left for Washington on 17 February 1963.

While these preparations were under way doubts persisted in Conservative circles about the independence of the proposed deterrent. Members of the Conservative Party Defence Committee saw the Minister of Defence on New Year's Day 1963 to express their reservations about Polaris and sought assurances that the weapon would not be operated under a two-key system that gave the Americans a final say in its use. In the same month MoA suggested that it might still be possible to opt for a wholly British programme based on the Black Knight missile or on a new research and development effort. Obviously the speed at which agreement had been reached had left domestic opinion far behind, and options which had backers in the defence community still continued to be actively considered for some time. But Nassau was a *fait accompli* and the government was determined to go forward with it. Backbench opinion was gradually contained (Snyder 1964: 71); MoA proposals were simply not followed up. Nassau was in a peculiar degree the personal achievement of the Prime Minister and he was unlikely to set his face against it for the uncertainties of a new research effort.

Some idea of the speed at which the programme was moving ahead is conveyed by looking at developments in organisation. By the time the negotiations began in February considerable progress had been made, within the Admiralty in particular, in setting up the Polaris Executive (PE), in clarifying its tasks, and in establishing contacts with SPO.

On Christmas Eve 1962, less than a week after the Nassau meeting, the Board of Admiralty decided to implement the Le Fanu scheme of 1960. PE was to be a project-type organisation, with a particular set of responsibilities placed in the hands of a small group within the Admiralty. The staff began taking shape almost immediately. By early February PE was sufficiently well established for the Chief Polaris Executive (CPE) to begin refining the programme's aims, and extending its relationships outside the Admiralty.

A sense of urgency permeates contemporary records, reflecting no doubt the unusually specific time-limit that was incorporated in the stated aim of the programme. The first submarine, with 16 missiles and with full support, was to be deployed on station by July 1968; the remaining boats were to follow thereafter at six-monthly intervals. The Board had stated categorically that these dates would not be allowed to slip. The V-bombers were coming to the end of their useful lives and Polaris was needed by 1969 at the latest, though actually the Vulcans continued in their strike role into the 1980s. Ordinarily, implementers can avoid strict time-limits, especially where research and development into high technology is involved. In the military field in particular, where the drive to win the fruits of advanced technology is intense, governments have been exceptionally tolerant of uncertain outcomes, delays and cost over-runs. In this case, however, there was to be no delay. PE was led to believe that time was more important than money.

The scope of the project was beginning to emerge. The UK government would order four 16-missile submarines; the decision on the fifth was expected later in 1963. The missiles would most probably be the advanced A3 type but no formal decision had been taken as yet. The submarines were to be of British design and construction, based on the Valiant class hull and propulsive machinery, but lengthened to incorporate the Polaris weapons system. The complete weapons system would be procured from the USA. The warhead would be of British manufacture; research and development and procurement associated with it would be the responsibility of MoA, which would also be responsible for the re-entry vehicle for the warhead. Clearly, the project lacked a dominant research and development function and this was to prove a distinct advantage as far as its implementation was concerned. The areas of invention were limited to the development of the re-entry system, and to a number of submarine systems such as the propulsive machinery, the control gear and the high-quality welding that would be required. For the rest it would be a procurement operation.

Close contacts between the two national teams preceded the formal negotiations and were even in some danger of overtaking them. Contemporary documents urge that all requests for information, action, sponsorship of missions and so forth should be severely restricted until the government-to-government agreement establishing the terms under which the missiles system was to be purchased had been signed. Close contacts and visits had obviously helped clarify aims. The actual negotiations went ahead smoothly on the whole, and the fact that they took as long as they did (about four weeks of actual talks, followed by signature on 6 April) bears testimony to the determination of the negotiators to reach a detailed and workable agreement which would provide a favourable basis for the subsequent process of implementation.

During the negotiations major differences arose from the restrictions that the Americans wished to place on the manufacture of equipment in the UK, and from their proposed financial terms. American reluctance to allow the manufacture of a wide range of standard items of equipment stemmed from the fact that the Polaris system could not be tested by frequent test firings and that its reliability could be established only by maintaining high standards of quality control for the entire system. All equipment had, therefore, to be made under identical conditions and monitored continuously. The representatives of the SPO took care to explain that the US government could not ensure the reliability of the entire system except by restricting the manufacture of equipment abroad. On a political level, the American negotiators wished to avoid domestic, and especially congressional criticism that the deal had been too generous, or had transferred technical knowhow or resulted in job losses at home.

The desire to avoid domestic and congressional scrutiny also led the British team to agree to certain unexpected and cumbersome financial terms and conditions. After prolonged negotiations the British side agreed to pay a sum of $17.5 million as compensation to the Americans for the increased overheads resulting from the additional UK programme, over and above the 5 per cent research and development levy agreed at an earlier stage. In the event the Polaris Sales Agreement had an easy passage through both legislatures. Its adoption not as a full treaty but as an 'agreement' (Cmnd 2108 and 2336 1963) meant that it was merely laid before the British Parliament on 9 April 1963 and treated as a Presidential or 'executive agreement' in the USA. Thus it escaped many of the problems which beset treaty-making, and the auguries were set fair to smooth the passage towards the implementation phase.

The Polaris Executive (PE)

In Britain the executive traditionally enjoys a monopoly in the conduct of defence and foreign affairs which enables it to move towards implementation with little interference from domestic pressures. This is not to deny the government's sensitivity to domestic political pressures but to assert its dominant position. In constitutional law foreign affairs and defence are Crown prerogatives, and in practice policies concerned with the nation's security are accorded a high priority. As a consequence, military programmes enjoy very considerable political support at the centre of government. They are often the subject of decision-making by senior members of Cabinet (in consultation with their military advisers and senior civil servants) whose conclusions become politically unassailable. Such concentration of authority and power ensures the forceful direction of policy and makes it easier to entrust a policy to a small group of implementers. The PE symbolised commitment by the government to the new joint programme as well as playing a crucial part in its management and coordination.

The Board of Admiralty were left in little doubt about the importance attached to the successful implementation of the programme, and they in turn devised and sanctioned the most effective means of carrying it out. CPE, as head of PE, was placed on the staff of the Controller of the Navy. He had a naval assistant, technical staff covering ship and weapon issues, and a senior civilian assistant to deal with the finance and general policy. There were liaison staff in Washington, and links with MoA (see Table 11.1). The prime function of PE was the coordination of tasks rather than direct involvement in management; but the details of its powers were not as important as the distinctiveness of its remit. 'It was as if the blessings of the Admiralty Board were on it,' as one official put it. CPE had access to every member of the Board of Admiralty and met them regularly; if dissatisfied with progress or co-operation he could raise the matter at ministerial or Board level. His mandate was reinforced too by the method adopted for selecting personnel. Staffing was carried through remarkably quickly by means of a flexible system of recruitment. A very

Table 11.1: The Polaris Executive, 1963–7

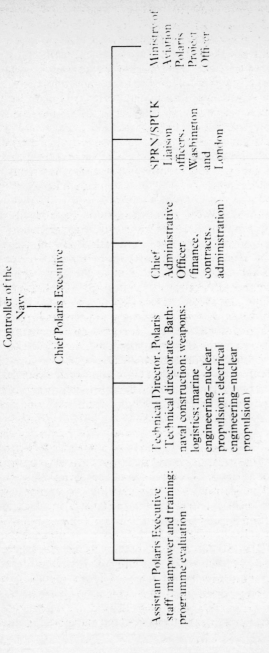

Controller of the Navy

Chief Polaris Executive

Assistant Polaris Executive (staff, manpower and training: programme evaluation)

Technical Director, Polaris (Technical directorate, Bath: naval construction: weapons: logistics: marine engineering–nuclear propulsion; electrical engineering–nuclear propulsion)

Chief Administrative Officer (finance, contracts, administration)

SPRN/SPUK (Liaison officers, Washington and London)

Ministry of Aviation Polaris Project Officer

small number of staff was directly allocated to PE; a larger group of 'dedicated' personnnel worked full-time for it while remaining attached to their own divisions in the Admiralty; and there were part-time liaison staff, acting as links with other parts of the Admiralty. By these means CPE's contacts reached every part of the Admiralty, while the priority attached to his tasks ensured prompt attention to his needs.

Timing was as important as the distinctiveness of the remit. Rear-Admiral Mackenzie's initial briefing as CPE about the aims of the programme, as conceived by the Board and ministers, took place in early January 1963 at a time when the details of the programme had yet to be worked out. By all accounts his briefing was far from comprehensive. However, his early appointment gave him the opportunity to begin the process of refining the aims of the programme by discussion and argument.

Within the Admiralty, PE encouraged the development of a relevant body of strategic doctrine, appropriate to the requirements of deterrence based on naval force. At another more mundane level, the staff strove to prepare the managerial basis for Polaris: ensuring the recruitment and training of submarine crews, and planning the Polaris base.

Outside the Admiralty, PE's most crucial relationship was with MoA. Alone among the service departments the Admiralty had retained control of its research and development and supply functions, except that procurement of aircraft and missiles was the responsibility of MoA. This division of tasks gave rise to negotiations of some delicacy over the Polaris programme. According to its statutory rights, MoA would buy the missiles from the USA (later transferring the costs of the transaction to the Navy vote) and ensure that the interface between the missile and the re-entry system (which still had to be designed) was provided for. In other words, MoA would be responsible for some of the central tasks of the programme. The Admiralty felt that this division of responsibility needed to be altered in the Polaris case. The urgency of the programme had indicated a project-type organisation; it made little sense to allocate some of the central tasks to a different agency. The identification with the US programme also indicated Admiralty primacy. Besides, the technology involved argued for a reduced MoA role. The system was conceived as a single integrated entity embodying the ship and the weapon; to separate the two would create difficulties. Behind these reasonings lingered another consideration. MoA, like the RAF, was still suffering from the shock of the sudden Skybolt cancellation: some of its personnel found it difficult to generate much enthusiasm over Polaris and, as was noted above, proposals were still being put forward for alternative all-British systems. An agreement was worked out therefore that the Admiralty would assume effective responsibility for procuring the missiles and associated equipment, except the re-entry system, and that it would be the 'design approval authority'. MoA sensitivities were soothed by giving it full representation on the whole range of ministerial and interdepartmental committees set up to assist PE; and by the courtesy and consideration unfailingly extended by Lord Carrington, the First Lord. Here, as in the US programme, co-optation was an important means of obtaining compliance (Sapolsky 1972).

PE's early pre-eminence stemmed from the soundness of its judgements. It was CPE's holistic approach, that is, his concern for the complete programme, that gave his arguments the edge over rival conceptions. The debate over the choice of missile illustrates this point. In March 1963 the earlier version of the Polaris missile, A2, had been in service for over a year, whereas firing trials of the bigger and more advanced A3 were still going on. These trials moreover were not an unqualified success. Nevertheless, CPE and his masters in the Admiralty definitely favoured A3. They believed that US commitment to its success was so great that the UK government could safely choose it; they were impressed in particular by the determination of SPO to stay with A3 even if difficulties persisted. MoA, given its special responsibility for the development of the re-entry system, objected that a re-entry system designed to fit the A3 missile would create many problems. The Admiralty were concerned with the overall advantages of the A3 system, and pointed out that the Americans were determined to phase out A2 production by 1965, and that the UK programme was in danger of adopting an obsolescent system. (The circumstances were rather similar to the ones that led another UK government 19 years later to ask the US government for Trident II instead of Trident I [Cmnd 8517 1982].) The formal decision to go for A3 was not taken until June 1963, but the intellectual argument was won by the Admiralty and CPE long before that.

The ability of government to give forceful direction to policy through a small group of implementers is a necessary but not a sufficient condition for success. Certainly the achievements of PE were due to the high-level support that it enjoyed; but they are also attributable to a number of other factors. To timing – PE was established sufficiently early in the life of the programme to exert a decisive influence on it during the formative stage. To initiative – CPE assumed a leadership role and commensurate responsibilities extending beyond his original remit. Finally, these things were possible because the Polaris project had relatively well-defined aims. These aims and the tasks involved in achieving them were established through a process of discussion and negotiation. Only subsequently did it become a question of following through in a programmed fashion. As one former PE official put it, the ideas and innovations came in the early stages, though the files grew thicker later on.

Implementation and its modes

What appears at first sight as a sudden and dramatic policy development was a speeded-up evolutionary process. The complex structures, arrangements and understandings necessary for carrying out the programme developed by stages, though relatively swiftly. Implementation was a running argument, a chain of linked problems and their tentative solution. Innovation and a willingness to learn proved crucial factors in evolving the design for executing policy: through adaptation, with the development of the project management idea; through a process of familiarisation, by establishing contacts with US officials; and through critical feedback, with the adoption of American management techniques. The PE displayed all of these qualities, in recognition of the risks of assuming that the British part of the programme could simply be modelled on an American blueprint.

Polaris was a large, high-priority programme requiring a massive initial investment of political support and a firm commitment of financial and administrative resources. Such programmes have an all-or-nothing quality about them and do not fit easily into any model of incrementalism in which the policy process advances disjointedly. Instead, they must be established by the rapid development of policy followed not by incremental or piecemeal commitments but by the equally swift creation of an appropriate institutional setting (Schulman 1975). This is why the initial stages of the Polaris programme have been examined in some detail here. The discussion which follows focuses on the main strategies of implementation which took shape in order to overcome the problems of implementing policy across national frontiers. Broadly speaking, the British programme got by on a combination of bold imitation and careful innovation.

The borrowing of innovation

Implementation presupposes a measure of familiarity with a common set of rules, procedures and values. This proposition is self-evident in domestic cases of implementation where a background of shared reality unites all participants. It is a different story in the international context, where establishing the requisite basis of commonality is no simple matter. The implementation of the joint programme involved becoming a little like the Americans – borrowing the US model, adopting their management practices, understanding the federal system of government. Importing a novel technology involves not only the acceptance of new machinery but also a commitment to the bundle of ideas that accompany it. For a technology comes with its own procedures and institutions; it imposes on all participants certain ways of thinking, organising and behaving.

Hence the difficulties: where a set of innovations accompanying a new technology are 'borrowed' by one state from another they are likely to be less effective because of various differences between the two countries (Walker 1969). If implementation depends upon a series of such borrowings, then ensuring their effectiveness and adjusting them to national needs becomes an important part of the policy process. Within the framework of this general rationale, the need to borrow and adapt arose from a variety of specific causes in the Polaris programme.

In some cases, the pressure of time and the excellence of the US model made imitation unavoidable. The management structure of PE, for instance, was in a sense predetermined by the prior existence of SPO. With the pressure of time at the beginning of the programme British planners could not possibly survey other management structures, and the Admiralty had to build on what was ready to hand. The Polaris Sales Agreement too, in delegating effective control of the joint programme to designated project officers on each side, seemed to hint that some similarity of structure could facilitate exchanges and co-operation. But, as we shall see, the structure of PE was adapted in important ways in order to fit British requirements. Broadly speaking powers correspond to responsibilities. SPO was in a very real sense a pioneer of under-sea missile development; it was concerned from the start with research and development and production. PE on the other hand was concerned with coordinating the UK programme and ensuring the development necessary to resolve system interface problems. The Director of SPO had extensive executive powers and virtual control over his own budget. CPE fitted more modestly into the Admiralty structure, under the Controller of the Navy, and did not enjoy financial autonomy. While it was the intention of the Board of Admiralty to give the programme high priority, it maintained sufficient control to ensure that it would not acquire automatic priority over other projects. In important respects therefore the SPO model was altered to suit British needs.

Similarly, many of the management techniques developed for the US programme were borrowed by the British in the belief that they gave the Americans a successful and effective management system. Although these techniques in their adapted form did help impose time and financial control on the UK project (Simpson 1970) some observers have remained sceptical about the efficacy of the original model and pointed to their public relations role.

An alchemous combination of whirling computers, brightly coloured charts, fast talking public relations officers gave the Special Projects Office a truly effective management system. It mattered not whether the parts of the system functioned or even existed. It mattered only that certain people for a certain period of time believed that they did. (Sapolsky 1972: 129)

The success of the techological development confirmed the effectiveness of the management system whether or not the latter truly deserved such acclaim. The Admiralty, having examined the operations of SPO closely for a long period, 'discovered the fabrication but also its value':

> Its representatives were initially surprised that the Special Projects Office's documented management philosophy did not match its management practice. Nevertheless, they too recommended the adoption of the entire management system as advertised since they recognised the advantages in terms of organisational independence and resource support that such a system could provide. (ibid.)

In fact, PE was quite impressed by the claims made by SPO, and only gradually grew more selective in its use of such techniques as network analysis or critical path scheduling. Initially, CPE spent a year trying unsuccessfully to develop a 'master network' that would spread control downwards from the top. A more workable approach, it was realised, would have been to develop a method of control from the bottom up – if there had been the time and resources to do that. Later, small-scale networks were successfully devised for specific areas, and apparently proved useful there.

Other mechanisms were created in order to provide a systematic but flexible means of managing the joint programme. Chief among these was a forum for PE–SPO meetings, the Joint Steering Task Group (JSTG). The model for this was the Steering Task Group which SPO itself had established. It was, as the name suggests, a committee of senior representatives from the two organisations. Its main function was to keep them abreast of developments and focus attention on any problems without itself assuming responsibility for any specific problem or negotiation. The benefits of this arrangement accrued in particular to the British side. During the period of collaboration the USA completed 41 Polaris-equipped submarines compared with the UK's programme of four. During most of this time SPO's senior management was understandably preoccupied with its own problems. To have an arrangement whereby several days were set aside three or four times a year for considering the UK programme was certainly an innovation worth supporting especially when the suggestion for its creation came from the American side in the first place.

Finally, there were some other cases in which the adoption of certain procedures on American insistence, such as joint procurement of equipment, did make life difficult for the British side. The joint procurement or common contracting procedures were contained in the original Sales Agreement. Although there were some resulting advantages of scale for the UK these were outweighed in the event by a number of other difficulties. UK orders often had to be placed before they were strictly necessary, which created difficulties with the Treasury. PE also had to work closely with SPO, depending on its advice about what was necessary, especially in the early months of the programme. Most tiresome of all, it also had to learn to deal with the idiosyncratic administrative system that SPO had evolved.

As a net beneficiary from the Polaris deal, and as the recipient of an entire weapons system, the UK was hardly in a position to refuse the procedures and techniques that accompanied the new system. But it was not so much a case of being forced to adopt innovation as resisting the temptation to make decisions by analogy. There is in such cases a tendency to look for similarities between the situation confronting the administrator in the recipient state (in this case the UK) and the situation in the donor state (the USA) where the problems associated with the development and production of Polaris had been successfully solved. In the event, the British side could be discerning as well as diplomatic, accepting American practices but modifying them to its own needs. It was a considerable achievement, given the degree of British dependence on the US programme. To some extent British planning was helped by the development of clear ideas about the priorities of its programme.

Establishing a hierarchy of intent
The attempt to combine acceptance of US missiles and equipment with retention of a measure of independence over their manufacture and use raised fundamental questions of priorities. It also illustrates the importance of ensuring that the differing objectives of a programme are compatible and mutually supportive, forming a hierarchy of intent.

The major principle on which the Polaris programme moved forward was compatibility or commonality: as far as possible the UK programme should adhere to the US weapons system, and adopt it unaltered even when substitutes were available in Britain. This way the Polaris system's reliability, which is based on elaborate US test programmes and guarantees, could remain unimpaired. Such a principle also made engineering sense, in that it saved time; and economic sense, in that it saved money, thereby avoiding the 'penalties of uniqueness'.

However, independence remained an important formal consideration. Therefore, while PE strove to achieve maximum compatibility with the American system it never lost sight of the other objective, which was to acquire sufficient technical mastery over the system to maintain it independently of the USA should the need ever arise. Accordingly, PE made certain that the British Polaris Fleet enjoyed complete mastery over the working system, both in a technical sense by ensuring that it kept a good stock of spares and supplies, and in an operational sense by making certain that Britain could use the system independently if it wished, without any form of external interference.

Adherence to the principle of commonality also posed problems for the USA. On the one hand, it committed them to accepting technical responsibility for ensuring that the equipment installed in the submarines and support facilities in the UK was fitted satisfactorily and checked out. On the other hand, there was a wish to restrict the transmission of information for the manufacture of weapons in other countries; in fact there were specific statutory limitations on such transfers in the US Atomic Energy Act 1954. The conflict between these two aims became most acute over the development of the re-entry vehicle. This was primarily a UK (specifically an MoA) responsibility and stemmed from the move to the A3 system. The US government had undertaken to supply data on the interface between the missile and the re-entry system, but it was not clear to what extent this could be supplemented with additional information or hardware.

A special committee was set up to provide a forum for discussion and a channel by which information could be passed. With its assistance, the UK decision on the type of re-entry system was made by March 1964. This committee also proved useful later in the development of the approved design, and in the support that it provided in the stages leading up to the testing and manufacture of the system. It is a nice question whether the British could confidently assume that, if it ever became the decisive issue, US guarantees about the success of the UK system would outweigh the restrictions on transfer of information. Such a calculation was not without risk. But then, as Helen Wallace reminds us in Chapter 8, international co-operation does not operate on very large margins of certainty.

Mechanisms of social control

The absence of the stable political and legal framework that normally supports domestic policy renders implementation additionally difficult in the international sphere, but not impossible. International society is an 'anarchical society', that is, a society without an explicit form of government (Bull 1977). However certain informal devices for social cohesion and control do operate in the international sphere, and constitute the political and social basis for co-operation.

A number of these devices can be identified in the case of Polaris. One was competition. The spirit of rivalry between the two national teams helped to move the joint programme forward. This was particularly evident from the work of the engineers. The British team operated under conditions that appeared somewhat galling to them. Because the principle of commonality operated throughout the programme, they could not indulge in the favourite pastime of engineers everywhere of messing about with specifications, incorporating modifications and improvements along the way. They were confined to the strict implementation of US plans according to US specifications. They could better the Americans only by carrying out their tasks more efficiently and cheaply, wherever this was possible. And, where equipment such as communications and sonar was to be of UK design and manufacture, the British technical team tended to go for simpler design and more elegant solutions than their American counterparts, which provided a basis for satisfaction. The constant striving for superiority had a beneficial effect on the quality of their work.

Peer group evaluation was another motivating factor. It affected PE's senior management in their relations with the rest of Whitehall. The Polaris project was novel and, within Whitehall, politically salient. PE staff were aware of their own and their programme's vulnerability to the extent of feeling that they were operating in an adverse environment. At the same time they were deeply committed to the success of the programme. Both novelty and saliency forced upon them the need for coherent and purposeful action. In order to meet these challenges adequately, PE's senior management made sure, through extensive delegation, that they had sufficient time to think and to plan. This unusual habit was forced on them in part by the requirements of PE's international role. PE had to explain policy to the Americans as well as defend it at home. It was necessary to argue coherently across different political arenas, and the requirements of operating in an international environment with a high level of visibility forced a degree of articulation which would not have been necessary in a purely domestic programme.

The relationship between SPO and PE also promoted a mutual loyalty and created a coalition of interests which helped advance the joint programme. The SPO link was particularly advantageous to PE in its various bureaucratic struggles at home, and a discreet and timely word from the US Navy tipped the balance more than once in its favour. This was especially true in the early years of the relationship.

Maintaining agreements on a continuing basis
However, the passage of time has an eroding effect on relationships. It wears down the sense of obligation; it brings about changes in personnel; the original agreement becomes a familiar thing on which both sides begin to impose exceptions and restrictions. Above all the international climate may change, or the relative position of the powers shift, profoundly affecting the basis of co-operation. Interests then begin to diverge. Having a formal agreement offers little assurance that standards of compliance will be maintained over the years.

In the Polaris case there was a definite falling-away in the intensity of the relationship once the two sides had sorted out the major problems. 'From 1966 a diminution of interest on the American side could be detected' (Freedman 1980: 42). In fact the US programme had begun to move from Polaris to Poseidon as early as 1965. At the administrative level this posed few problems; both sides had to decide what quantities of A3 equipment were needed on a once-and-for-all basis before production lines were shut down, and this was easy enough to settle. Both sides were also keen – at Navy-to-Navy level – to switch from Polaris to Poseidon. But this was a larger question. It was difficult to justify such a move in strategic or political terms. In strategic terms, as Freedman notes, the American move had come at least five years too early. The Americans planned to use Poseidon to replace the older single warhead A1 and A2 missiles but not the more advanced multiple warhead A3, and their decision weakened the argument for replacing the British A3. In any case, the Labour government was in no position to sanction such a move having recently accepted Polaris against the wishes of many backbenchers. To go over to Poseidon so soon would have provoked considerable dissent in the party. Besides, Mr Wilson was anxious to portray his rejection of Poseidon as a Nassau in reverse in order to demonstrate Britain's 'Europeanness' (Wilson 1971: 408).

Polaris as precedent
Alternatives to Poseidon were likely to be costly. Close collaboration with the US had served, as we have seen, to keep the UK Polaris programme lean and efficient so that it had been completed on time and within budget. The missiles had actually cost 42 per cent less than was first estimated, and the percentage decrease in cost for the submarines and missiles combined had been 13 per cent (HC 1972/3: vii). The submarines had been delivered on time. The first, HMS Resolution, was commissioned in October 1967 and went on patrol in June 1968. The fourth and last, HMS Revenge, was commissioned in December 1969 and went on patrol in September 1970 (Freedman 1980: 142). In 1980 terms, the force cost the UK £1.7 billion.

The prevailing view in the British government was that something had to be done to maintain the credibility of the Polaris system in the face of prospective Soviet advances in ballistic missile defence. As a substitute for collaboration with the US, Britain gradually, and secretly, committed itself to designing and producing a new re-entry vehicle for the Polaris missile. Initial studies of the improvement programme, known as Chevaline, began in 1967; and a formal feasibility study was authorised in 1970. In contrast to Polaris, the Chevaline programme failed to keep within costs – the 1972 estimate of £175 million having to be revised upwards more than once until it reached £530 million at 1972 prices or £1 billion at 1980 prices (HC 1981/2).

Senior MoD witnesses appearing before the House of Commons Public Accounts Committee in December 1981 offered several reasons for the Chevaline programme 'going bananas', to use the colourful phrase of the Secretary of State for Defence, John Nott. The defence scientists had undertaken a pioneering research programme and had pushed the state of the art beyond known frontiers; the programme had lacked both political support and a competent management system in its early years, when it was a model of hesitant incrementalism, lacking some of the essential dynamism of the Polaris programme (HC 1981/2).

The experience of Chevaline underlines the point previously made that Polaris is not necessarily typical. But nor is it unique. Large-scale, 'non-incremental' programmes have often enjoyed a high and central priority in British defence policy. Trident is likely to be just such a programme and the similarity between it and Polaris is quite striking. In July 1980 it was announced that agreement had been reached through an exchange of letters between Mrs Thatcher and President Carter for the purchases by the UK of Trident I C4 missiles, equipment and supporting services, on a basis similar to that on which Polaris missiles were supplied under the 1963 agreement (Cmnd 7979 1980). This was apparently the culmination of lengthy and sensitive bilateral discussions which paralleled closely the negotiations of 1962–3 (Baylis 1981). As before, soon after the original agreement was reached the US government decided to phase out Trident I C4 in favour of Trident II D5. The UK followed suit in March 1982, in order *inter alia* to maintain commonality (Cmnd 8517 1982). The adoption of the new missile was accompanied by a decision to ensure that the missile-carrying submarines should be of the latest design and equipped with the most advanced propulsion and tactical weapon systems. Changes in submarine design affected the estimated cost of the new system more significantly than the change of missile (Freedman 1982). But one of the UK successes in the negotiations was the agreement on a charge of only

$116 million towards research and development for Trident II. This charge was expected to remain fixed in real terms even though the missile's development was not yet complete.

At the same time there are two notable differences between the Polaris and Trident agreements. The first concerns the re-entry vehicle. The UK built its own for Polaris, but will now be buying the highly accurate D5 'front end'. In her letter of 11 March 1982 Mrs Thatcher wrote specifically of purchasing 'missiles complete with multiple, independently targettable re-entry vehicles but without the warheads themselves' (Cmnd 8517 1982).

The second difference concerns the disposition of fleet maintenance and service facilities. In one of its earliest decisions PE had established a service depot at Coulport in the Clyde estuary. With the coming of Trident it was expected that the Coulport base would undergo further expansion. But MoD's proposals for enlargement, and in particular the substantial amounts of additional land required to provide a safety zone for the bigger missiles, aroused opposition from local councils and anti-nuclear campaigners. A bitterly contested public inquiry over the purchase of public land was in prospect when it was announced in September 1982 that the new missiles would be serviced in the US Navy's King's Bay facilities in Georgia. Mr Nott gave assurances that servicing the Trident fleet in the USA would not affect the independence of the British deterrent (*Financial Times*, 1982). In 1963 the UK government was keen to demonstrate operational freedom for its deterrent; there are fewer sensibilities on this point now. Certainly a number of considerations have altered somewhat in the past 20 years. But, whatever the political, economic and strategic differences between then and now, Polaris remains a valid and possibly an encouraging precedent for the implementation of the new programme.

Acknowledgement

The author would especially like to acknowledge his indebtedness to Professor Peter Nailor whose work on the UK Polaris programme as well as his advice were of great value to him in writing this chapter.

References

Baylis, J. 1981, *Anglo-American defence relations, 1939–1980*, London, Macmillan

Bull, H. 1977, *The anarchical society*, London, Macmillan

Cmnd 1915 1962, *Bahamas meetings December 1962: texts of joint communiqués*, London, HMSO

Cmnd 2108 1963, *Polaris sales agreement*, Treaty series no. 59, London, HMSO

Cmnd 2336 1963, *Index to the treaty series*, London, HMSO

Cmnd 7979 1980, *The British strategic nuclear force*, London, HMSO

Cmnd 8517 1982, *The British strategic nuclear force*, London, HMSO

Financial Times, 10 September 1982

Freedman, L. 1980, *Britain and nuclear weapons*, London, Macmillan

Freedman, L. 1982, 'The Trident decision', in *Strategic nuclear weapons policy*, First Special Report from the Defence Committee, HC 266, session 1981–2, pp. 23–31

HC 399 1972–3, 12th Report from the Expenditure Committee: *Nuclear weapon programme*, London, HMSO, p. vii

HC 269 1981–2, 9th Report from the Committee of Public Accounts, *Chevaline improvement to the Polaris missile system*, London, HMSO

Macmillan, H. 1973, *At the end of the day*, London, Macmillan, pp. 356–63

Neustadt, R. 1970, *Alliance politics*, Columbia University Press

Pierre, A.J. 1972, *Nuclear politics*, Oxford, Oxford University Press

Sapolsky, H.M. 1972, *The Polaris system development*, Harvard University Press, Cambridge, Mass.

Schulman, P.R. 1975, 'Nonincremental policy-making: notes towards an alternative paradigm', *American political science review*, vol. 69, pp. 1354–70

Simpson, J. 1970, 'The Polaris executive: a case study of a unified hierarchy', *Public administration*, vol. 48, pp. 379–90

Snyder, W.P. 1964, *The politics of British defence policy*, Columbus, Ohio University Press

Walker, J.L. 1969, 'The diffusion of innovations among the American states', *American political science review*, vol. 63, pp. 880–99

Wallace, W. 1975, *The foreign policy process in Britain*, London, RIIA

Wilson, H. 1971, *The Labour government 1964–1970*, London, Weidenfeld & Nicolson/Michael Joseph

12 Conclusion
Improving implementation
David Lewis

This concluding chapter focuses on the language in which policies are expressed and discussed, and the difficulties of translation into more concrete language, in order to elucidate the processes by which policies evolve in the course of implementation. It then considers what constitutes successful implementation, and suggests ways in which the probability of success could be increased in future cases.

As a starting-point, let us review the essential nature of policy implementation in the light of earlier chapters. The evolutionary model described in Chapter 1 seeks to represent the way in which policies must be interpreted, adapted and extended in the course of implementation in order to cope, on the one hand, with the complexity and variety of interests and circumstances and, on the other hand, with the tendency of the environment to change during implementation, whether in response to the policy or for other reasons. These modifications affect not merely detailed aspects such as the timetable (which could occur under the most tightly programmed strategy for implementation), but potentially any part of the content of the policy. In some fields, this phenomenon may be especially apparent: education is an example (Chapter 2) because of the emphasis on consensus and local autonomy. Indeed, Chapter 5 concludes that, in the California school improvement programmes, policy was largely formulated through the process of implementation. At the opposite pole, Chapter 11 describes a policy which was implemented through a closely defined system of project management, but emphasises that this system should not be seen in isolation, and should rather be regarded as itself the outcome of a process of evolution through negotiation. In some fields the processes of adaptation and negotiation become routine and largely anticipatory, as with food standards, a field in which Chapter 9 described policy as 'almost self-implementing'.

The evolutionary model remains a simplified account of real-life processes. A policy normally consists of a number of different 'dimensions'

(Hill 1981: 214–15, citing Knoepfel and Weidner 1979), for example organisation, financing, standards, enforcement. Feedback and modification may therefore take place simultaneously on different dimensions, but at different speeds, and perhaps at different levels of organisation. These complications do not detract from the validity and usefulness of the evolutionary model, but they are a warning against trying to apply it in too crude a way, and expecting the policy process to be neatly divisible into a succession of discrete cycles of the kind adopted in Chapter 1 for clarity of exposition. The extent to which a policy can be shown to have evolved will also depend on the length of the period chosen for study: Chapter 4 found relatively little evolution over the 15 months of the Job Creation Programme, but the lessons of that period had a considerable effect on the Manpower Services Commission's subsequent Special Programmes.

Implementation was described in Chapter 1 as a running argument, a chain of linked problems and tentative solutions. Elsewhere it has been described as a 'chain within which issues are increasingly solidified', and it has been suggested that we may in fact find it impossible to say where policy-making stops and implementation begins (Hill 1972, esp. ch. 10, 1981). However extensive the links and overlaps between the two stages, there are nevertheless good reasons (in addition to the ordinary usage of words) for drawing a distinction between them. In the first place a policy belongs to a specific organisation or body of people: we need to be able to say *whose* policy it is. Implementation is often the responsibility of a separate group of people, or at least a larger group. Other things follow from this separation. The implementers may not necessarily accept that the would-be policy-makers have the authority to fulfil that function. Either there is dispute about whether there should be a policy at all in that field (for example, race relations in Chapter 3, or Industrial Strategy in Chapter 7) or there is disagreement about the respective functions of different levels of government (central and local government, the European Community, or the different levels of US government). The values of the implementers may differ from the values of the policy-makers, and that can considerably affect the way a policy is carried out, as in the case of the Job Creation Programme in Chapter 4. The group of people who are from one point of view the implementers of a policy may have policies of their own on the matter, or on certain dimensions of the matter: in that sense, policy and implementation can become superimposed in their activities, but not in a way that undermines the validity of the distinction between the two.

A policy is a hypothesis which must be tested, and implementation is the process of testing. Implementation requires an 'implementation structure' (Hjern and Porter 1980), 'appropriate mechanisms' a 'delivery system', 'institutional capabilities', an 'appropriate institutional setting' (Chapters 3, 4, 7 and 11). It is not sufficient to borrow such a structure ready-made from another policy or another country, as Chapter 11 emphasises. Several of the case studies in this book also show how the implementation of a policy can bring about structural changes which are not part of the initial policy; or at least not directly or obviously or unquestionably so. Chapters 5 and 6 show this happening in California, and Chapters 9 and 10 in the European Community. The wish to be able to discuss implementation structures and consequential structural changes is another reason for distinguishing clearly for analytical purposes between a policy and its implementation.

Implementation will not proceed creatively and purposively through an evolutionary process unless there is an adequate level of political support (using that as a general concept which subsumes factors like authority, legitimacy and credibility). Chapter 8 stresses the importance of political impetus in implementation across national boundaries. Chapters 3, 5, 6 and 7 identify it as also an important factor at the national or state level. Chapter 11 shows how organisations can cope with a withering-away of political support if the structures for co-operation are already in place and well established, but also draws attention to the significance of political support in the initial stages of a policy. In further discussion of the processes by which policies evolve, we must keep political factors very much in mind.

Implementation as translation

It is quite common to write of 'interpreting' or even 'translating' policies. The difference between a 'translator' and an 'interpreter' is that the former works at his or her own pace to achieve the most exact equivalent in one language of what has previously been written in another language; the interpreter, working at forced pace and under greater uncertainty, aims to give the general sense of what has been said in another language. It can be taken as a basic axiom that no language is ultimately and completely translatable into any other language, but the practical extent of the translation problem will vary from case to case.

As a statement of a hypothesis, a policy is likewise subject to interpretation or translation. The discussion here will be in terms of 'translation', as the more rigorous of the two activities. In practice, however, the 'interpretation' of policies is no doubt the more common activity.

The different groups of people involved in the implementation of a policy are likely to have not merely different values and different interests, but motivations and perceptions which constitute a different cognitive structure. This will give them different ideologies, 'frames of reference' or 'assumptive worlds' (Berger and Luckman 1966; Vickers 1970; Young 1979; Young and Mills 1980), and will determine the meanings they attach to the policy. The relevant cognitive structures are incorporated in, and can be studied through, the language used by each group.

In examining the effects and implications of differences in language, it is simplest to begin with the normal colloquial sense of the word ('foreign languages') and consider languages such as English, French or German. Most international agreements involve translation from one language to another. The European Community is a particularly striking example of the routine use of multiple languages. Identifiable errors in translation can be eliminated, but there remains the problem of translating concepts which are embedded in a particular administrative and cultural tradition, and have no exact equivalent in another language. Some examples of French terms which have caused difficulties of this kind are 'controle', 'surveillance' and 'correspondent'; an English example would be 'waste disposal'; a German example, 'Verhältnismässigkeit'.

At the same time, the English language itself has various forms ('parallel languages') incorporating different cognitive structures, and corresponding to different human activities (for one such distinction, see Ramsey 1961). This is not simply a matter of vocabulary but of the fundamental logic of the language. Although the differences are less obvious than those between English and, say, French they are even more important in the policy process.

Let us look first at implementation within a single organisation such as a government department. Dunsire (1980) describes a process he calls 'operationalising': 'turning a message or idea into a set of specifications you can actually work from.' To the extent that this involves more than one parallel language, it will involve 'translation', with consequent risk of difficulties of communication, either between parts of the organisation at the same level or between different levels within one part of the organisation.

Dunsire describes the difficulties between different levels as follows:

Each level, top management, middle management, shop floor – or whatever we call them – has its characteristic 'universe of discourse', sphere of interests, working vocabulary, style of going about things, outlook and mental set. Those whose daily work constantly brings them up against 'what Ministers will think of it', or the vagaries of the Parliamentary timetable, live (as it were) in a different world from those whose concerns are with time and motion studies, production indices, and clerical staff turnover. . . . Those at about the same level in the cognitive hierarchy can communicate fairly easily even if in different grades of rank (any superior with his own immediate subordinates, for example); those vertically remote from one another do so only with difficulty.

Of course, there may well be differences of motivation between different levels in the organisation (Tullock 1965; Downs 1967). However the difficulties Dunsire describes are also a direct implication of the classical theory of bureaucracy: top management uses concepts which are a good deal more general than those used at lower levels.

Nevertheless the requirement for translation in this situation does not make implementation an essentially problematic process, at least in Dunsire's view. The whole purpose of a bureaucratic organisation is to achieve a cascade of operationalisations, from level to level and section to section, in order to implement an initial policy or some other instruction. In this book however we have looked at cases which involve not a single organisation but a number of more or less autonomous organisations. One might expect translation to loom larger in such cases on the ground that people in different organisations are more likely to have different cognitive structures. On the other hand, Dunsire argues that communication may be easier horizontally – between people at the same level in different organisations – than between different levels in the same organisation: top managers in different organisations may find that they 'talk the same language', even when they have conflicting objectives. What do our cases show?

Problems of communication do loom large in several cases. In order to implement Industrial Strategy, a 'communications exercise' was mounted from NEDO. The main function was to communicate the recommendations of sector working parties to individual firms and their employees. Chapter 7 concludes that the exercise was a failure because there was no real attempt to deal with differences of perspective either between the different partners (government, management, unions) or between levels. Communication was also a factor in the implementation of race relations policy (although the detailed argument is presented elsewhere, Nixon 1980a). One reason why progress was slow was that the Home Office did not communicate the policy effectively to the other organisations involved, but action does not seem to have been carried forward to the point where translation would have emerged as a major factor. Communication is also problematic in the case of some European Community funds (Chapter 10), because of the concepts and detailed rules involved, and not simply because of foreign languages. On the other hand, Chapters 9 and 11 reveal fluent communication between people within specialised fields, not only in different organisations but in different countries.

In general it would seem that, if difficulties of communication are often as great between organisations as within a single organisation, this is because the situation is more complex and less well defined. There may not be accepted and familiar channels of communication, there may be a failure to use whatever channels do exist, or there may be a problem in selecting the organisational level or levels at which communication can most profitably take place. Translation between different parallel languages is not necessarily the main problem. On the other hand, where a language links together individuals in different organisations, and especially where it is the language of a particular 'policy community', communication between people at roughly the same level in different organisations may be as easy as Dunsire suggests.

The language of politics

Although problems of translation are encountered in other contexts, it is the problem of translating between the language of politics and the language of administration which is of central importance in studying implementation. The 'language of politics' is the language in which policies are expressed, discussed, defended and attacked in political systems. In the last couple of years the word 'rhetoric' has come to be widely used not only to mean 'false, showy, artificial, or declamatory expression' (a dictionary definition) but with a very specific implication of a 'gap between the rhetoric and the reality of public policy' (Walker 1983). More even-handedly (and although he does not himself regard it as corresponding to the policy/implementation distinction), Hill (1981: 219) has drawn attention to the split, for social policies, 'between the kinds of controversy which arise at the political level, in which economic interests have been prominent, and the issues which arise in connection with their day-to-day administration.'

Political language has its own internal logic (Vedung 1982). Some of its characteristics are of a kind already mentioned earlier in this chapter. Policies are often expressed in general or abstract terms, and in advance of working out the methods of implementation, especially where there is a wish for speed. In addition, the language used often conceals the interaction of interests and the actual operation of inter-organisational relations, as happened with Industrial Strategy. There is a prudent wish to avoid precise statements which would carry the risk that a policy could be incontrovertibly judged a failure (Blowers 1980: 109–10; Pollitt 1980: 156). These are perhaps factors which operate rather more strongly in Britain than in other countries, as Chapter 4 suggested. Furthermore, there is very frequently a degree of ambiguity in the statement of policies. This may be acknowledged and justified as 'flexibility' or 'keeping options open', or it may for the time being remain latent.

Political actions, including the act of stating a policy, are frequently symbolic, either in themselves (Burke 1950: 161; Wynne 1982) or in the language employed. For the individual, symbolic representations of the world are part of his or her 'most generalised, most taken-for-granted, and most enduring assumptive world' (Young and Mills 1980: 7). The term 'symbol' is used here in the sense derived from anthropology and defined by Cohen (1974: 23–4):

> Symbols are objects, acts, relationships or linguistic formations that stand *ambiguously* for a multiplicity of meanings, evoke emotions, and impel men to action. . . . Symbols tend to be grouped together within the frameworks of dynamic ideologies, or world-views, that are developed and carried by specific groupings. In these ideologies the symbols of interpersonal relationships, like kinship and friendship, are integrated with those of ritual, which deal with such perennial problems of human existence as the meaning of life and death, illness and health, misery and happiness, fortune and misfortune. These two symbolic complexes support one another within the ideology and are made to express and validate the political organisation of these groupings.

There is a parallel with the concept of 'myth' used by Levi-Strauss (1963: 229): 'a logical model capable of overcoming a contradiction'.

The ambiguities and the symbolic content of political language feed upon and reinforce each other. Writers who have drawn attention to these characteristics have often done so in order to criticise the workings of particular political systems, and highlight what they see as the trivialised and ritualised quality of the language (notably Edelman 1971, 1977). However it can be argued that the general nature of political language is inevitable, and even in principle desirable.

First, specialisation in the functions of language can be regarded as essential if human action is to have an impact on the complexities of the real world. Some persuasive parallels can be drawn. Designers of large-scale computer systems have found it necessary to devise not only 'multilayer', but 'multilevel' systems, in which the different levels perform quite different functions (Findeisen *et al.* 1980). Scientists in the field of artificial intelligence are pursuing the notion that the rules of reasoning in an 'expert' computer system must be tied to a particular domain of discourse (Kolata 1982). Even within a subject like economics, discussion may be conducted in practice on two levels; and there may be considerable difficulty in translating from one level, which has a high symbolic content, to the other (Leontief 1982). A similar point is made specifically about public expenditure policies in Chapter 6.

The characteristics of political language are necessary in order to achieve political communication. Symbols are employed and manipulated because they are meaningful to a wide audience, as Chapter 6 emphasised in analysing the campaign for Proposition 13. A relatively low factual content and a high symbolic content are necessary in order to achieve communication in the mass media (Johnston 1982) and within legislatures (Foot 1973). There is a similar requirement even in more restricted contexts. Chapter 2 notes that the formation of a larger local authority area increased the symbolic element in discussion of educational issues. Even where communication is primarily with those directly affected by a policy, the characteristics of political language may still be required to a greater or lesser extent in some circumstances. Chapter 7 suggests that industrial policies must have stated objectives, which must be 'consistent and comprehensible to those at the sharp end', and regarded by them as feasible. Although these objectives will need revision from time to time they should be sufficiently broad and general to prevent that happening frequently. Symbolism and idealism were major elements in the presentation of the California school improvement programmes. All these features are apparent in political language because its functions are to mobilise, motivate and build coalitions; and generality, ambiguity and symbolic content are essential for those tasks.

Indeed, the symbolic content of the language in which it is discussed may determine whether an issue appears at all on the general political agenda. If the symbolic content is low, an issue may nevertheless provide an example of something more limited: 'interest group politics'. In that case an objective of some of those concerned might be to prevent the issue making the transition from interest group politics to symbolic politics. Food standards are perhaps an example.

Finally, in the ambiguities of political language lie the seeds of change (Mannheim 1936: 112–13). As Burke (1945: xix) puts it:

> Instead of considering it our task to 'dispose of' any ambiguity by merely disclosing the fact that it is an ambiguity, we rather consider it our task to study and clarify the *resources* of ambiguity. For . . . it is in the areas of ambiguity that transformations take place; in fact, without such areas, transformation would be impossible.

The ambiguities of political language reflect the difficulty of obtaining agreement on policy between conflicting and competing interests, especially when a number of parties are involved. It is no accident that, in the reports of committees, the crucial passages are frequently written in an obscure and Delphic way. Not that 'Community language has attained heights of obscurity which some countries have taken centuries to achieve' (Kaiser *et al.* 1983: 8). In fact the use of foreign languages can have advantages: because there are equally authoritative texts in the different languages, it is not unknown to end up, whether by accident or design, with unresolved discrepancies between them.

Where ambiguities and discrepancies do cause problems of course is at the implementation stage. The implementation of the compromise policy has to satisfy all the conflicting interests, and they in turn are expected to fulfil the commitments they made in the process of bargaining which led to the statement of the policy. But this means translating ambiguous words and symbols into unambiguous, or at least less ambiguous, reality. In addition to operational requirements for greater precision, those directly affected by a policy may want the rules about its application set out in detailed language in order to limit the discretion of staff at the working level who may have quite different values (a point made in Chapter 4). It seems almost inevitable that some of those concerned will end up disappointed or discontented.

The points made above about the nature of political language are not new ones, but their central importance in explaining the problematic nature of implementation has not been sufficiently emphasised. To those involved in implementation on the ground, concepts like 'worthwhile employment' in the Job Creation Programme may look 'almost meaningless' (a description used in Chapter 4); but in political terms they usually have clear and important meanings. That does not mean however that it is necessarily feasible to put them into practice on the ground. From the centre, on the other hand, the difficulties may not be readily apparent, and it may look as though policies are being frustrated by only shadowy and suspect obstacles (Wheare 1955: 40).

This doctrine of two languages, and the argument that their separation is actually a more effective way of achieving the desired outcomes, may seem like another version of the traditional distinction between 'politics' and 'administration', which has been severely criticised by academic writers. However, whether or not it is desirable, the case studies in this book clearly demonstrate that there is a separation, and that the linkages between the two languages give rise to complex and significant problems. Several of the chapters have studied the process of translation in detail: Chapter 2 for 'comprehensive education'; Chapter 4 for 'worthwhile employment' and other phrases such as 'community benefit'; Chapter 5 for 'school improvement'; Chapter 7 for 'Industrial Strategy'; and Chapter 11 for 'independent deterrent'. In other cases translation was halting or abortive: 'positive discrimination' (Chapter 3); a 'more relevant curriculum' (Chapter 5); and 'cutting out the waste' (Chapter 6). Having demonstrated that there are translation problems, we must now look for a general criterion of accuracy in translation. This amounts to saying that we must decide how we want to define success in implementation.

Successful implementation

The case studies support the view (Smith 1978) that recognising successful implementation is not necessarily an easy matter. Chapter 4 judges that the original intentions of the Job Creation Programme were distorted, but it was nevertheless 'a remarkable success'. Chapter 6 suggests that the question of success has to be considered at several levels. Chapter 8 argues that in implementation across national boundaries the concept has a special meaning: '"Success" often lies in the gradual and often painful learning process through which national practices and attitudes are marginally adjusted to take account of external influences.' Chapter 10 concludes, after discussing the implementation of Community funds, that in their case no single judgement can be offered about success: major changes may have taken place, and execution may have been efficient, but so long as the purposes of the funds remain controversial or obscure there will be conflicting judgements about them.

If we set out to identify a general criterion for judgements about success, two basic difficulties are immediately apparent. If policies are modified and developed during the process of implementation, what should determine whether such modifications are regarded as indicating 'success' or 'failure'? This difficulty parallels what Wildavsky says about planning: 'Planning is everything, and non-planning can hardly be said to exist.' In principle, the solution is the same: 'The determination of whether planning has taken place must rest on an assessment of whether and to what degree future control has been achieved' (Wildavsky 1973: 129–30). It is the practical application of the solution that gives rise to difficulty. Secondly, because we are dealing with more than one language and more than one logic, it is not clear in which language the criterion for success ought to be expressed.

Some simplification can be introduced by treating implementation as a morally neutral concept, and deciding not to take into account in this particular context the justice or fairness of the original policy (Pollitt 1980). Success thus becomes equivalent to effectiveness. The problem can then be approached by listing the possible criteria for success, and examining them in turn:

1. the policy has been carried out exactly, and without any variation;
2. the policy has achieved its objectives;
3. the implementation of the policy has resulted in the best possible outcome;
4. the implementation of the policy has produced the best outcome for the organisation(s) responsible for the policy and/or its implementation:

5. implementation has not been accompanied by undesirable and unexpected side-effects;
6. the measures taken to implement the policy have been appropriately designed and are cost-effective;
7. implementation has met with general public assent;
8. implementation has satisfied the expectations aroused by the policy.

The criterion that the policy has been carried out exactly and without variation would be sufficient in some cases; but its limitations will be obvious from the earlier parts of this chapter. First, policies are not normally expressed in a way that makes this feasible, they are very often in general or abstract terms, and contain inherent ambiguities. Moreover this criterion disregards the possibility that, either because of changes in circumstances or because of defects in the original policy, punctilious implementation may fail to produce the intended outcome; and a better outcome would have been achieved if the policy had been extended and adapted. In other words, this criterion ignores the factors which the evolutionary model highlights. Proposition 13 is a classic example of a policy which was implemented in exact terms but failed to achieve the objectives sought by most of the people who supported it.

That might suggest that 'successful implementation' ought to be defined in terms of achieving objectives. Again, this would be sufficient in some cases: we often speak of the *unintended* consequences of a policy, as in Chapter 6. However, if the objectives are not stated explicitly in the policy itself, we have to rely on inference to discover what they were, and it may be difficult to do that with confidence. Moreover, in any given case, different actors may have quite different intentions, as with the expenditure of Community funds. Where a policy has been in existence for some time, it is all the more likely that there will be no one identifiable and paramount set of intentions associated with it. Moreover the objectives of a policy should not be regarded as protected from evolution and revision: Industrial Strategy would have benefited from such a process (Chapter 7).

The third of the possible criteria listed above attempts to overcome the difficulty about inferring intentions by defining as 'successful' implementation which results in the best possible outcome. This form of words allows for modifications of the policy in that these could contribute to 'success', instead of automatically diminishing it as they would under the first (and sometimes under the second) criterion. The objection is that this criterion fails to provide any direct link between outcomes and intentions. Moreover we run once again into a difficulty about subjectivity. From whose standpoint do we judge that the outcome is the 'best possible'? A good outcome for one group may be a long way short of the best outcome for other groups.

The fourth criterion attempts to overcome this last difficulty by specifying the most favourable outcome for the organisation(s) responsible for the policy and/or its implementation. There are certainly cases where the effect of implementation on an organisation's general credibility or standing is a significant factor; Chapters 2, 3 and 11 provide examples. However if we interpret this criterion literally (so that it covers, for example, larger staff or budget) it is unacceptable. If we adopt a wider interpretation, on the ground that the organisations responsible for public policies exist to serve the public interest (in some sense), then we arrive back at the third criterion.

The fifth criterion was the avoidance or minimisation of side-effects on other policies. Obviously such side-effects have to be considered: policy-making is more compartmentalised than the real world. They may in fact be the most important constraint on the implementation of some policies. But whether any given side-effects are desirable or undesirable may well depend on one's standpoint. Some policies (race relations is an example) cannot be successfully implemented unless they interact with and modify policies in other areas in ways that may seem undesirable if they are viewed solely from the standpoint of those other policies. We might try to narrow this criterion by disregarding side-effects which are intended, but that would land us again in the difficulties about whose intentions, and how we can infer them.

The sixth criterion suggested defines success in terms of the appropriateness and cost-effectiveness of the measures taken. Tests that might be applied include the right choice of strategy in terms of the 'situational parameters' (Berman 1980: 213ff); whether the necessary 'performance programmes' have been established (March and Simon 1958); whether the expenditure involved in implementation was justified in terms of the results obtainable; and whether there is appropriate provision for feedback, about the progress of implement-ation, about changes in the external environment, and about the results of carrying out the policy. Nevertheless it would be paradoxical to adopt a sole criterion for success which is internal to the implement-ation process, and thus was not affected by the actual outcome. In any case, we should ultimately be driven back to other criteria in order to prove what are the 'appropriate measures' in given circumstances.

The next possible criterion for success was that implementation of the policy should meet with general public assent. If a particular policy requires public 'approval' in order to be adopted, then by definition such approval will have been secured before implementation begins. 'Assent' is deliberately a weaker word (one might almost say that the policy should not provoke public dissent). As Chapter 1 points out, policies attract very different amounts of public attention, and in some cases only certain groups directly concerned will have any real knowledge of, or opinion about, their implementation. However the criterion is framed in terms of the general public, for two reasons. The views of groups directly concerned may differ, and there may also be controversy about which groups are directly concerned. (For example, in the case of a school, is the local community such a group?) The second, and more important, reason is that the views of groups directly concerned will have been taken into account, to a greater or lesser extent, in negotiations which form part of the evolutionary process; and it is the outcome of that process that we are trying to assess, from some independent standpoint. In the event we are left with a rather negative criterion about retaining general public assent, which has only a limited usefulness.

The final criterion suggested is that the implementation of a policy must satisfy the expectations aroused by it. Not only is it very much subject to extrinsic changes in the external environment, there are practical difficulties in applying it: in obtaining evidence about expectations, and because these may be based on misunderstandings and poor information, and may alter over time. Nevertheless it is in an important respect more precise than the previous criterion: we can confine our attention to those groups in whom the policy has aroused some expectation (for example, those given temporary employment under the Job Creation Programme). The expectations aroused will not necessarily be identical for each group. Because of the ambiguous nature of political language, it is often very difficult or impossible to fulfil everyone's expectations simultaneously, more especially so where different countries are involved.

We can now review the list of possible criteria at the beginning of this section. As we are looking for a general criterion for successful implementation, (4) and (5) are too narrow, and can be discarded. So can (1) and (2), which are too restrictive, and do not allow for the modifications and developments of policy which are the central feature of the evolutionary model; and (3), which is too vague to be useful. That leaves the last three criteria, of which (6) highlights administrative factors while (7) and (8) highlight political factors.

In order to obtain a plausible general criterion, we have to find a way of blending the administrative and the political. Combining the three remaining criteria produces the following definition. *The 'successful' implementation of a policy is the cost-effective use of appropriate mechanisms and procedures in such a way as to fulfil the expectations aroused by the policy and retain general public assent.* By combining administrative and political factors this definition bridges the gap between the two languages. It also re-establishes a link with the justice or fairness of the policy, because that is likely to enter to a greater or lesser extent into the expectations aroused and the retention of public assent. It is not without its difficulties: the practical difficulties in discovering expectations, and the imperfect state of understanding about what are 'appropriate mechanisms and procedures'. Nevertheless it brings together in a coherent way the most significant points about implementation. And it is independent of the observer's own role or viewpoint.

Improving implementation

In this book a good deal of attention has been devoted to the difficulties of implementation. Chapter 1 pointed out that it was widespread failures which made the subject one of general interest. There is a natural tendency for failures to attract more attention than successes: even in a hostile environment many, perhaps most, policies are successfully implemented in terms of the criterion just proposed. Nevertheless it is relevant to ask whether the success rate could be increased. In order to discover whether that is feasible, some possible ways of increasing the success rate will be considered under three headings: the form of the policy, the mechanisms for implementation, and the translation process. These correspond broadly to three of the aspects of implementation identified in Chapter 1: strategy, limits and style.

The policy

The evolutionary model emphasises the progressive modification of policies, largely in response to environmental factors, and this chapter highlights the roles of participation, expectations and assent. In a pluralistic political system, in which power is spread relatively widely and evenly, all these factors can be expected to favour consensus and continuity in policies (Blowers 1980: 114–15). As a result, the evolutionary model might be mistaken for a restatement of the 'incrementalist' view of the policy process (Lindblom 1959). Nothing in the model implies that changes in policies are normally, or ought to be, gradual: discontinuous change may be caused either by feedback from within the policy process or by external factors. An adaptive strategy, leaving the maximum scope for evolution during implementation, can be regarded as particularly appropriate to an innovatory policy which, in social policy for example, can amount to 'a new way of perceiving society and the rights and duties of its citizens' (Donnison 1978: 49; Hall *et al.* 1975).

Although not all government activity is subject to explicit policies (Keeling 1972; Hyder 1979), it is wrong to regard such policies as evidence that implementation has broken down or as merely an assertion of a power relationship by one organisation over others (Hill 1981: 213). Explicit statement of a policy is necessary for the efficient operation of the evolutionary model because it provides the baseline for feedback and evaluation. Moreover it fosters accountability and openness (Garrett 1980), and thus confers important benefits by opening the way to independent checks on the quality and completeness of the feedback and evaluation.

As a policy is an explicit statement, it might be thought that the probability of successful implementation would be maximised if the statement was as precise as possible. Indeed, the notion of 'quasi-administrative limits' (Hood 1976: 12) seems to imply that. A detailed and unambiguous policy would ease the problems of translation, and provide the best possible baseline for subsequent stages. Within the European Community there have also been strong pressures, partly generated by the Court of Justice, towards precision of language and clarity of objectives, even in the case of directives, which are specifically the form of Community legislation designed to leave an element of discretion to national governments.

Precision can be a disadvantage, however, as should be clear from the earlier discussion of political language. In the first place the effort devoted to seeking it will be misplaced if it is in fact unattainable because the political problems of reaching specific agreement are too great. Within the European Community governments often seek to insert escape clauses into legislation to protect themselves from the general precision of the language. Secondly, it may deter radical changes, in that the initial statement of innovatory policies is likely to require ambiguity and symbolism, as was argued earlier in this chapter. The Great Debate in education provides an example: Chapter 5 concluded that only very slow progress was made towards a more relevant curriculum because the policy was stated in too detailed a form at too early a stage. Thirdly, precision in the content of a policy may be 'spurious', in that it may conceal, and even be associated with, uncertainty or absence of agreement about objectives (Pollitt 1980: 156). Chapter 6 showed that Proposition 13 was one such case, and others would be the various Community funds and the legislation on school governing bodies in England and Wales.

There are other disadvantages of precision which are more directly linked with the evolutionary model and the definition of successful implementation suggested above. It reduces the extent to which the policy can evolve and develop in the course of implementation, and thus reduces the usefulness of feedback. It also reduces the scope for further innovation at the periphery, which may be a serious loss if (as

Chapter 2 said of education) that is where innovations normally occur. At the same time a precisely stated policy will arouse both strong and specific expectations among those affected by it, and thus automatically make that part of the definition of successful implementation which related to expectations more difficult to fulfil: again, Proposition 13 is an example.

Implementation can be handicapped either by too much precision in the statement of a policy, or by too little. In race relations (Chapter 3) or the California school improvement programmes (Chapter 5), greater precision would have made it easier to translate the policy into detailed requirements for action and to reach judgements about performance. The optimal degree of precision will vary from case to case and from level to level. Successful implementation is facilitated when the initial statement of policy is sufficiently general to leave scope for modification in the light of experience, but provides a firm basis for creative translation or interpretation, so that successively more precise policies can be promptly derived from it as and when required.

The mechanisms

In looking at the mechanisms for implementation, we can complement the main themes of this chapter, and the book, by looking briefly at other factors which have been extensively discussed in earlier literature. Whether the eventual strategy of implementation is programmed or adaptive, it is desirable to draw up an implementation plan in parallel with the formulation of a policy. The purpose of the plan is not to ensure that the policy will necessarily be easy to implement (Hill 1981: 208), but to ensure that it is at least possible to implement, and to provide a proper baseline for monitoring the process. The plan must include a careful assessment of the resources of all kinds required for implementation, so that adequate assurances can be obtained that these will be provided. The most obvious categories of resources are personnel and money, which were important in Chapter 11, and also significant on a much smaller scale in the comprehensive education policy in Humberside. The organisations concerned must also be capable of using such resources efficiently (Cmnd 8616 1982). However, implementation failures do not necessarily stem from a lack of resources, or even from failure to use them properly. Only Chapter 3, on race relations, mentions such a lack as significant; and even there the most important element seems to have been a modest shortfall in staffing. Here, and in other cases, a more important factor was the presence or absence of another kind of resource: political support.

Organisational mechanisms are a further category of resources. The characteristics of the required mechanisms may go well beyond the limits of a classical bureaucratic organisation, to which reference was made in Chapter 1. As well as translating and interpreting the policy, provision is required for adapting it to particular situations: for maintaining political support; for negotiating with groups directly concerned; for monitoring all the relevant circumstances (but especially the effects of implementing the policy); for communicating and evaluating the results of monitoring; and for modifying and extending the policy in the light of the results of negotiations and evaluations. These requirements will not necessarily be met in particular cases, and Chapter 4 showed how the existence of a particular administrative structure predetermined the way in which the Job Creation Programme evolved.

If an adaptive strategy of implementation is adopted, there will be an especially demanding requirement for a capability to manage inter-organisational relations in an atmosphere of confidence and mutual trust. Chapter 7 showed that the lack of such a capability was the major factor accounting for the failure of Industrial Strategy. Our cases illustrate two other kinds of situation in which it is likely to be lacking: where the organisation responsible for implementation is of the traditional bureaucratic kind (the Home Office in Chapter 3), and where the political and legal infrastructure is weak (as with implementation across national boundaries).

In practice, the 'engineering' approach is often adopted in creating an 'implementation structure': 'The more one can adapt and make use of existing "offices", existing programmes and rules, and existing command structures, the cheaper and quicker the implementation of the decision will be' (Dunsire 1980: 32–3). However this amounts to avoiding the translation problem in the short term by making maximum use of existing cognitive structures, and it can introduce a significant distortion in the direction of maintaining the *status quo*. In contrast, the California school improvement programmes sought to bypass the existing organisations as far as possible, and in this they were following the precedent of the Great Society programmes (Hill 1981: 210–11). A calculation has to be made of the relative costs of these two approaches in a particular case (Williams 1979, who calls the approaches 'synchronic' and 'diachronic').

Feedback is an essential characteristic of the mechanisms, and may be of two types: 'negative', which corrects deviations from an original objective, and 'positive', which amplifies deviations (Maruyama 1963). In some circumstances positive feedback will be appropriate, for example where the objective of a policy is to secure movement away from the *status quo* or to promote local initiative or structural change. Thus Chapter 3 referred to bringing about 'cumulative changes in the environment'. In general, however, given the nature of policy as an explicit statement, negative feedback will be required. In considering the necessary mechanisms, the costs of obtaining information will have to be taken into account, and also the time-scales. The best mechanism is not necessarily the quickest acting and most sensitive one. Feedback which is strong and rapid may produce over-correction, and hence instability; and it has been suggested that this is in fact happening in advanced industrial societies (Pippard 1981). Finally, the mechanisms for evaluating the information received and ensuring that appropriate use is made of it are the subject of an extensive literature, and no attempt will be made to summarise that here (but see Pollitt 1980; Smith 1981).

The translation process

This chapter has described the implementation of policies as translation from political language to administrative language. That is more than a metaphor. Different groups of people involved in implementation have different cognitive structures, incorporated in different languages (more often 'parallel languages' than 'foreign languages'). Policies are explicit statements, and language is the vehicle for the interplay of different cognitive structures within the implementation process. Almost any conceivable action relevant to policy implementation depends to a greater or lesser extent on the use of language. The ways in which language is used are therefore of fundamental importance in the process. Chapter 11 notes the advantages derived from the high degree of articulateness forced on officials when they were operating in a difficult political environment.

Effective translation depends on the existence of people who are fluent in both languages. Even before that, it demands people who are aware of the duality, because we normally 'remain unconscious of the prodigious diversity of all the everyday language games because the clothing of our language makes everything alike' (Wittgenstein 1967: 224). More particularly they must be able to analyse the ambiguities and symbolic content of political language, and what these entail in terms of expectations.

There must also be the motivation to undertake the translation. Those involved in the policy process ought not to be guilty of the indictment urged by Burn (1978: 303):

> One gets the impression that those responsible for policies (Ministers and their Civil Service and economic advisers) regard the adoption of their policy as the 'end of the affair'; its outcome, which is the important thing socially, is not of interest to them. In political terms this is understandable: to secure the acceptance of a policy is an exercise of power for the Minister and his advisers,

it often results in a transfer of power to friends and supporters, and for the government it is expected to gain some immediate additional voting support.

Given the existence of fluency and motivation, can structures and procedures also contribute to accurate translation? Obviously translation is facilitated if, at least within organisations, the same people are responsible for a policy at the formulation stage and at the implementation stage. That tends not to happen in the British civil service, and there is presumably a similar tendency in other large organisations. The civil service is also marked by rather frequent changes of staff, as Chapter 7 noted.

Translations can also be facilitated by the adoption of a participative style. At one level this would involve close and continuing contacts with other organisations, or other parts of the same organisation, which have responsibilities in implementation. At another level it would involve consultation with those directly affected by the policy. The relative emphasis placed on the two levels will depend on circumstances. The review of the Supplementary Benefits scheme in the late 1970s was an example of very extensive consultation at both levels (Nixon 1980b). A participative style can be valuable in establishing whether a policy remains coherent when translated into administrative language. As with food standards (Chapter 10), it makes possible 'feasibility testing' or 'conjectural feedback' (Dunsire 1980): impossibilities in the policy can be identified and removed, and difficulties can be ironed out, even before it is formally stated. In contrast, there was apparently very little participation and debate in the drawing-up of the Job Creation Programme. A participative style is also beneficial in relation to the expectations aroused by a policy: it facilitates an accurate assessment of those expectations, and can also help to make them more realistic. Moreover if those concerned are known to have been consulted, or to have participated, this helps ensure that the condition about retaining general public assent is not breached. The consultative bodies described in Chapter 2 are a good example. The conflicts and ambiguities in a proposed policy need to be identified, not necessarily to eliminate them (although it may well be possible to eliminate some), but to give us the ability to manage their consequences during the implementation stage. The function of the civil servant has been described as 'to enable disputes to be carried on within reasonable bounds' (Heclo and Wildavsky 1974).

Understanding implementation

One model of decision-making which has been put forward is a 'cybernetic paradigm' (Simon 1962), in which the decision-maker does not have a picture of his environment, or necessarily any notion in advance of what the outcome of his actions will be, but performs an established repertory of operations and monitors the feedback from a few selected variables. It is important to distinguish this model from the evolutionary model, not only because we have emphasised the nature of policy as an explicit statement, but also because that hypothetical statement is in turn based on other, implicit hypotheses about the world. Indeed, these hypotheses determine what the perceived problem is, to which the policy is an intended solution. In exposing the policy to testing and possible falsification, we also expose these other hypotheses to falsification, although (if implementation fails) it may be very difficult in practice to determine which of the hypotheses are false – in other words, whether the policy is mistaken or it has been badly executed.

In our case studies, the importance and salience of hypotheses about the world vary considerably. They were high for distributive policies like the Job Creation Programme, Proposition 13 and Community funds, and also for Industrial Strategy; and in several of these cases some hypotheses were shown to be false. They were moderate for race relations, and low for educational policies, because (as Chapter 5 notes) education is a field in which many important propositions are hard to substantiate in terms of factual evidence. They were very low for food standards (because of the extent of prior consultation) and in the remaining case (Chapter 9) because the nature of the policy meant that only limited feedback could be obtained. In general, however, a broad merit of the evolutionary model is that it allows our knowledge of the world to extend and develop, so that this greater knowledge can be reflected in our policies.

Knowledge of the world depends on many kinds of expertise. Underlying this book is a belief that a more specific kind of understanding is also necessary: understanding of the implementation process itself. The case studies provide a number of examples of success based on a conscious understanding of the requirements for successful implementation (Chapters 2, 5, 10 and 11), and of varying degrees of failure associated with a lack of understanding (Chapters 3, 4 and 7). In addition, Chapter 8 emphasised the tendency of international organisations to select a programmed strategy for implementation (in order to limit the discretion of national governments) when an adaptive strategy was really required. So far as the contents of this book and the prescriptions offered are concerned, the proof of the pudding must be in the eating. The evolutionary model and the concept of implementation as translation are intended as a means of codifying and systematising understanding of the subject, and making it more widely and readily available. One aspect of such understanding is to identify the circumstances in which other kinds of expertise are required; Chapter 4 provides an example of a failure to do that.

There are a number of further tasks which need to be undertaken in order to apply and extend our understanding of implementation. We end by identifying some of them:

1. Techniques need to be developed for drawing up and applying implementation plans (this chapter) which are both rigorous and comprehensible, which utilise the concept of a 'hierarchy of intent' (Chapter 11), and which can accommodate adaptive strategies as well as programmed ones. The preparation of adequate implementation plans presupposes adequate theoretical understanding, and the use of a suitable vocabulary.
2. More detailed studies need to be made of the cognitive and linguistic structures of different groups of actors in the policy process, and the implications need to be identified, both within particular fields of policy and generally.
3. More exact knowledge ought to be obtained of the differences between different countries and over time, especially in the content of political symbolism and in the expectations generally held about the results of government actions. Do similar policies require different implementation strategies in different countries?
4. Work already undertaken on designing and creating the necessary capability to deploy adaptive strategies of implementation successfully must be further developed and extended when appropriate to the international level.

References

Barrett, S. and Fudge, C. (eds) 1981, *Policy and action: essays on the implementation of public policy*, London, Methuen

Berger, P. and Luckman, T. 1966, *The social construction of reality*, New York, Anchor Books

Berman, P. 1980, 'Thinking about programmed and adaptive implementation: matching strategies to situations', in Ingram, H.M. and Mann, D.E. (eds), *Why policies succeed or fail*, London, Sage Yearbooks in Politics and Public Policy, vol. 8

Blowers, A. 1980, 'The administrative politics of planning', in Open University, op. cit., pp. 89–132

Burke, K. 1945, *A grammar of motives*, Englewood Cliffs, N.J., Prentice-Hall

Burke, K. 1950, *A rhetoric of motives*, Englewood Cliffs, N.J., Prentice-Hall

Burn, D. 1978, *Nuclear power and the energy crisis: politics and the atomic industry*, London, Macmillan (for the Trade Policy Research Centre)

Cmnd 8616 1982, *Efficiency and effectiveness in the civil service*, London, HMSO

Cohen, A. 1974, *Two-dimensional man: an essay on the anthropology of power and symbolism in complex society*, Berkeley and Los Angeles, California University Press

Donnison, D.V. 1978, 'Research for policy', in Bulmer, M. (ed.), *Social policy research*, London, Macmillan

Downs, A. 1967, *Inside bureaucracy*, Boston, Little, Brown

Dunsire, A. 1980, 'Implementation theory', in Open University, op. cit., pp. 5–54

Edelman, M. 1971, *Politics as symbolic action*, Chicago, Markham (Institute for Research on Poverty Monograph Series)

Edelman, M. 1977, *Political language: words that succeed and policies that fail*, London, Academic Press (Institute for Research on Poverty Monograph Series)

Findeisen, W. *et. al.* 1980, *Control and coordination in hierarchical systems*, Chichester, Wiley (International Series on Applied Systems Analysis, 9)

Foot, M. 1973, in Granada TV, *State of the nation*, quoted in *New Statesman*, 14 November 1980, p. 6

Garrett, J. 1980, *Managing the civil service*, London, Heinemann Educational Books

Hall, P., Land, H., Parker, R. and Webb, A. 1975, *Change, choice and conflict in social policy*, London, Heinemann

Heclo, H. and Wildavsky, A. 1974, *The private government of public money*, London, Macmillan

Hill, M.J. 1972, *The sociology of public administration*, London, Weidenfeld & Nicolson

Hill, M.J. 1981, 'The policy-implementation distinction: a quest for rational control?', in Barrett and Fudge, op. cit., pp. 207–23

Hjern, B. and Porter, D.O. 1980, 'Implementation structure: a new unit of administrative analysis', Berlin, International Institute of Management, unpublished mimeo (paper prepared for a conference, Institute of Advanced Studies, Vienna)

Hood, C.C. 1976, *The limits of administration*, Chichester, Wiley

Hyder, M. 1979, *Parliament and defence affairs: a critique of the major decisions approach*, Civil Service College Working Paper 11

Johnston, M. 1982, 'The "New Christian Right" in American politics', *Political quarterly*, vol. 53, no. 2, pp. 181–99

Kaiser, K., Merlini, C., de Montbrial, T., Wallace, W. and Wellenstein,

E. 1983, *The European Community: progress or decline?*, London Royal Institute of International Affairs

Keeling, D. 1972, *Management in government*, London, Allen & Unwin

Knoepfel, P. and Weidner, H. 1979, 'The formation and implementation of air quality control programmes: patterns of interest consideration', IIUG (Berlin) preprint 79/25

Kolata, G. 1982, 'How can computers get commonsense?', *Science*, vol. 217, 24 September, pp. 1237–8

Leontief, W. 1982, Letter, in *Science*, vol. 217, 9 July, pp. 104–7

Levi-Strauss, C. 1963, *Structural anthropology*, New York, Basic Books

Lindblom, C.E. 1959, 'The science of muddling through', *Public administration review*, vol. 19, no. 1, pp. 79–88

Mannheim, K. 1936, *Ideology and Utopia*, New York, Harcourt Brace

March, J.G. and Simon, H.A. 1958, *Organisations*, New York, Wiley

Maruyama, M. 1963, 'The second cybernetics: deviation – amplifying mutual causal processes', *American scientist*, vol. 51, pp. 164–79

Nixon, J. 1980a, 'The importance of communication in the implementation of government policy at local level', *Policy and politics*, vol. 8, no. 2, pp. 127–44

Nixon, J. 1980b, *The review of the Supplementary Benefits scheme: a case study*, Civil Service College Working Paper 25

Open University 1980, *Social sciences: a third level course. Policies, people and administration (D336), block 3, Implementation, evaluation and change*, Milton Keynes, Open University Press

Pippard, B. 1981, Inaugural address to the 150th meeting of the British Association for the Advancement of Science, reported in *The Guardian*, 1 September

Pollitt, C. 1980, 'Evaluation', in Open University, op. cit., pp. 133–66

Ramsey, I.T. 1961, *Religious language*, London, SCM Press

Simon, H.A. 1962, 'The architecture of complexity', *Proceedings of the American philosophical society*, vol. 106, pp. 467–82

Smith, G. 1978, 'The meaning of "success" in social policy: a case study', *Public administration*, vol. 56, autumn, pp. 263–81

Smith, R. 1981, 'Implementing the results of evaluation studies', in Barrett and Fudge, op. cit., pp. 225–45

Tullock, G. 1965, *The politics of bureaucracy*, Washington DC, Public Affairs Press

Vedung, E. 1982, *Political reasoning*, London, Sage

Vickers, G.C. 1970, *Value systems and the social process*, Harmondsworth, Penguin

Walker, M. 1983, 'Charity goes on the dole', *The Guardian*, 30 March

Wheare, K.C. 1955, *Government by committee*, Oxford, Oxford University Press

Wildavsky, A. 1973, 'If planning is everything maybe it's nothing', *Policy sciences*, vol. 4, pp. 127–53

Williams, B.A. 1979, 'Beyond "incrementalism"', organisational theory and public policy', *Policy studies journal*, vol. 7, no. 4, pp. 683–9

Wittgenstein, L. 1967, *Philosophical investigations*, Oxford, Basil Blackwell

Wynne, B. 1982, *Rationality and ritual: the Windscale inquiry and nuclear decisions in Britain*, British Society for the History of Science Monographs no. 3

Young, K. 1979, 'Values in the policy process', in C. Pollitt *et al.* (eds), *Public policy in theory and practice*, Sevenoaks, Hodder & Stoughton

Young, K. and Mills, L. 1980, *Public policy research: a review of qualitative methods*, London, Social Science Research Council

Index of Authors

Index of Main Concepts